Summer was approaching and each year, since 1970, we have mounted an important historical exhibition. What should we do this year, 1985? Suddenly it became clear that we, Annely Juda and Alex Gregory-Hood had spent almost a lifetime in gallery work and for me it was 25 years since I had started the Molton Gallery in 1960, went on to the Hamilton Galleries in 1963 and finally emerged in 1968 as Annely Juda Fine Art. The changes I have witnessed over these 25 years have been enormous. A variety of artists and art have passed through the galleries and finally a face, a kind of being has emerged which has its own life, its own force, its own identity.

The exhibition this year is a combined effort. On the Annely Juda Fine Art side we are showing important historical paintings, on the Juda Rowan Gallery side contemporary works from the three decades, the Sixties, the Seventies and the present decade, the Eighties. Each month we will be exhibiting the work of one decade.

I would like to thank all my friends, supporters, collectors and especially the artists who have made these last 25 years possible and I dedicate this exhibition to all the artists who have been with us over the years, some of whom are still with the gallery today. My gratitude to our colleagues, Thomas Gibson, James Kirkman, Leslie Waddington, Tokyo Gallery, Mr A. Venema, The British Council, and The Tate Gallery, as well as the many private lenders who wish to remain anonymous, but who have entrusted us once again with their paintings. Special thanks to Margaret Pedley, Eve Guttentag and Anne Goldsmith for working so hard on this catalogue and exhibition, Mr and Mrs Douglas Upton, our printers, George Meyrick for taking most of the photographs and Keith Thomas for installing our exhibitions. My thanks also to Wyn Chalmers for her long years of hard work in the gallery, her new assistant, Teresa Rubey, and to Celia Garrick who was my assistant for many years.

Only the dedication and hard work of my son, David, has made it possible to arrive at the point the gallery is at today. Without him I might often have foundered, as indeed I did in my first seven years. Instead, together we have been going from strength to strength. The merger with the Rowan Gallery three years ago put our contemporary side on a wider footing and we have added a great number of artists, who are of national and international importance. We are very happy to have Ian Barker who recently joined the Juda Rowan Gallery and who will no doubt greatly further our future contemporary policies.

Looking back at my time at the Rowan Gallery, I am indebted to Diana Kingsmill, because together we started the Rowan Gallery and for the first ten years jointly built it up. I am also very indebted to all the artists with whom we had, or still have, the honour to work. Also to Celia Plunkett, Francie Pritchett and Alan Tinkler, all of whom devoted many years to the gallery.

This catalogue with its extensive Chronology and a description of the decades preceding the controversial Eighties, will show some important works which have passed through our hands, together with the artists who played a vital part in the Sixties and Seventies. We feel sure that the Eighties will continue to bring both new and exciting work from them and perhaps from other new artists that may join the gallery in the future.

The object of this catalogue is to tell the story of our two galleries and, in the telling, to chronicle a fragment of art history over the last two and a half decades. During this time we have between us mounted 442 exhibitions and have been responsible for numerous exhibitions abroad of our artists.

We are both very grateful for the interest and support that we have had over the years from the art critics, particularly, on this occasion, Norbert Lynton, Bryan Robertson, Marina Vaizey and Waldemar Januszczak, who have written important essays in the catalogue.

Last but not least, we would like to thank the various establishments, museums and private collectors both in this country and abroad for their support which has played such an important role in enabling us to continue to do the work we both love and enjoy so much.

Annely Juda — Alex Gregory-Hood

TWENTY FIVE YEARS

Annely Juda Fine Art/Juda Rowan Gallery

11 Tottenham Mews (off Tottenham Street)
London W1P 9PJ
Telephone: 01-637 5517/8/9
Mon–Fri: 10 am–6 pm Sat: 10 am–1 pm

Masterpieces of the Avantgarde

17 September – 20 December, 1985

Three Decades of Contemporary Art

THE SIXTIES: 17 September – 19 October, 1985

THE SEVENTIES: 22 October – 23 November, 1985

THE EIGHTIES: 26 November – 20 December, 1985

ISBN 0 9504121 6 3 (hardback)
ISBN 0 9504121 7 1 (paperback)

Printed by Creasey Flood Ltd, Tower Road, Lowestoft, England

Contents

Chronology of the Galleries

Molton Gallery
1960–1963

Rowan Gallery (Lowndes Street)
1962–1967

Hamilton Galleries
1963–1967

Rowan Gallery (Bruton Place)
1968–1981

Annely Juda Fine Art
1968—

Juda Rowan Gallery
1982—

Rowan Gallery
Loxley Sculpture Garden
1976—

Unless otherwise stated all works illustrated are in Private Collections or courtesy of the gallery/artist.

Molton Gallery

1960

	Opening Exhibition
27 April–May	Emilio Pettoruti Paintings 1914–1959
May–June	E. R. Nele Sculptures
June–July	Friedlaender Etchings and Aquatints
July	Francisco Borès Paintings
Aug–Sept	William Turnbull Paintings
Sept–Oct	Avinash Chandra Paintings
Oct–Nov	Baram Paintings and Collages
Nov–Dec	Erich Kahn and Margarete Brauer Paintings
December	Small Paintings and Sculpture by International Artists

Borès, Untitled 1946
watercolour 89 × 72 cm

Margarete Brauer, Capernaum 1960
oil on canvas 70 × 85 cm

Avinash Chandra, Untitled 1960
oil on board 60 × 80 cm

Emilio Pettoruti, Le Siphon 1915 collage on paper 48 x 35 cm

Molton Gallery *Continued*

1961

Jan–Feb	Ossip Zadkine Sculpture, Drawings and Lithographs
Feb–March	Five Painters from the Galerie Massol Paris Busse, Clerte, Cortot, Lagage, Key Sato
March	Alfred Aberdam Paintings and Gouaches
March–April	Ecole de Paris Appel, Bryen, Gischia, Le Moal, Manessier, Singier, Sugai, Zao Wou-Ki Watercolours and Drawings
April–May	William Turnbull Sculpture
May	Jannis Spyropoulos Paintings
May–June	Francis Rose Paintings
June–July	Paul Klee Paintings and Watercolours
July–Aug	John Plumb Paintings
August	Luichy Martinez Sculpture
September	Duncan Paintings
October	Michael Werner Abstracts for Architecture
Oct–Nov	Ann Cole Phillips Paintings
Nov–Dec	Robyn Denny Paintings
Dec–Jan	Black and White a selection of Drawings and Lithographs Walter Nessler Metal Reliefs

Paul Klee, Gruppe macht Augen 1938 gouache and oil 33 x 49 cm

Jannis Spyropoulos,
The Variation No. 37 1960
oil on paper 60 x 50 cm

Ossip Zadkine, Three Beauties 1953
bronze 75 cm

Luichy Martinez, Composition marble 30 cm

1962

January	Gillian Ayres Paintings
February	Bernard Cohen Paintings and Drawings
March	Baram Paintings and Gouaches
March–April	Avinash Chandra Paintings
April–May	Four American Painters Hedda Sterne, Paul Feeley, Minoru Kawabata, Jesse Reichek. In collaboration with Betty Parsons Gallery, New York
May–June	Gerald Gladstone Metal Sculpture
July	E. R. Nele Sculpture
July–Aug	Painters of the Gallery
August	Peter Coviello Paintings
September	Oliffe Richmond Sculpture and Drawings
October	John Barnicoat Paintings
November	Mario Samona Paintings
December	Pastels by Turuoka Gouaches by Duncan

Rowan Gallery

1962

4 July	Opening Exhibition 5 Young British Artists Antony Donaldson, Jeffrey Harris, Terry Jones, John Rich, Brian Young
Aug–Sept	Summer Exhibition of Contemporary Artists Coleman, Conn, Hubbard, Snow, Thompson, Tirr
October	Garth Evans Reliefs in White Brian Fielding Paintings
November	Anthony Green Paintings Peter Upward Paintings
December	Christmas Exhibition Contemporary Work Including Trevor Coleman, Garth Evans, Brian Fielding, Geoffrey Grinling, Margaret Mellis, Gerald Moore, Sushila Singh, Michael Snow, Brian Yale

E. R. Nele
bronze 25 x 30 x 12 cm

Antony Donaldson
with his paintings 1962

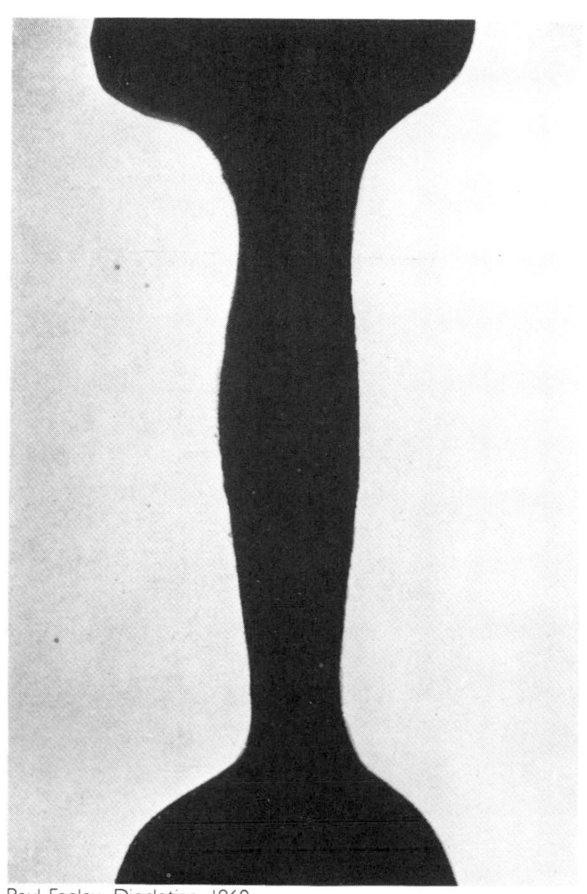
Paul Feeley, Diocletian 1960
oil on canvas 80 x 54 cm

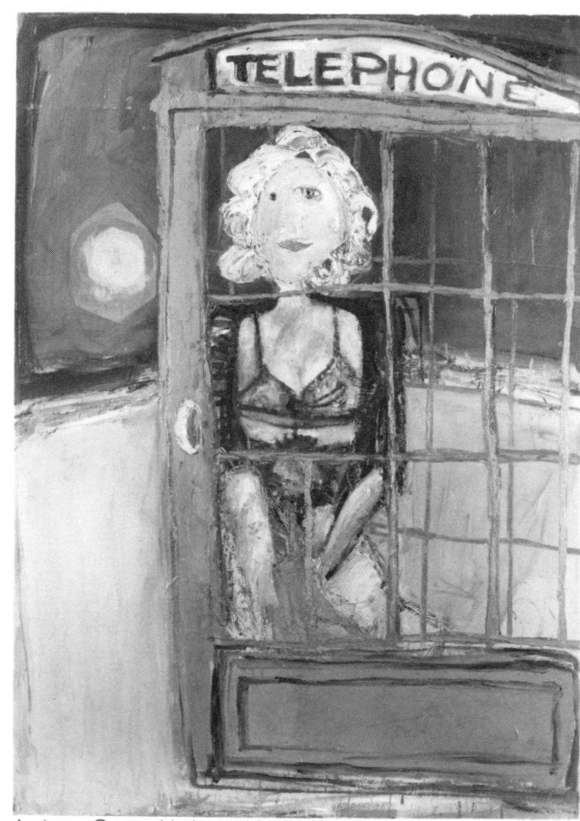

Anthony Green, Undressed Lady 1961
oil on board 124.5 x 91.5 cm

Gerald Gladstone, System A 1962
welded steel 79 x 91.5 cm

Brian Young, Tilt 1961
oil on canvas 152.5 x 152.5 cm

Molton Gallery *Continued*

1963

January	Maurice Jadot A Retrospective Exhibition of Paintings, Wood Reliefs and Sculpture
February	Roy Ascott Diagram Boxes & Analogue Structures
March	Max Chapman Paintings
March–April	Denis Bowen Dedicated to the Astronauts
April–May	Nicholas Georgiadis Paintings and Watercolours

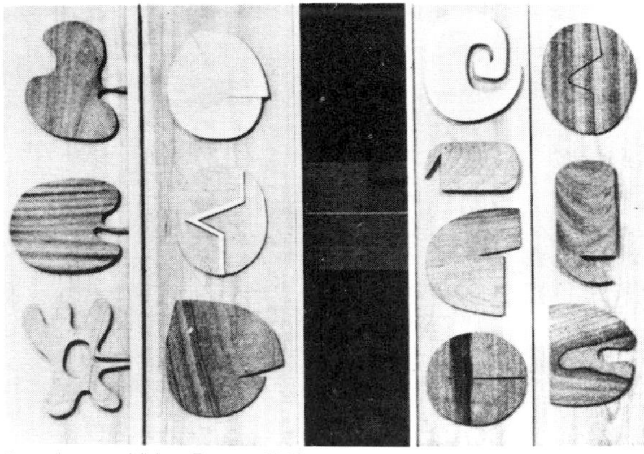

Roy Ascott, Video-Roget 1962
wood, perspex, glass 127 x 89 cm

Hamilton Galleries

1963

	Opening Exhibition
17 July–Aug	Klaus Friedeberger Paintings
Aug–Sept	Hamilton painters: Gillian Ayres, Avinash Chandra, Peter Coviello, Robyn Denny, Klaus Friedeberger, John Hart, Nicholas Georgiadis, Michael Michaeledes with guests, Anne Hagen and Sally Scott
	Hamilton Sculptors: Anthea Alley, Oliffe Richmond with guests, Michael Werner and Kadishman
Sept–Oct	Gillian Ayres Paintings
October	John Hart Paintings
November	Gunther Gumpert Paintings, Gouaches, Monotypes
December	Avinash Chandra Drawings and Watercolours

Rowan Gallery *Continued*

1963

January	Group Show
February	Paul Huxley Paintings Alistair Park Paintings
March	Jeffrey Harris Paintings Jane Beeson Paintings
April	Hayman Chaffey Paintings
May	Antony Donaldson Paintings
June	Jon Thompson Paintings
July	William Tucker Sculpture
August	David Taggart Paintings Jeremy Moon Paintings 61–63
September	John Rich Reliefs
October	Asher Bilu Paintings
November	Isaac Witkin Sculpture
Dec–Jan	Winter Exhibition House Artists Antony Donaldson, Paul Huxley, Jon Thompson, William Tucker, Peter Upward, Brian Young

Paul Huxley, Untitled No. 21 1963
oil on canvas 203 x 203 cm

Gillian Ayres, Drawing 1962
oil, charcoal, pastel, pencil on paper 20 x 25 cm

Jeremy Moon, Trellis 1962 oil on canvas 137 x 106.8 cm
coll. The Tate Gallery, London

Gunther Gumpert, Composition 1962
mixed media 63.5 x 45.8 cm

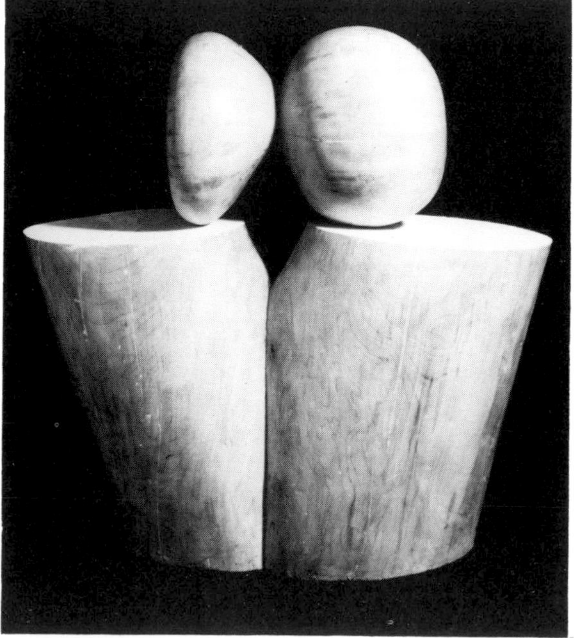

Isaac Witkin, Birth 1963
wood 81.5 x 81.5 x 81.5 cm

William Tucker, Search 1963 wood 76 x 117 cm

Hamilton Galleries *Continued*

1964

Jan–Feb	Francisco Toledo Paintings and Gouaches Ado Paintings
February	Gerald Gladstone Spacist Sculpture
March	Key Sato Paintings
March–April	Anthea Alley Paintings and Sculpture
April–May	Michael Werner Sculpture
May	Patrick Scott Paintings
June–July	Shinkichi Tajiri Sculpture
July–Sept	The Blue Four Klee, Kandinsky, Feininger, Jawlensky
Sept–Oct	Hamilton Painters and Sculptors
October	Michael Rothenstein Collages
November	Tony Underhill Figure Painting
December	Friederich Werthmann Sculpture

Rowan Gallery *Continued*

1964

February	Phillip King Sculpture
March	William Tirr Paintings
April	Michael Snow Paintings
May	Austin Wright Sculpture
June	Garth Evans Reliefs
July	Anthony Green Paintings
September	Roger Cook Paintings
October	Brian Fielding Paintings
November	Peter Upward Paintings
Nov–Dec	Group Show

Toledo, No. 1 1963
watercolour on paper 25 x 30 cm

Garth Evans, Pale Blue/Pink No. 32 1964
plywood, hardboard, polyurethane 115.5 x 123 cm

Key Sato
with one of his paintings 1964

Anthony Green, Tower of Babel 1964
oil on hardboard 183 x 122 cm

Paul Klee, Stimme aus dem Aether: 'Und du wirst dich satt Essen' 1939 oil and tempera on paper 50.5 x 38 cm.
By courtesy of the Board of Trustees of the Victoria and Albert Museum, London

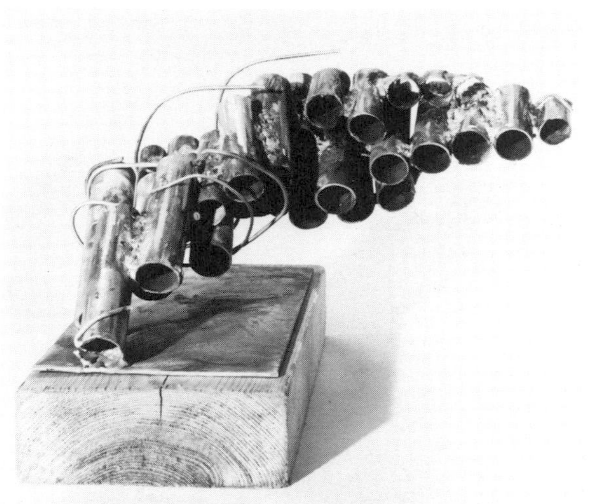

Anthea Alley, Pipe Composition I 1963
brass 25.5 x 40.5 cm

Roger Cook, Painting 1965
acrylic on canvas 137 x 137 cm

Michael Werner, Structure I 1963
iron and polyester 76 x 40.5 cm

Brian Fielding, Sign 1964
acrylic on canvas 152.4 x 152.4 cm

Phillip King, Sculpture, February 1964

Hamilton Galleries *Continued*

1965

Jan–Feb	Frank Hodgkinson Paintings and Collages
Feb–March	Roy Ascott Recent Works
March	Avinash Chandra Paintings and Drawings
March–April	Frank Roth Paintings
April–May	Tess Jaray Paintings
May–June	Ann Cole Phillips Recent Paintings
June–July	Nicholas Georgiadis Paintings
July–Aug	30 Centuries of Iranian Art: Amlash, Luristan and The Islamic Period
September	Peter Coviello Paintings Commonwealth Gallery Artists: Hodgkinson, Friedeberger
October	Oliffe Richmond Recent Sculpture
November	Stephen Gilbert Structures 1962–65
Nov–Dec	Marc Vaux Paintings
Dec–Jan	Antanas Brazdys Sculpture

Rowan Gallery *Continued*

1965

February	David Taggart Paintings
March	Paul Huxley Paintings
April	Jon Thompson Paintings
May	Antony Donaldson Paintings
June	Jeremy Moon Paintings 1964–65
July	Alistair Park Paintings
August	Derek Southall Paintings
September	Hayman Chaffey Paintings
October	Jan Diederen Paintings
November	Mark Lancaster Paintings

Marc Vaux, Equinox 1965
acrylic on canvas 183 x 183 cm

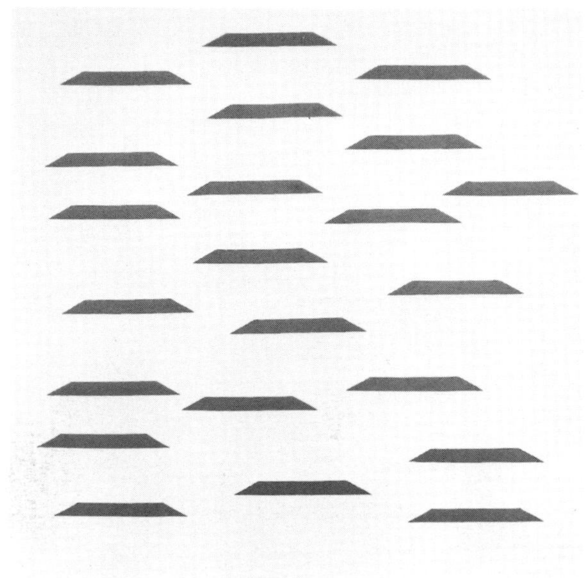

Mark Lancaster, Host 1965
acrylic on canvas 152.4 x 152.4 cm

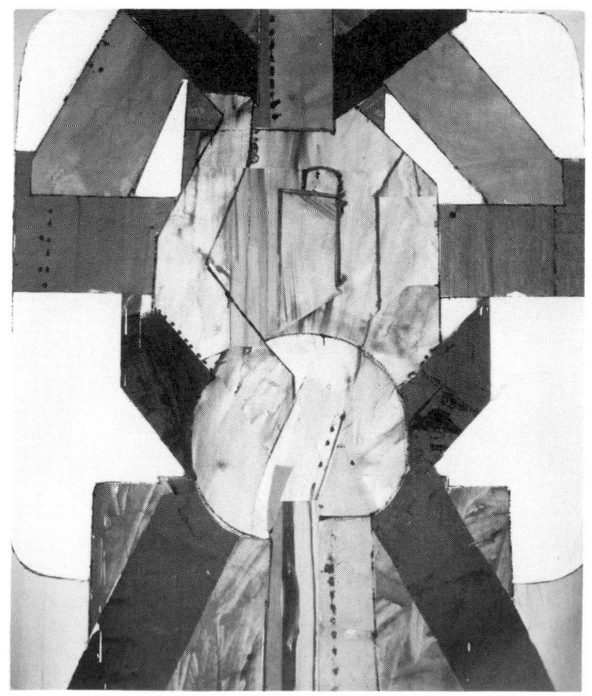

Nicholas Georgiadis, The Inmate 1964
mixed media 152.5 x 183 cm

Anthony Donaldson, Summershot 1965
acrylic on canvas 172.8 x 172.8 cm coll. The British Council

Frank Roth Paintings
March–April 1965

Paul Huxley Paintings
March 1965

Oliffe Richmond with his sculpture 1965

Jeremy Moon in his studio c. 1964

Hamilton Galleries *Continued*

1966

Jan–Feb	Margaret Neve Constructions Guy Burn Paintings
Feb–March	Sculpture and Sculptors' Drawings at the Hamilton Galleries
March–April	Michael Kenny Sculpture
April–May	Bernard Schottlander Sculpture
May–June	Patrick Scott Paintings
June–July	E. R. Nele Sculpture and Collages
August	Trends and Movements: Appel, Francis, Pollock, Tapies, Johns, da Silva, de Stael
Sept–Oct	Michael Rothenstein Constructions and Prints
Oct–Nov	Friederich Werthmann Sculptures
Nov–Dec	Michael Michaeledes Paintings
Dec–Jan	Mixed Show

Rowan Gallery *Continued*

1966

February	Asher Bilu Paintings
March	Anthony Green Paintings
April	Michael Thorpe Paintings
May	William Tucker Sculpture
June	Roger Cook Paintings
July	Jeremy Moon Paintings 1965–66
August	Barry Flanagan Sculpture
September	Garth Evans Sculpture
October	Roy Conn Paintings
November	Antony Donaldson Paintings
December	Group Show

Barry Flanagan in his studio 1966

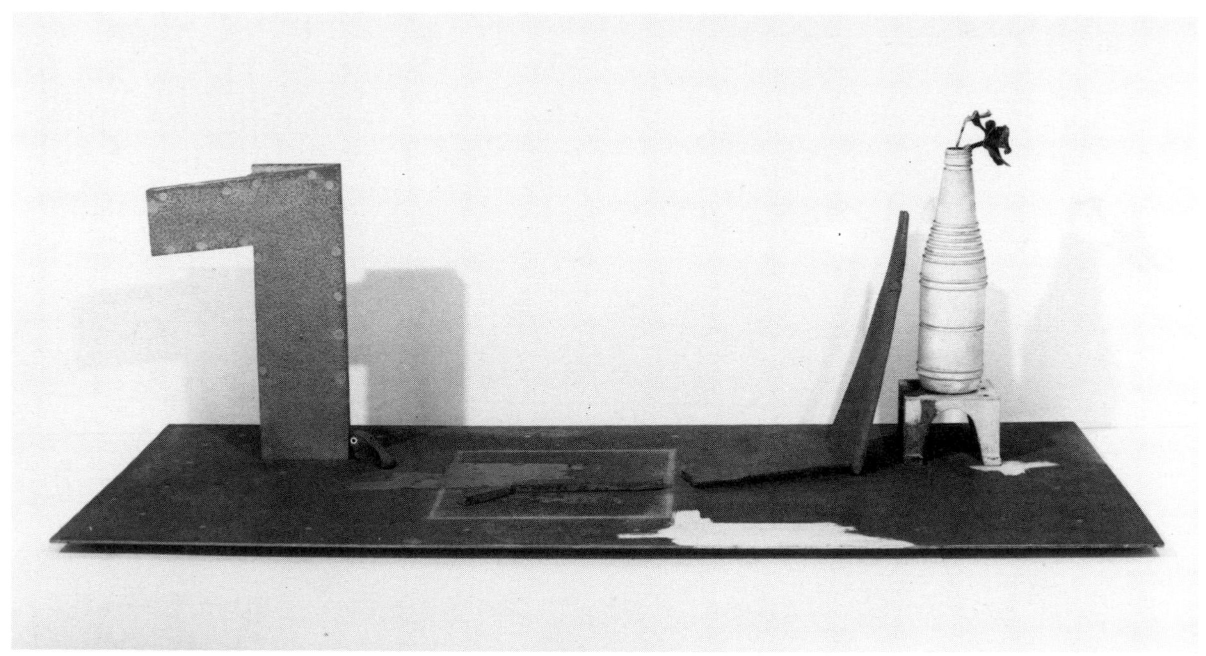

Michael Kenny . . . Place 1966/67 aluminium, oilpaint and found objects 41 × 109 × 46 cm

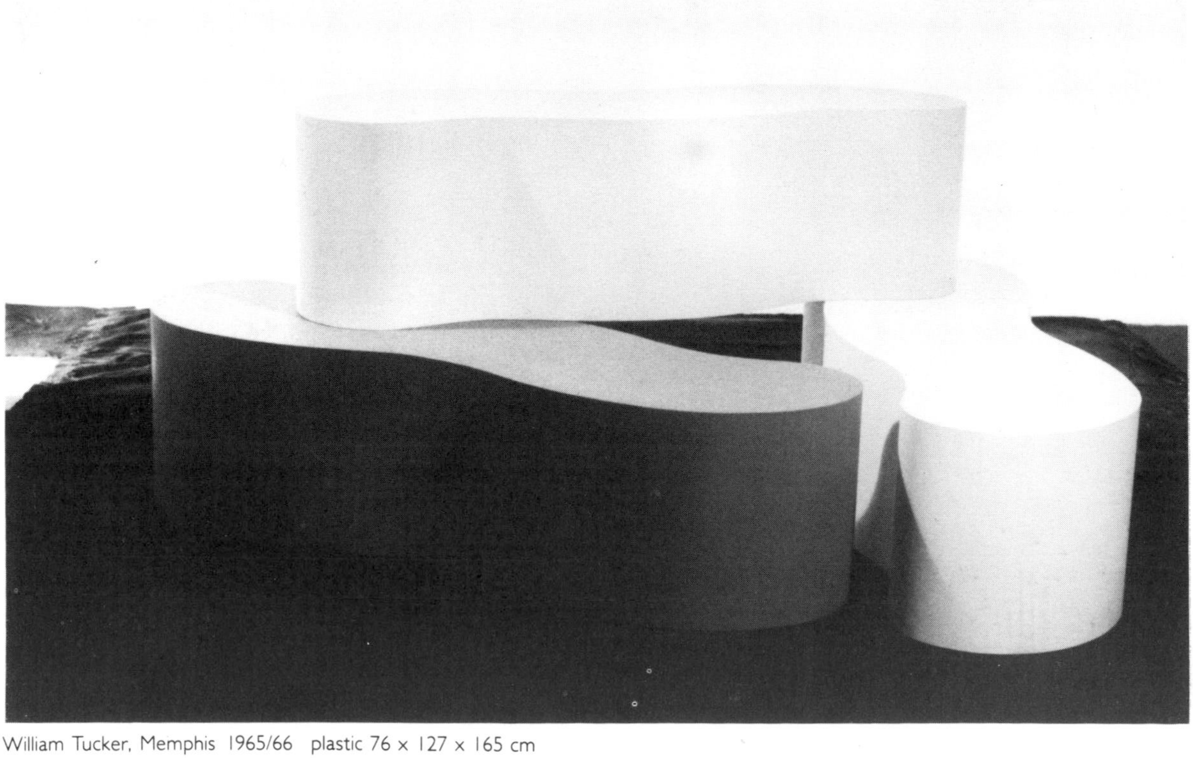

William Tucker, Memphis 1965/66 plastic 76 × 127 × 165 cm

Tess Jaray, Haven 1966 oil on canvas 114 x 274 cm

Antanas Brazdys, Sculpture, December 1965–January 1966

Jackson Pollock, Composition No. 13 1950 oil on pavatex 56.5 × 56.5 cm

Hamilton Galleries *Continued*

1967

Jan–Feb	Tony Underhill Paintings
Feb–March	Avinash Chandra
March–April	David Partridge Sculpture and Reliefs
April–May	Frank Roth Paintings Barbara Pniewska
May–June	Tess Jaray Paintings Buky Schwartz Recent Sculpture
June–July	Vic Gentils Sculpture and Assemblage Juuko Ikewada Paintings
July	Roy Ascott New Work Allen Jones Lithographs
Aug–Oct	Homage to Silence De Chirico, Giacometti, Balthus, Morandi etc.
Oct–Nov	The best of the Hamilton Painters and Sculptors
Nov–Dec	Edith Galliner Paintings and Collages

Rowan Gallery *Continued*

1967

February	John Edwards Paintings 1966–67
March	Anthony Green Paintings
April	Thomas Lenk Sculpture
May–June	Joe Goode's English Still Life on White Tablecloth
June–July	Mark Lancaster Paintings
July–Aug	Gallery Artists
September	Jon Thompson Paintings
December	Gallery moved to Bruton Place

David Partridge with his sculpture 1967

John Edwards, Blue Vertex 1966
polymer acrylic emulsions on canvas 167.5 x 167.5 cm

Vic Gentils, L'Imploration 3/67
wood 42 x 33 cm

Mark Lancaster, Motel 1967
oil and liquitex on canvas 183 x 172.8 cm

Tony Underhill in his studio 1967

Anthony Green, 8C 6216 New York 1967 oil on board 122 x 122 cm

de Chirico, Les Philosophes 1926 oil on canvas 146 x 114 cm. Homage to Silence, July 1967

Annely Juda Fine Art

1968

	Opening Exhibition
16 June–Sept	Now Open: Important Paintings of the 20th Century and Young Artists Bonnard, Leger, Rouault, Soutine, Giacometti, etc
Sept–Oct	Balthus Drawings
Oct–Nov	Nicholas Georgiadis Gouaches and Collages
Nov–Jan	The World of Naifs

Rowan Gallery *Continued*

1968

	Opening Exhibition at Bruton Place
9 Feb–March	Jeremy Moon Paintings
March	Andy Warhol Paintings and Silkscreens
April	Barry Flanagan Sculpture
May	Paul Huxley Paintings
June	Garth Evans Sculpture
July–Sept	Gallery Artists
Sept–Oct	John Edwards Paintings
October	Antony Donaldson Paintings
November	Antony Donaldson Reliefs

Giacometti, The Chair 1960 oil on canvas 61 x 50 cm
Now Open, June–September 1968

Warhol, Marilyn Monroe 1967
serigraph 92 x 92 cm

Rowan Gallery Opening Exhibition, February–March 1968

Annely Juda Fine Art Now Open:
Important Paintings of the 20th Century and Young Artists, June–September 1968

Balthus, Nude Woman on Chair, Cat on the Table c.1947 ink 28.5 x 43.5 cm

Paul Huxley, Paintings, May 1968

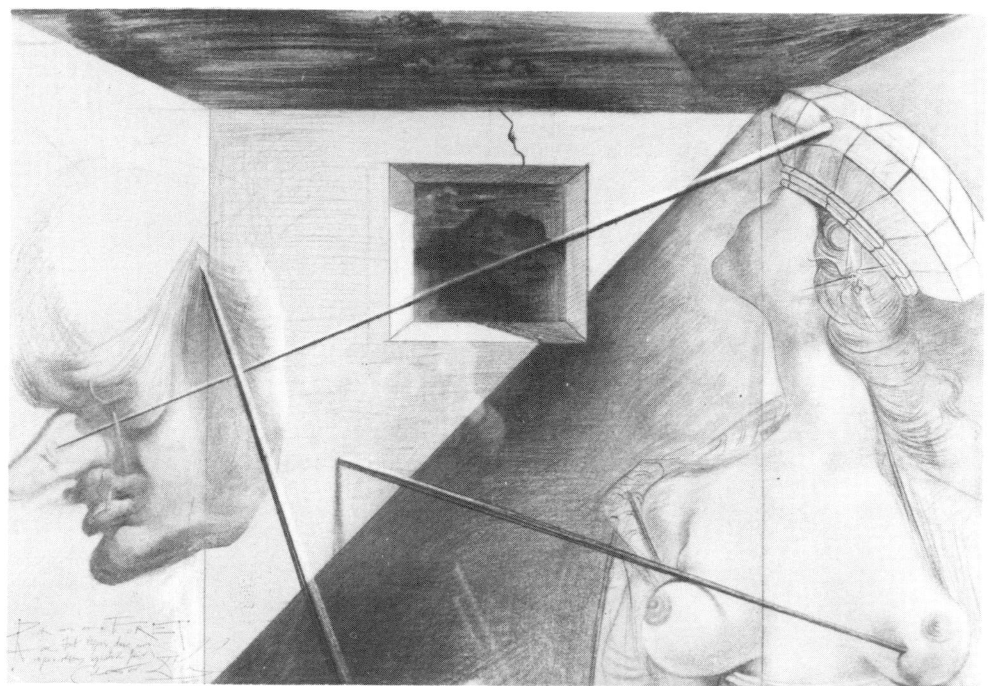

Dali, La Reine Salomé 1937 pencil on paper 62.5 x 93.6 cm
Annely Juda Fine Art Now Open: Important Paintings of the 20th C. and Young Artists, June–Sept. 1968

Barry Flanagan, Heap 1 1968 canvas and sand 46 x 76 cm

Annely Juda Fine Art *Continued*

1969

Feb–March	Print Show
April	Hilde Goldschmidt Monotypes
May–June	Surrealist Drawings: Bellmer, Brauner, Castillo, de Chirico, Dali, Ernst, Klee, Lam, Magritte, Moore, Paalen, Penrose, Picasso, Man Ray, Requichot, Tanguy
Sept–Oct	Sculpture and Drawings
Oct–Nov	Peter Hobbs Collages from Box
Nov–Feb	Modern Images in Ancient Times

Rowan Gallery *Continued*

1969

April	Jeremy Moon Paintings
May	Les Levine Constructions
June	Mark Lancaster Paintings
July	Bridget Riley Working Drawings
August	Garth Evans Sculpture
September	Michael Craig-Martin Sculpture – The Boxes
October	Anthony Green Paintings
November	Paul Huxley Paintings
December	Gallery Artists

Picasso, Untitled 1937 pencil on paper 40 x 30.5 cm
Surrealist Drawings, May–June 1969

Bridget Riley
with one of her paintings c. 1969

Modern Images in Ancient Times, November 1969–February 1970

Bridget Riley, Study for Cateract 1967
gouache on paper 48.2 × 35.5 cm

Garth Evans, 8 Cones Grey 1969
plastic 219.8 × 219.8 × 219.8 cm

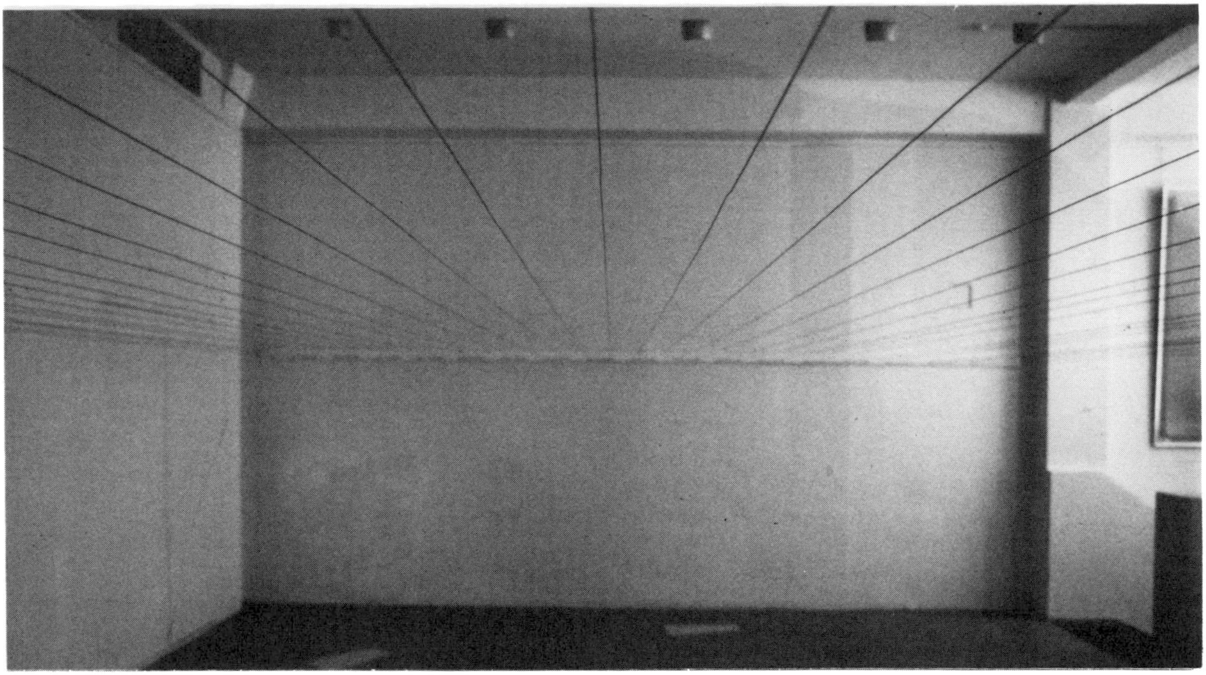

Les Levine Constructions, May 1969

Hilde Goldschmidt, Holy City IV 1968
monotype 50 x 40.5 cm

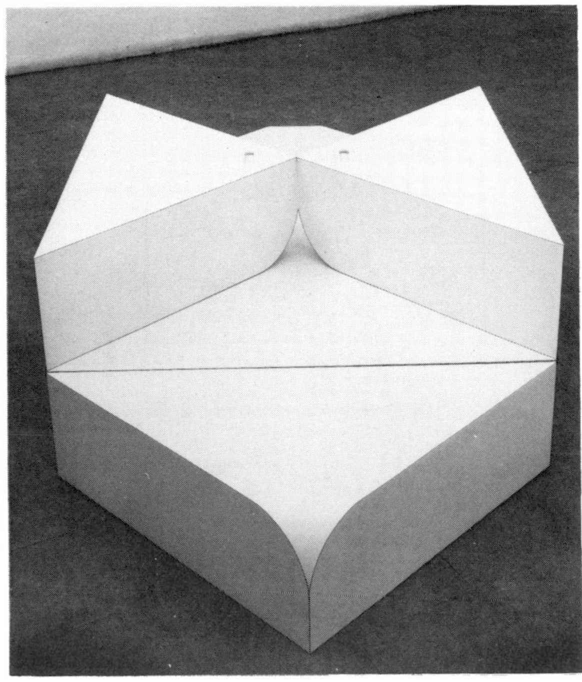
Michael Craig-Martin, Untitled No. 1 1968
formica 122 x 122 x 61 cm

Laurens, Baigneuse 1932 bronze 68.5 cm
Sculpture and Drawings, September–October 1969

Annely Juda Fine Art *Continued*

1970

Feb–March	Peter Kalkhof Environmental Paintings
April–May	Marcia Herscovitz Collages
May–June	Rudolf Bauer Paintings
June–Sept	The Non-Objective World 1914–1924
Oct–Nov	Alan Green Paintings
	Abraham Hadad Paintings, Gouaches, Lithographs
Dec–March	Mixed Christmas Show

Rowan Gallery *Continued*

1970

March	John Edwards Paintings
April–May	Barry Flanagan Sculpture
May–June	Jeremy Moon Paintings
July	Phillip King Sculpture
August	Gallery Artists
September	Michael Craig-Martin Sculpture – The Balances
October	Mark Lancaster Paintings
November	Antony Donaldson Sculpture and Lithographs
December	Gallery Artists

Phillip King, Green Streamer 1970 steel 111.8 x 363 x 236 cm coll. The Tate Gallery, London

The Non-Objective World 1914–1924, June–September 1970

The Non-Objective World 1914–1924, June–September 1970

Alan Green in his studio, St. Katharine's Docks 1970

Michael Craig-Martin, 8' Balance with 2 reinforced plywood sheets 1970, wood, mild steel 183 x 438 x 244 cm

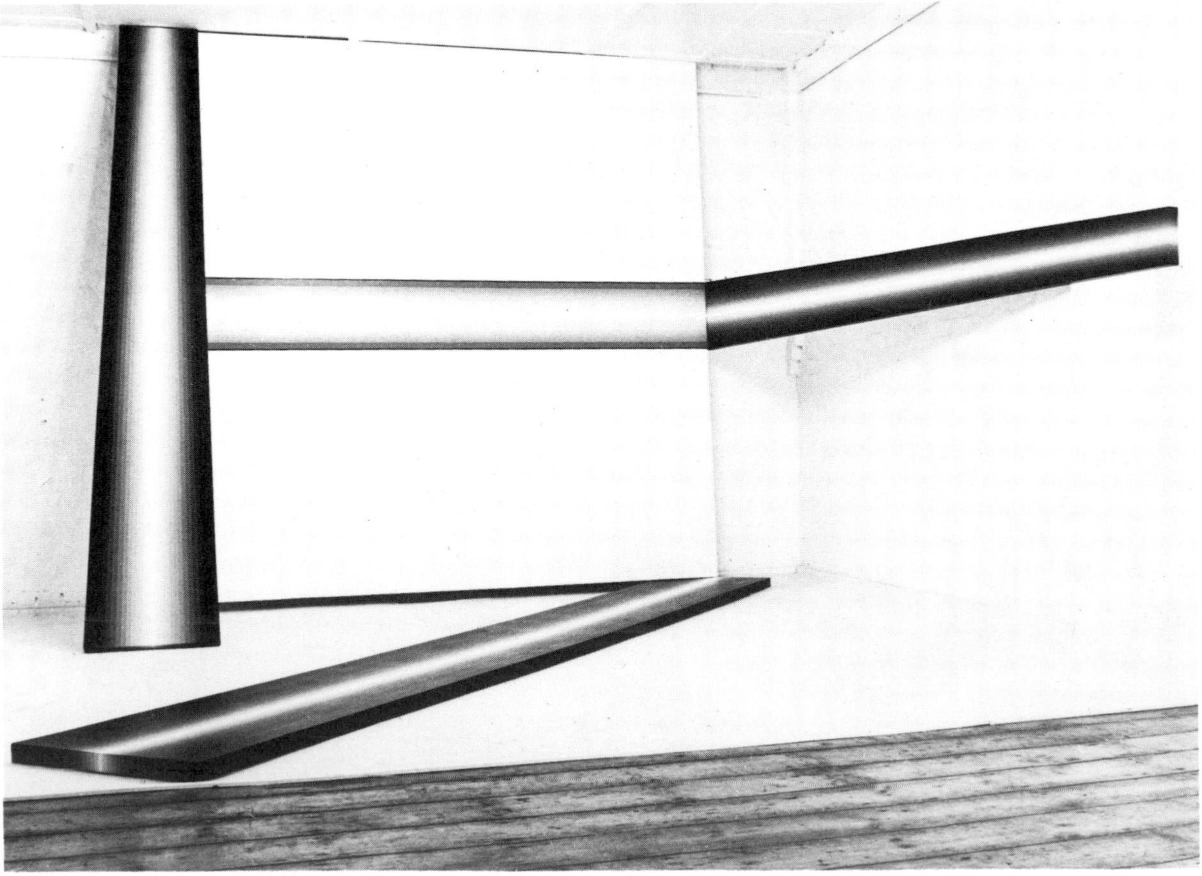

Peter Kalkhof, Environmental Colour Dimension 1969 acrylic on canvas 276 x 308 x 445 cm

Annely Juda Fine Art *Continued*

1971

March–April	Christo: Projects Not Realised
April–May	Hector Borla Paintings, Gouaches & Drawings Sergio Segre Paintings
June	Ancient Art from Persia
July–Sept	The Non-Objective World 1924–1939
Oct–Dec	Antanas Brazdys Sculpture
Dec–Feb	Modern Images in Ancient Times II

Rowan Gallery *Continued*

1971

Jan–March	Gallery Artists
April	Barry Flanagan Sculpture
May	Anthony Green Paintings
June–July	John Edwards Paintings
July–Aug	Bridget Riley Drawings
Aug–Sept	Paul Huxley Paintings
October	Mark Lancaster Paintings
November	Jeremy Moon Paintings

Moholy-Nagy, Composition with Symmetrical Circles 1932
gouache on paper 40 x 30 cm
The Non-Objective World 1924–39, July–September 1971

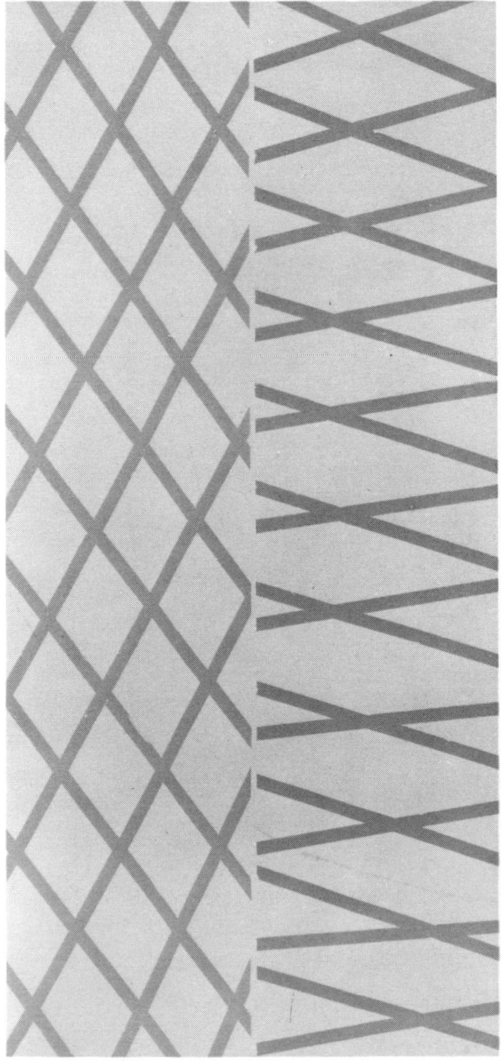

Jeremy Moon, Norway 1971
acrylic on canvas 195.5 x 91.5 cm
coll. The Government Art Collection, London

Bridget Riley Drawings, July–August 1971

Paul Huxley Paintings, August–September 1971

Christo, Allied Chemical Tower Packed 1968 collage 71 x 56 cm

Annely Juda Fine Art *Continued*

1972

Feb–March	Anna Mayerson Paintings
March–April	Michael Michaeledes Reliefs
May–June	Ella Bergmann-Michel, Robert Michel Retrospective 1917–1966
July–Sept	The Non-Objective World 1939–1955
Sept–Nov	Friedrich Vordemberge-Gildewart Retrospective
Nov–Jan	Sculpture and Sculptors' Drawings

Rowan Gallery *Continued*

1972

February	Garth Evans Sculpture
March	Michael Craig-Martin Wall Constructions with Mirrors
April	Gallery Artists
May	Antony Donaldson Portraits
June	Bridget Riley Drawings
July	Phillip King Sculpture
August	Gallery Artists
September	John Edwards Paintings
October	Anthony Green Paintings
November	Barry Flanagan Sculpture

Phillip King, Blue Between 1971 painted steel 220.8 x 457.5 x 366 cm coll. The Art Gallery of New South Wales, Australia

Ella Bergmann-Michel, Robert Michel Retrospective, 1917–1966 May–June 1972

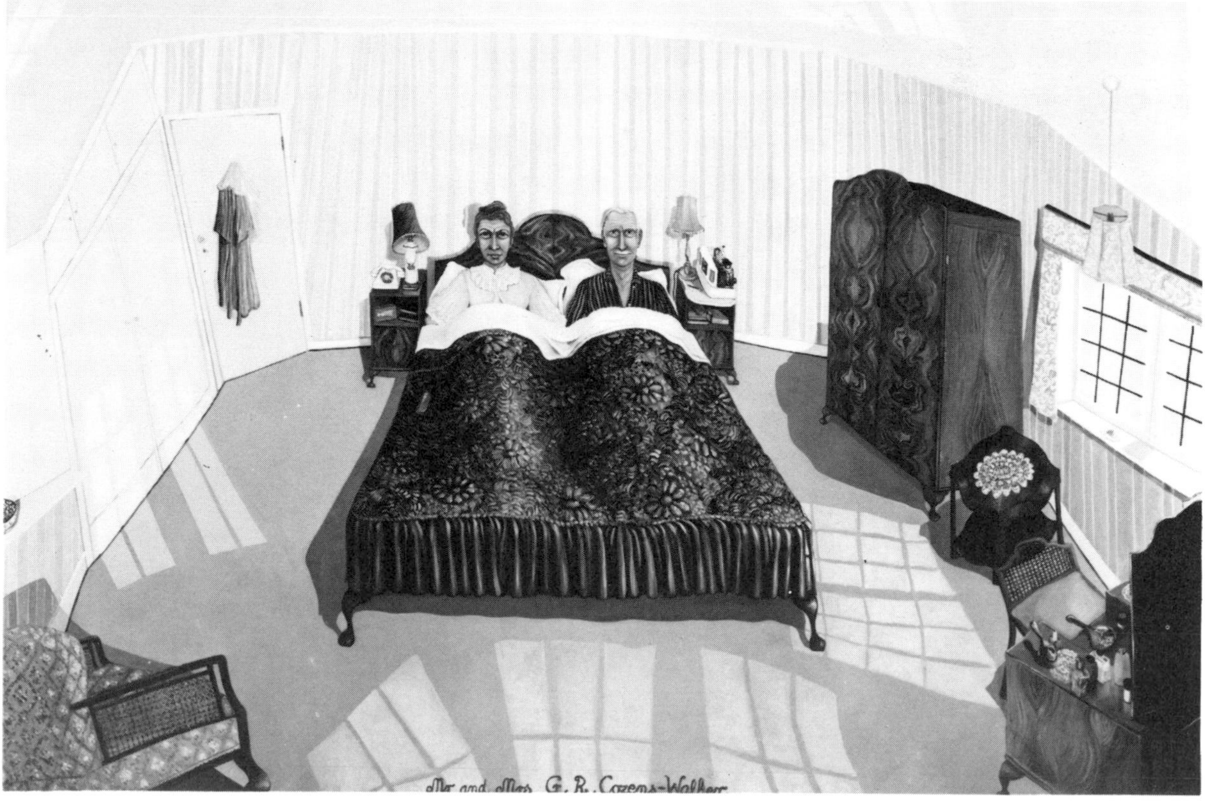

Anthony Green, Mr. and Mrs. Cozens-Walker 1972 oil on board 152.5 x 228.5 cm

Barry Flanagan Sculpture, November 1972

Michael Michaeledes, White Relief No. 5 1971
unprimed cotton duck 61 x 61 x 76 cm

Otto Freundlich, Composition (Paris) 1930
oil on canvas 130 x 97 cm

Friedrich Vordemberge-Gildewart, Komposition mit Reisschiene 1924
oil on board and assemblage 65 x 85 cm coll. Nationalgalerie, West Berlin

Annely Juda Fine Art *Continued*

1973

Jan–Feb	Paul van Hoeydonck Space Sculpture
March	Alan Green Paintings and Drawings
April	Amikam Toren Sculpture and Drawings
May–June	Cesar Domela Retrospective
July–Sept	The Non-Objective World 1914–1955
Sept–Oct	Gallery Artists
Nov–Dec	Pioneers of Abstract Painting in Belgium 1915–1930 De Boeck, Joostens, Servranckx
Dec–Jan	Friederich Werthmann Sculpture

Rowan Gallery *Continued*

1973

February	Graphics by Gallery Artists
March	Mark Lancaster Paintings
April	Gallery Artists
May	Jeremy Moon Paintings
June	Michael Craig-Martin Reflections
July	Barry Flanagan Sculpture
August	Gallery Artists
September	John Edwards Paintings
October	Phillip King Sculpture
November	Sean Scully Paintings

Sean Scully, East Coast Light I 1973 acrylic on cotton duck 226 x 254 cm

Amikam Toren Sculpture and Drawings
April 1973

Phillip King, Open Bound 1973
steel, aluminium, wood 167.8 x 366 x 366 cm
coll. Rijksmuseum Kröller-Müller, Otterlo, Holland

Jeremy Moon Paintings May 1973

The Non-Objective World 1914–1955 July–September 1973

Cesar Domela, Composition Neoplastique No. 5B 1926 oil on canvas 54 x 73 cm

Annely Juda Fine Art *Continued*

1974

Jan–Feb	Anthea Alley Sculpture
Feb–March	Jorge Stever Paintings
March–April	Don Kunkel Paintings and Drawings
April–May	Peter Kalkhof Paintings and Drawings
June	Charmion von Wiegand Retrospective
July–Sept	Vordemberge-Gildewart Remembered
October	Theatre – An exhibition of 20th Century theatrical designs and drawings arranged by Charles Spencer
Nov–Dec	Christo: Otterlo Mastaba, Project for the Rijksmuseum Kröller-Müller, Otterlo, Holland
	Christo Collages and Drawings

Rowan Gallery *Continued*

1974

January	Jeremy Moon Memorial Show
February	Martin Naylor Sculpture
March	John Golding Paintings
April–May	Michael Craig-Martin An Oak Tree
May	Gallery Artists
June	Anthony Green Paintings
July	Paul Huxley Paintings
October	Garth Evans Sculpture
November	Barry Flanagan Sculpture

Vordemberge-Gildewart Remembered, July–September 1974

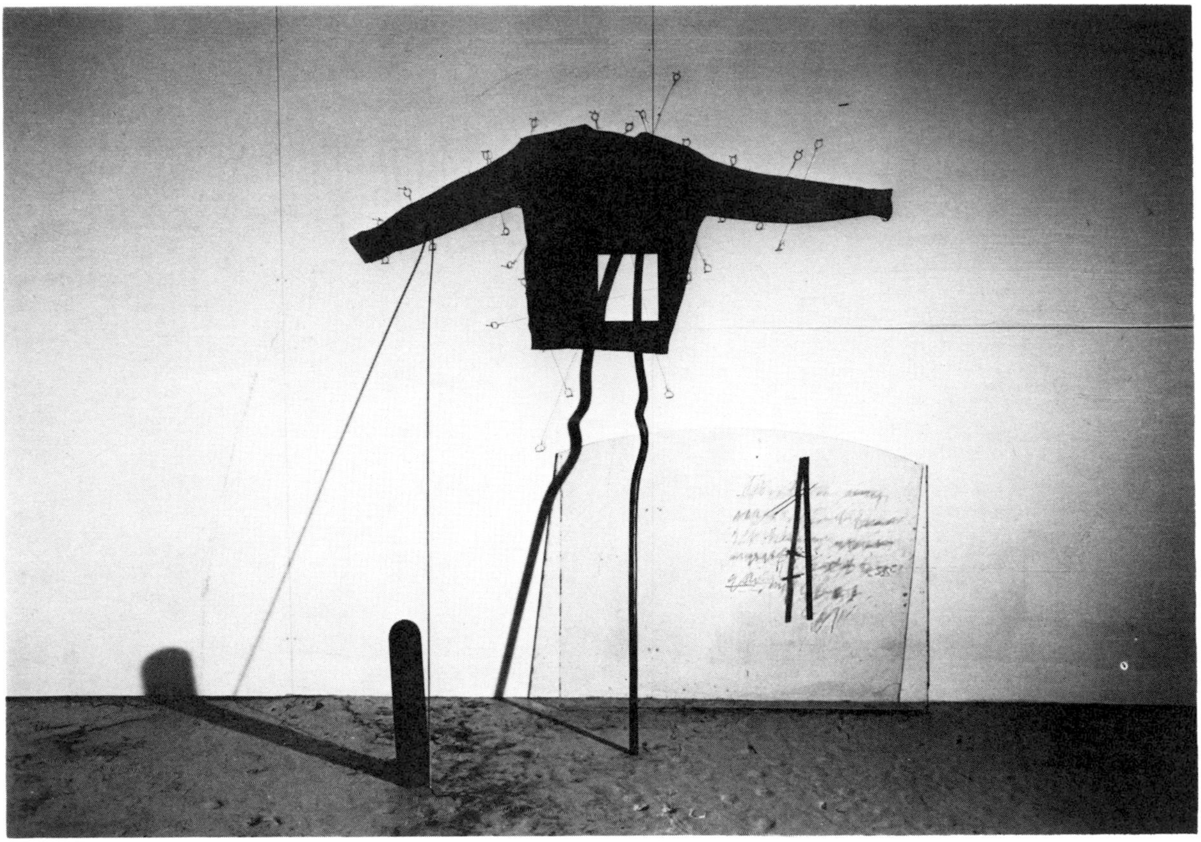

Martin Naylor, Discarded Sweater 1973 mixed media 218.5 x 205.8 x 82.5 cm

Charmion von Wiegand, Air Terminal 1954–5
oil on canvas 25 x 55 cm

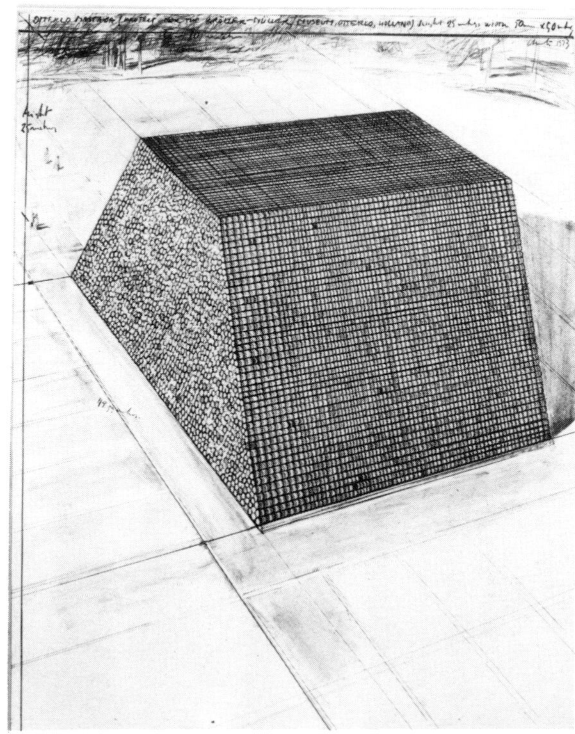

Christo, Otterlo Mastaba, project for the Rijksmuseum Kröller-Müller, Otterlo, Holland 1973
pencil, enamel paint, crayon and ink on paper 71 x 56 cm

Michael Craig-Martin, An Oak Tree 1973
glass, metal, water 12 x 30 x 15 cm
coll. National Gallery of Australia, Canberra

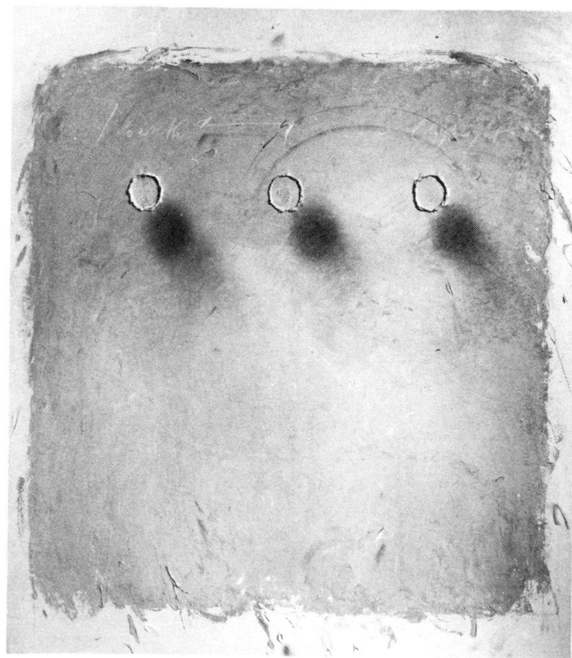

Jorge Stever, Untitled 1973
acrylic, oil on canvas and wood 161 x 141 x 7 cm

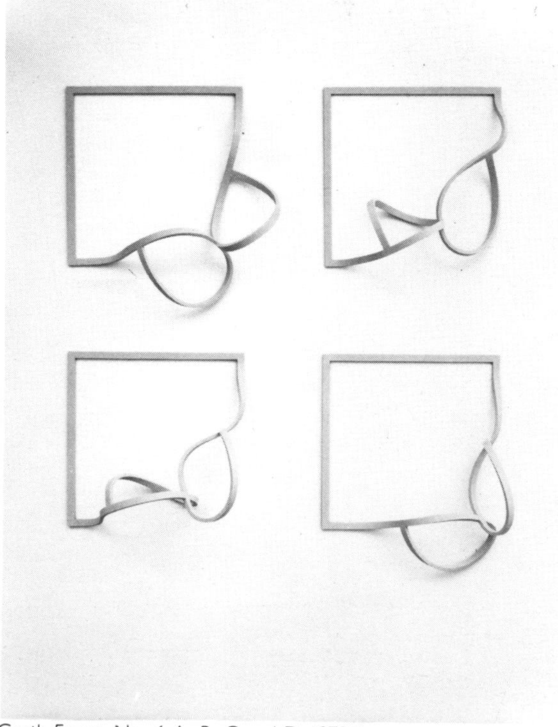

Garth Evans, No. 6 A, B, C and D 1973/4
painted wood 170 x 155 x 30.5 cm

Annely Juda Fine Art *Continued*

1975

January	Michael Werner Sculpture
February	Mixed Exhibition
March	Riccardo Guarneri, Giorgio Olivieri, Claudio Verna Paintings
April–May	Alan Green Paintings and Drawings
May–July	Russian Constructivism 'Laboratory Period' Reconstructions of Sculpture by the Sternberg Brothers
July	Gallery Artists
August	Joost Baljeu Twenty Years in Retrospect
Sept–Oct	Wendy Taylor Sculpture
Oct–Nov	Michael Michaeledes White Reliefs
December	Tony Underhill Figure and Landscape 1957–1975

Rowan Gallery *Continued*

1975

January	Tim Head Installation and Drawings
Feb–March	Phillip King Sculpture
April	Sean Scully Paintings
May	Martin Naylor Sculpture
June–July	John Edwards Paintings
July–Aug	Gallery Artists
September	Mark Lancaster Paintings
October	Michael Craig-Martin Neon Drawings
November	John Golding Paintings

Russian Constructivism 'Laboratory Period' 1919–21, May–July 1975

Alan Green Paintings and Drawings, April–May 1975

Tim Head Installation and Drawings, January 1975

John Edwards, Marco Polo 1975
acrylic on canvas 228.5 x 167.5 cm

Phillip King, Sculpture 1974
concrete, steel, steel mesh 254 x 315 x 175 cm

Claudio Verna, Pittura 1974
oil on canvas 140 x 180 cm

John Golding, D(CS) VI 1975 acrylic on cotton duck 183 x 244 cm
coll. The Arts Council of Great Britain

Reconstructions of Sculpture by the Stenberg brothers
May–July 1975

Joost Baljeu, Synthesist Construction R4 1955
painted wood 70 x 30 x 3 cm

Annely Juda Fine Art *Continued*

1976

January	Judith Rothschild Reliefs and Collages
February	Ulrich Erben Paintings and Works on Paper
March	Antonio Calderara Paintings and Watercolours 1959–1975
April–May	Ancient Art from Persia and Gallery Artists
June–Sept	Russian Pioneers at the Origins of Non-Objective Art
October	Alan Green Etchings 1973–1976
November	Edwina Leapman Paintings and Drawings
Dec–Jan	Mixed Christmas Exhibition and Gallery Artists

Rowan Gallery *Continued*

1976

Feb–March	Garth Evans Sculpture
March–April	Drawings by Gallery Artists
May–June	Anthony Green Paintings
June–July	Bridget Riley Paintings and Gouaches
August	Michael Craig-Martin Paintings
Sept–Oct	Gallery Artists
Nov–Dec	Tim Head Installation

Anthony Green with one of his paintings 1976

Bridget Riley, Shêng-tung 1974 acrylic on linen 96.5 x 229 cm

Edwina Leapman in her studio 1976

Liubov Popova, Pictorial Architectronic winter 1916–17 oil on canvas 105.5 x 70 cm
Russian Pioneers at the Origins of Non-Objective Art, June–September 1976

Annely Juda Fine Art *Continued*

1977

Jan–Feb	Peter Kalkhof Paintings and Drawings
March	Francois Morellet Paintings, Drawings and Objects 1954–1977
April	Jan J. Schoonhoven Reliefs and Drawings
May–June	Al Held Paintings and Drawings
July–Sept	The Suprematist Straight Line Malevich, Suetin, Chashnik, Lissitzky
October	Norman Dilworth Reliefs and Sculptures Malcolm Hughes Paintings and Drawings Peter Lowe Reliefs Jeffrey Steele Paintings and Drawings
November	Christo: Project for Wrapped Reichstag, Berlin
Dec–Jan	Friederich Werthmann Steelhenge 77

Rowan Gallery *Continued*

1977

Feb–March	Gallery Artists
April	Martin Naylor Sculpture
May	John Edwards Paintings
June	Phillip King Sculpture
July–Aug	Gallery Artists
September	Richard Kidd Paintings
October	John Golding Paintings
November	Sean Scully Paintings & Drawings

Al Heid with one of his paintings
Paintings and Drawings, May–June 1977

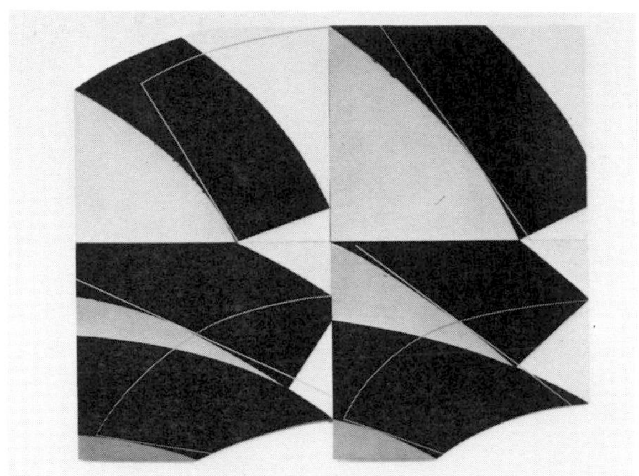

Richard Kidd, Of Things to Come 2 1977
acrylic on canvas 152.5 x 183.5 cm

Phillip King, Open Place 1977
slate and steel 332.8 x 597.8 x 683 cm
coll. National Gallery of Wales, Cardiff

Jan Schoonhoven, R77-7 relief
1977 82 x 61 cm

Christo with his scale model of the 'Wrapped Rechstag, Berlin' project, 1977

The Suprematist Straight Line, Malevich, Suetin, Chashnik, Lissitzky, June–September 1977

Annely Juda Fine Art *Continued*

1978

February	Alan Reynolds Reliefs and Drawings
March	Michael Kenny Sculpture and Drawings
April	Nancy Genn Handmade Paper Works Paul Rotterdam Drawings
May	Nigel Hall Sculpture and Drawings
June	Hans Hinterreiter A Theory of Form and Colour
July–Sept	The Non-Objective World Twenty Five Years 1914–1939
October	Alan Green Paintings, Panels, Drawings and Prints
Nov–Jan	The Twenties in Berlin: Johannes Baader, George Grosz, Raoul Hausmann, Hannah Hoch

Rowan Gallery *Continued*

1978

February	Jeremy Moon Paintings 1962–64
March	Julian Hawkes Sculpture
April	Tim Head Present, Installation and Photographs
June	Anthony Green Paintings
July–Aug	Garth Evans Sculpture
August	Gallery Sculptors
Sept–Oct	Paul Huxley Paintings
Oct–Nov	Michael Craig-Martin Wall Drawings
Nov–Dec	Martin Naylor New Work 'A View Beyond the City'

Johannes Baader, Der Mutter collage 11.5 x 16.4 cm
The Twenties in Berlin, Baader, Grosz, Hausmann, Hoch
November 1978–January 1979

Hannah Hoch, Staatshäupter 1918–20 collage 15.8 x 23.5 cm
The Twenties in Berlin, Baader, Grosz, Hausmann, Hoch
November 1978–January 1979

The Non-Objective World 1914–1939, June–September 1978

Tim Head, Present, Installation and Photographs
April 1978

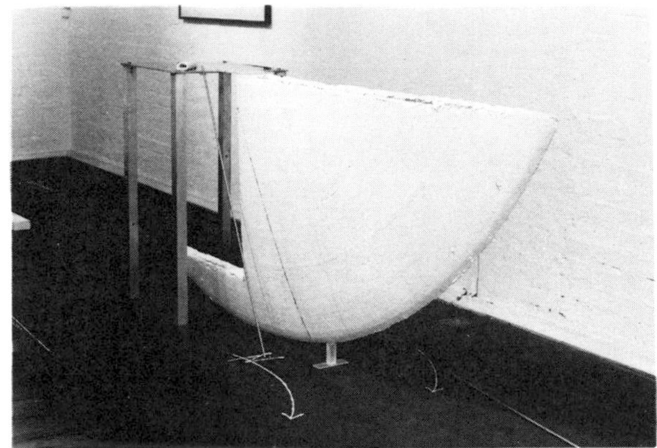

Michael Kenny, . . .Also Wounded by Love 1977/8
steel, wood, resin and aluminium 104 x 157 x 305 cm

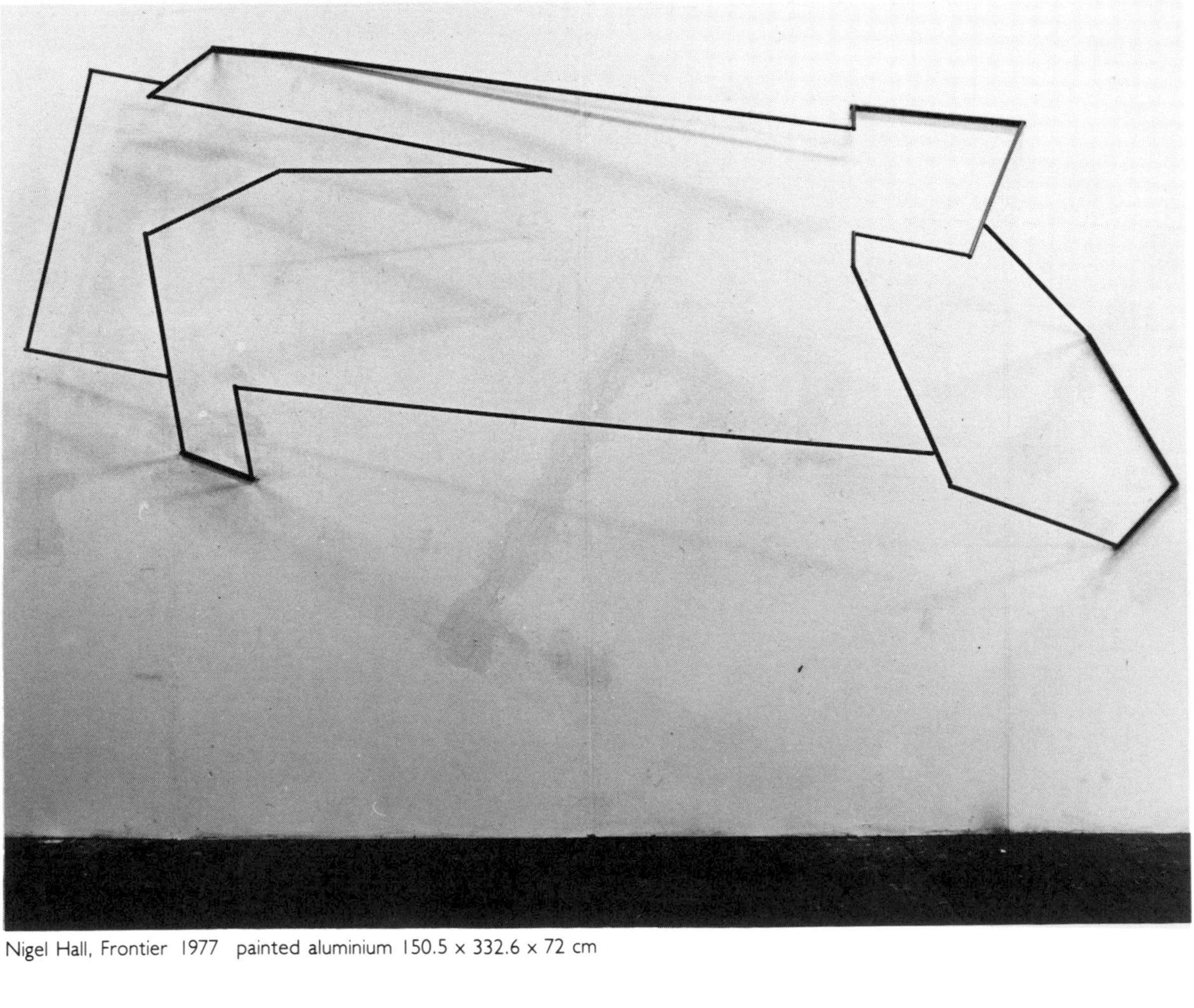

Nigel Hall, Frontier 1977 painted aluminium 150.5 x 332.6 x 72 cm

Julian Hawkes, Nexus 1976
leather, steel, stone and rope 167.8 x 205 x 61 cm

Martin Naylor, Important Mischief 1978
mixed media 208.2 x 360.5 x 216 cm

Alan Reynolds in his studio 1978

Annely Juda Fine Art *Continued*

1979

February	June Green Drawings, Jeff Hellyer Painted Panels, Colin Nicholas Sculpture, Trevor Sutton Paintings
March	El Lissitzky Chad Gadya and Four Mathematical Processes
April–May	Christo: Wrapped Walk Ways, Kansas City
May–June	Gottfried Honegger Paintings and Drawings
July–Sept	Line + Movement Mondrian, van Doesburg, van der Leck, Vantongerloo, Vordemberge-Gildewart, Domela and Moholy-Nagy
Oct–Nov	Peter Kalkhof Paintings and Drawings
Dec–Jan	Michael Werner Assemblage and Sculpture

Rowan Gallery *Continued*

1979

Feb–March	Richard Kidd Paintings
April	Phillip King Sculpture
May	John Edwards Paintings
June	Antony Donaldson Sculpture
July	Jeremy Moon Paintings 1966–67
Aug–Sept	Sean Scully Paintings
October	John Golding Paintings
Nov–Dec	Keith Milow Sculpture

Gottfried Honegger Paintings and Drawings, May–June 1979

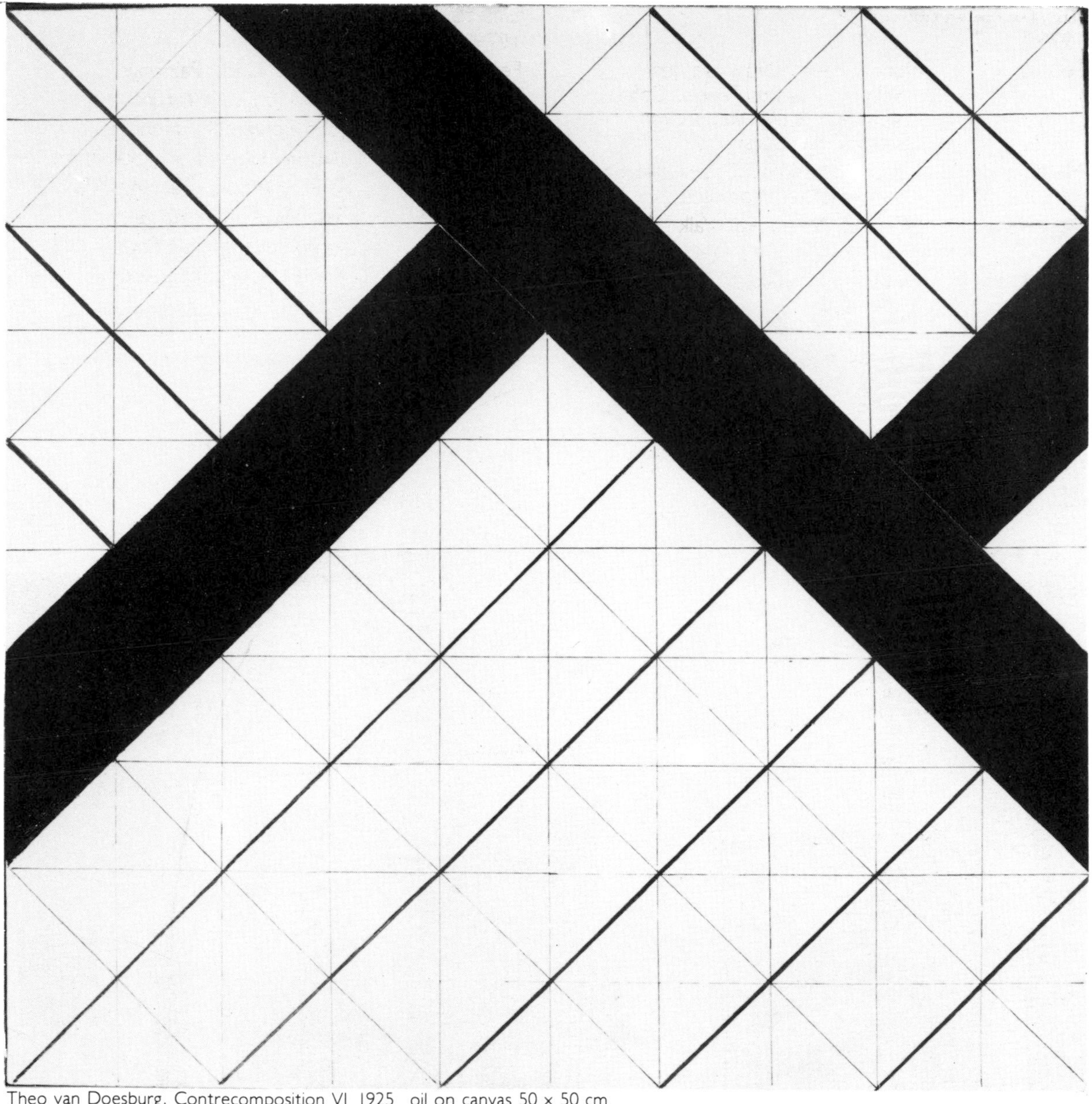

Theo van Doesburg, Contrecomposition VI 1925 oil on canvas 50 × 50 cm
Line + Movement, June–September 1979 coll. The Tate Gallery, London

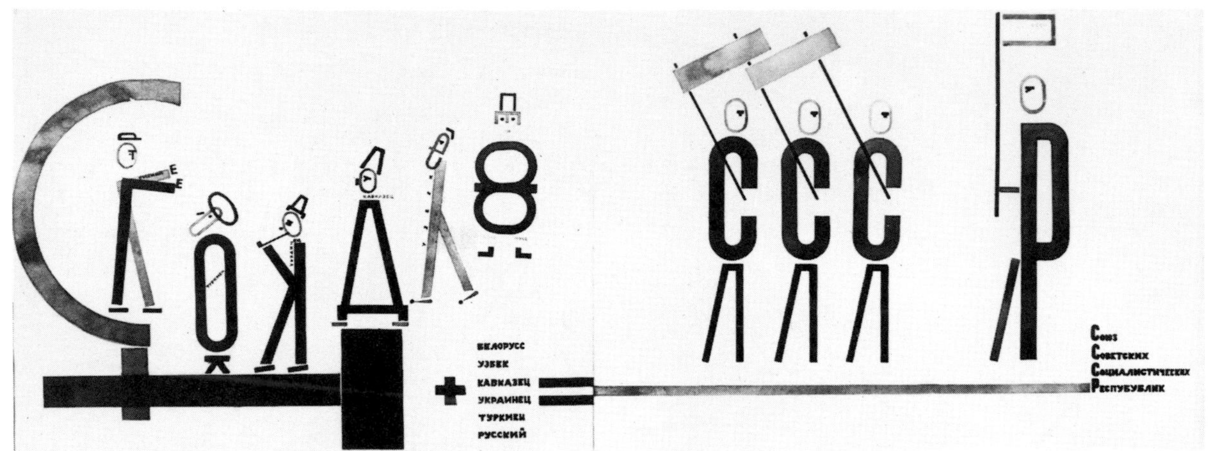

El Lissitzky, The Four Mathematical Processes 1928 pencil and gouache on paper 24.5 x 63.5 cm

El Lissitzky, Chad Gadya c. 1917 'A Dog Came and Ate the Cat' watercolour on paper 28 x 23 cm coll. Tel Aviv Museum, Israel

El Lissitzky, Chad Gadya c. 1917 'A Cat Came and Killed the Kid' watercolour on paper 28 x 23 cm coll. Tel Aviv Museum, Israel

Sean Scully Paintings, August–September 1979

John Golding, G(M.B.) IX 1979
acrylic on cotton duck 152.5 x 243.8 cm

John Edwards, Wild fire 1977
acrylic on canvas 183 x 167.5 cm

Richard Kidd, Still Inside 1978
acrylic and graphite on cotton duck 122 x 117 cm

Annely Juda Fine Art *Continued*

1980

February	Patrick Scott Paintings and Screens
March	Noriyuki Haraguchi Sculptures and Drawings
April–May	Al Held Recent Paintings
May–June	Eight + Eight Alan Green, Nigel Hall, Peter Kalkhof, Michael Kenny, Edwina Leapman, Michaeledes, Alan Reynolds, Michael Werner Norman Dilworth, June Green, Jeff Hellyer, Malcolm Hughes, Peter Lowe, Colin Nicholas, Jeffrey Steele, Trevor Sutton
July–Sept	Abstraction 1910–1940
October	Yoshikuni Iida Sculpture and Drawings
November	Edwina Leapman Paintings and Drawings
Dec–Jan	Accrochage Exhibition

Rowan Gallery *Continued*

1980

Jan–Feb	Gallery Artists
March	Michael Craig-Martin Wall Drawings
April	Martin Naylor Drawings
May–June	Julian Hawkes Sculpture
July	Mark Lancaster Paintings
Aug–Sept	Richard Kidd Paintings
October	Paul Huxley Paintings
November	Garth Evans Drawings

Paul Huxley, Paintings, October 1980

Michael Craig-Martin Wall Drawings, March 1980

Julian Hawkes Sculpture, May–June 1980

Yoshikuni Iida, Hexahedron-Rokumentai 2 1980
lead, stainless steel, coloured nylon rope 190 x 220 x 25 cm

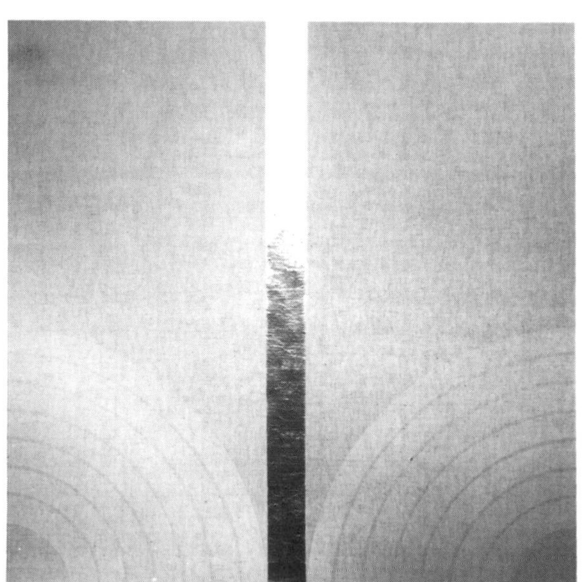
Patrick Scott Paintings and Screens
January–March 1980

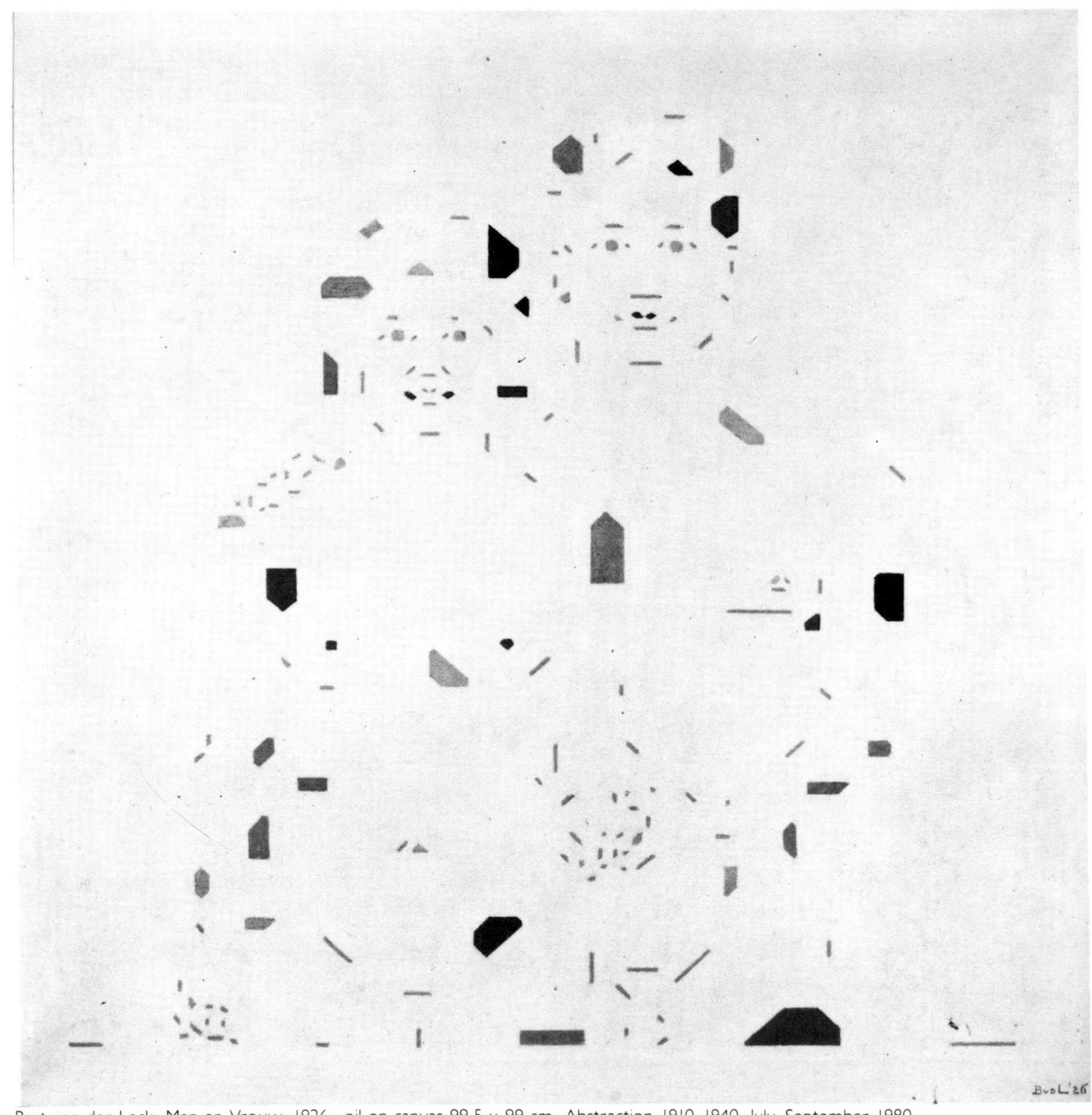

Bart van der Leck, Man en Vrouw 1926 oil on canvas 99.5 x 99 cm Abstraction 1910–1940, July–September 1980

Annely Juda Fine Art

1981

Jan–Feb

March–April

April–May

June

July–Sept

Oct–Nov

Nov–Dec

owan Gallery *Continued*

981

ʻeb–March	John Edwards Small Works
ꜛpril	Sean Scully Paintings
ʼlay	Antony Donaldson Paintings
ıne	Bridget Riley Paintings and Gouaches
ıly	Anthony Green Paintings
ꜛug–Sept	Gallery Artists
)ct–Nov	Martin Naylor Paintings
ɩov–Dec	John Golding Works on Paper

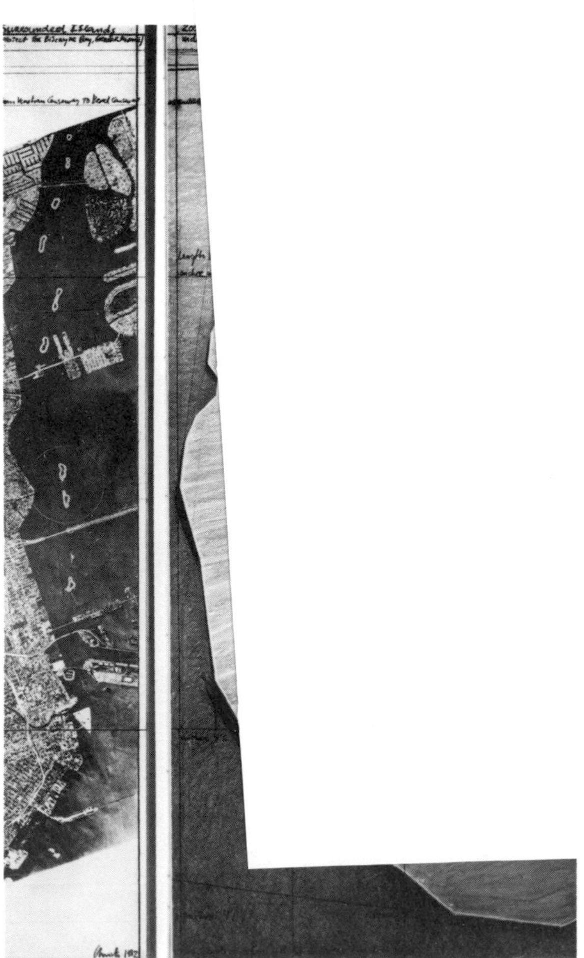

Christo, Surrounded Islands (project for Biscayne Bay, Greater Miami, Florida) 1981 2-part collage 244 x 38 cm, 244 x 106.5 cm

Sean Scully with his paintings, 1981

John McLaughlin Paintings 1950–1975, April–May 1981

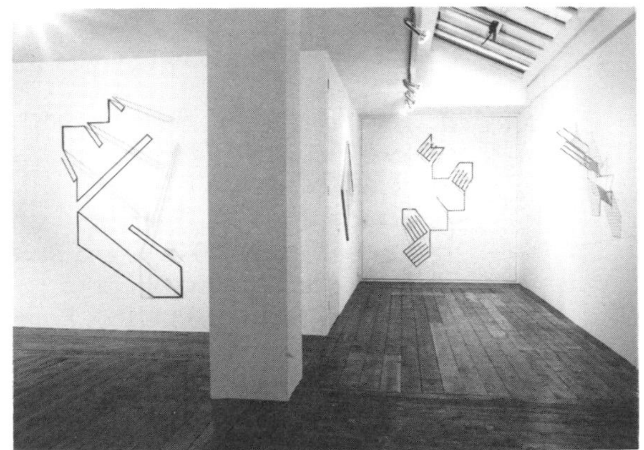

Nigel Hall Sculpture and Drawings, November–December 1981

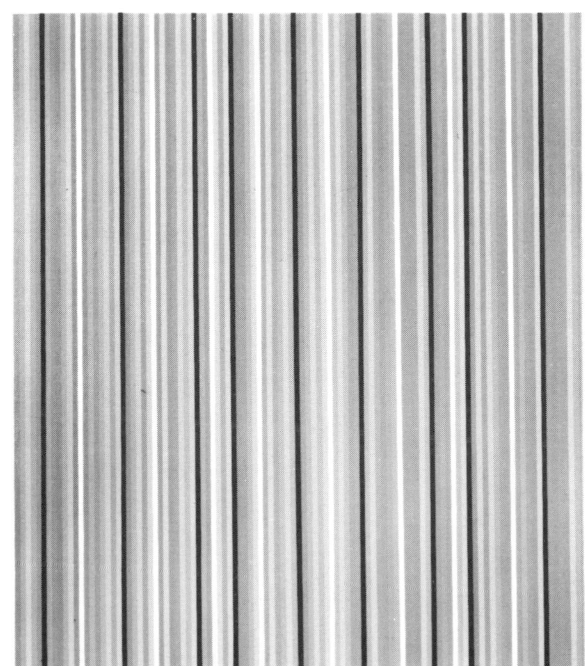

Bridget Riley, Achaian 1981
oil on linen 238.8 x 202.5 cm
coll. The Tate Gallery, London

Anthony Green, L'Heure du Thé – Argenton sur Creuse, Départment de l'Indre 1980 oil on board 198 x 221 cm
coll. The Tate Gallery, London

Judith Rothschild, Ogygia XV 1980
relief painting 76.2 x 101.6 cm

Tatlin Reconstructions, Configuration 1910–1940 and Seven Tatlin Reconstructions July–September 1981

Al Heid Recent Paintings
February–March 1982

Piet Mondrian, Composition 1927 oil on canvas 50 x 35 cm
Configuration 1910–1940 and Seven Tatlin Reconstructions, July–September 1981

1982

May–June	Robert Michel Collages 1918–1930
July–Sept	Collages and Reliefs 1910–1945 and Hiller Heliographs
Nov–Dec	Henryk Stazewski Paintings and Reliefs

Juda Rowan Gallery

1982

February	Al Held Recent Paintings
March	Alan Reynolds Reliefs, Constructions and Drawings
April	Alan Green Recent Paintings and Drawings
May	Gallery Artists
June	Jeremy Moon Paintings and Drawings from 1968
July–Sept	Gallery Artists
October	Michael Michaeledes Shaped Canvas Reliefs and Works on Paper
Nov–Dec	Paul Huxley Recent Paintings

Michael Michaeledes
Shaped Canvas Reliefs and Works on Paper, October 1982

Paul Huxley Recent Paintings, November–December 1982

Alan Green Recent Paintings and Drawings, April 1982

Alan Reynolds Structures – Group II (U) 1981 relief construction – prepared card on wood base 117 x 117 x 1.5 cm

Jeremy Moon, 17/68 1968
acrylic on canvas 122 x 137 cm

Henryk Stazewski, White-Black
oil on wood relief 57 x 56.8 cm

Robert Michel, Untitled 1923–24
pencil, ink, wash and collage 42.5 x 47 cm

Giacomo Balla, Linea di Velocita + Paesaggio 1915 collage 35 x 28 cm
Collages and Reliefs 1910–1945 and Hiller Heliographs July–Sept. 1982

Karol Hiller, Composition 1939 heliograph 30.6 x 20.8 cm
Collages and Reliefs 1910–1945 and Hiller Heliographs July–Sept. 1982

Annely Juda Fine Art *Continued*

1983

Sept–Nov — The First Russian Show
A Commemoration of the van Diemen Exhibition, Berlin 1922

Martin Naylor, Between D & D (Rites of Passage) 1982
pastel, pencil, oil and ink on paper 204.5 x 101.5 cm

Juda Rowan Gallery *Continued*

1983

Feb–March — Juda Rowan Gallery's Selection from Tokyo Gallery
Minoru Kawabata, Lee U-Fan, Yoshishige Saito

March–April — Peter Kalkhof Recent Paintings
Martin Naylor Works on Paper Paris 1982

April–May — Noriyuki Haraguchi Sculpture and Drawings
Malcolm Hughes Work in Progress

June — Gottfried Honegger Paintings and Drawings
Phillip King Sculpture

July–Aug — Bridget Riley Gouaches

September — Gallery Artists

October — Julian Hawkes Sculpture

Nov–Dec — Richard Kidd Work done in New York 1982–1983

Julian Hawkes, Lovelock 1982–83
sandstone, oak and powder colour 17.8 x 25 x 28 cm

Saito, Triangularly 1982 painted wood and bolts 280 x 460 x 360 cm coll. Rijksmuseum Kröller-Müller, Otterlo, Holland

Bridget Riley Gouaches, July–August 1983

Peter Kalkhof Recent Paintings, March–April 1983

The First Russian Show, A Commemoration of the van Diemen Exhibition Berlin 1922, September–December 1983

Noriyuki Haraguchi, Untitled No. 6 1983
paper and copper 113.5 x 85 x 28.5 cm

Phillip King, Head 1982/3
painted steel 221 x 237 x 223 cm

Alexandra Exter, Composition 1916 oil on canvas 78.5 x 59.5 cm
The First Russian Show. A Commemoration of the van Dieman Exhibition Berlin 1922, September–December 1983

Annely Juda Fine Art *Continued*

1984

May–June	Ella Bergmann-Michel Collages and Drawings 1917–1931
Sept–Dec	Dada-Constructivism, The Janus Face of the Twenties

Juda Rowan Gallery *Continued*

1984

February	John Edwards Recent Paintings and Works on Paper Garth Evans Recent Wall Sculpture
March	Michael Kenny Sculpture, Reliefs and Drawings Bridget Riley Dance Boxes
April	John Golding Recent Paintings and Drawings Martyn Chalk Reliefs and Drawings
May	Antony Donaldson Sculpture
June	Anthony Green Recent Paintings and Drawings
July–Aug	Christo Objects, Collages and Drawings 1958–1984
Sept–Oct	Five Sculptors Garth Evans, June Green, Nigel Hall, Phillip King, George Meyrick
Nov–Dec	Sean Scully Paintings and Drawings

Sean Scully Paintings and Drawings, November–December 1984

John Golding, SH 5 (Ming) 1984
mixed media on cotton duck 122 × 152.5 cm

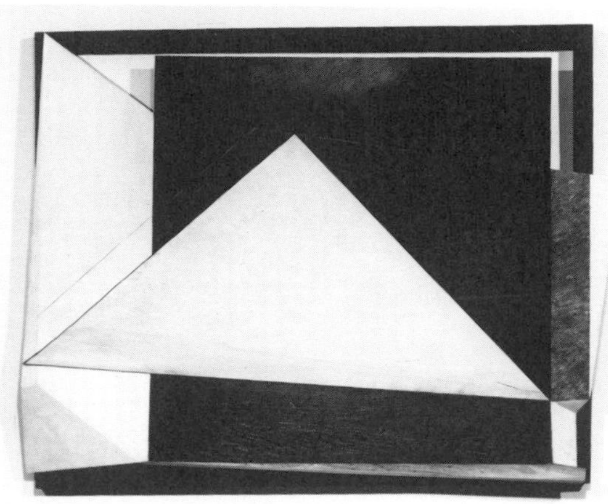

Martyn Chalk, White Triangle Black Square 1983
gesso and paint on wood and oil treated steel 72.5 × 93 × 8 cm

Christo Objects. Collages and Drawings 1958–1984, July–September 1984

Michael Kenny Sculpture, Reliefs and Drawings
March 1984

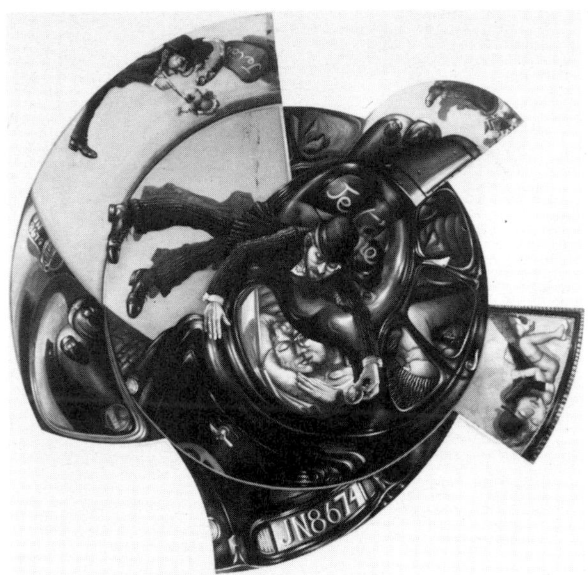

Anthony Green, JN 8674, Kissing and Cuddling 1983–84
oil on board, diam. 198.2 cm

Garth Evans, Canal No. 33 1982
laminated wood 77.5 x 44.5 x 26 cm

Antony Donaldson, Four 1984
bronze, stone, plastic, oil paint 22.5 x 41 x 34

Theo van Doesburg, Dadasophie 1920 poster for Dada Soirée made together with Kurt Schwitters 30.2 x 30 cm
Dada – Constructivism, September–December 1984

Annely Juda Fine Art/Juda Rowan Gallery *Continued*

1985

February	Small Works
March–April	Nigel Hall Sculpture and Drawings
May–June	Judith Rothschild Collages
July–Aug	Alan Green Recent Paintings and Drawings

Juda Rowan Gallery *Continued*

1985

Sept–Dec	Annely Juda Fine Art–Juda Rowan Gallery 25 Years Masterpieces of the Avantgarde and Three Decades of Contemporary Art, The 60's, 70's and 80's

Nigel Hall in his studio 1985

Alan Green with his paintings 1985

Nigel Hall Recent Sculpture and Drawings, March–April 1985

Alan Green Recent Paintings and Drawings, July–August 1985

Masterpieces of the Avantgarde

ASPECTS OF MODERNISM
radical art in Annely Juda Fine Art exhibitions

We are only beginning to understand Russian Modernism, the most profound, the most radical and in several respects also to this day, the most challenging chapter in the history of modern art. The subject is still screened from us by gaps in our knowledge and by the inaccessability of key works, in spite of all the research and in spite of the paintings and other things that have become visible in the West, in permanent public collections (a fine Malevich in the Tate, the Hack collection in Ludwigshafen, etc.) and in exhibitions such as the 1979 'Paris-Moscou' show at the Pompidou Centre and Annely Juda's sequence of major historical exhibitions, starting with 'The Non-Objective World 1914–1924' in 1970. In 1971 'Art in Revolution' at the Hayward Gallery provided a great contextualising experience for Russian Revolutionary art, with vivid displays of architecture, typography, textiles and theatre design, and a vast model of Tatlin's *Monument to the Third International* erected on one of the sculpture courts, looming over Waterloo Bridge.

Where information is concerned things have changed a great deal in the last fifteen years. In 1962, when Camilla Gray published *The Great Experiment: Russian Art 1863–1922*, we leapt on it with excitement and gratitude but came away with an infinity of questions. The cut-off point itself was unsatisfactory. 1922 was the year of voluntary and involuntary emigration from the Soviet Union by many intellectuals. Camilla Gray's ending on it suggests that her information and in some measure her sympathy for her subject ended there. 1922 was also the year, as Annely Juda's show of 1983 reminded us, in which Russian Modernism came West in the form of the '1st Russian Show' in Berlin and Amsterdam, and in the even livelier form of El Lissitzky, cultural activist extraordinary, busying himself in Central Europe until 1925. The subsequent story of the Soviet government's rejection of what seems to us the most brilliant and also ideologically apt artistic contributions to the Revolution has in the end given the subject a false glamour in western eyes. The Hayward exhibition was reviewed in the daily press more in terms of what could not be shown than of what was there. The issue feels less loaded today. There seems to have been some relaxation on the Soviet side; there has certainly been much sympathetic enquiry on ours. It may not be long before Russia opens up her treasury of works and documents and lets us benefit from the close research into the art and design of the period that has long been pursued by scholars in Moscow and Leningrad. The (literally) obscene will at last take the centre of the stage.

But there is one kind of screening that we ourselves could help to remove and should take the lead in removing. Western interest in the subject has had its characteristic admixture of colonialism. Marvellous what those Russsian fellows did in the years before and after the Revolution, but of course they had busied themselves studying modern art in the West, in many cases actually spending months and years in Paris and other centres, sending and bringing back home information of all sorts. And didn't those Moscow tycoons, Shchukin and Morosov build up their great collections of Post-Impressionism, Fauvism and Cubism? So Russian Modernism was a growth out of the cultural stew of Paris . . . with a touch of Whitman and William Morris and Theosophy thrown in, plus the Yankee dream of a great technological leap forward. That well-known photograph of Grosz and Heartfield in the Berlin Dada exhibition, holding a placard saying 'Art is dead. Long live the machine art of Tatlin' sums it up. Tatlin=Picasso in 1913+the technological dream. Russian Modernism is seen as a growth – by some as an extravagant, false growth – out of the Modernism of Paris, and in praising it we often seem to be praising ourselves.

Malevich's *Head of a Peasant* represents his first maturity. He has come out of Russian Symbolism, and has been impressed by the Gauguins and Matisses available to him in Moscow. He is a member of the circle around Larionov, then leader of a primitivizing movement in Moscow art, and he is especially close to Gontcharova. Larionov's primitivism takes him close to a Dubuffet-like *art brut*; Gontcharova and Malevich turn to the muscular, solemn traditions of Russian religious painting, murals and icons. These traditions had in some measure survived among the schismatic sects, suppressed yet powerful, that had formed in the seventeenth century, survived as pockets of resistance to Russian authority and were currently under renewed attack at the behest of the leaders of the Orthodox Church. But the last decades of the nineteenth century had also seen artists working as archaeologists to rediscover, uncover, clean, repair, record these traditions of church art which were also very much Russian traditions, close to the heart of true Russian-ness. Western influence had done its best to terminate them by imposing a veneer of classicism and realism, but by about 1910 many Russians had come to see the future of their country's art as held by those traditions more than by western ways. In 1911 the great leader of Paris Modernism, Matisse, announced to the Moscow art world that Russian icon painting was superior to anything the West had to offer. In 1912 Kandinsky's *On the Spiritual in Art* and the *Blaue Reiter Almanach* offered a global view of art and art's true purposes that ignored the Renaissance and its aftermath. In 1913 Moscow saw a great exhibition of icon painting in celebration of 1613 when the Romanov dynasty was established and in celebration of a Russia not yet divided by church reforms and by Peter the Great's dictatorial imposition of western ways.

Malevich exhibited paintings of this sort in 1911–12: peasants, a peasant funeral, peasants in church, also paintings he called *Saints*. He was turning away from more urban and socially uncertain themes such as the *Argentine Polka* and also from a partly Fauvist way of painting to a firmer but also ungraceful style that makes his figures look as though they were assembled of bits of cones and cylinders. In this new manner he goes on portraying peasants, individual figures in close-up, peasants in the fields and the village, peasants at work. Malevich said later that he and Gontcharova had been working with a social purpose or programme. This would be clear from his images anyway. Hers, though even more visibly indebted to church traditions, tended towards a classical, decorative, less affirmative character. His look like polemics, especially if one knows that blessing oneself with two fingers instead of three brought down the anathema of the Orthodox Church upon the so-called Old Believers, and if one has hearkened to the political and social ambitions associated with the Populist movement of the second half of the nineteenth century. That *Woodcutter's* axe says revolution.

The blotchy technique of *Head of a Peasant* is part Fauvist but also suggests the (Fauvism-inspired) technique of Kandinsky, whose work was frequently seen in Russia. In 1912 Malevich sent another fine head to the Blaue Reiter exhibition in Munich. In his titles he uses the word *krestyanin* (peasant), *krestyanka* (peasant woman) etc., echoing words almost identical but not from the same root that mean Christian: *khristianin*, *khristianka*. He is reiterating in his images the well-established association of the Russian peasant with piety and profound human virtues, and thus representing an item of faith that has been marked among Russians since the days of Alexander Herzen: national renewal will come from the adoption of rural ethics and rural forms of communal self-government. Tolstoy had recently given priority to peasant values in his well-publicized moral and aesthetic homilies, denying even the name of art to the highbrow masterpieces he had himself loved and learned from. *What is Art?* (1890) is a blunt statement that what is not art to the populace cannot be art to anyone. His death in 1910 brought renewed discussion of his uncomfortable doctrines. Malevich's peasant subjects show him representing the Russian peasant, especially the Old Believer peasant, untarnished by westernism and remote from capitalism, as possessor of essential truths. Some of those peasant families, like sectarian groups in the West, had meanwhile become eminent enough through industriousness and discipline, emerging in the cities as leading industrialists. The Morosovs, for example, were not only rich art collectors. They supported liberal cultural work of several kinds, and a religious-philosophical debating society. In addition they provided funds for revolutionary work behind the scenes.

All this is written into Malevich's peasant subjects, as well as the Old Believers' additional role as protectors of the pre-Schismatic canons of icon painting, undisturbed by the western forms that began to creep into Russian church art even in the seventeenth century. They denounced any departure from those canons as the work of Antichrist, come to destroy Russia's God-appointed role as the Third Rome, last guardian of the true faith ever since Constantinople, weakened by *rapprochements* with western Christianity, had fallen to the Turks in 1453. They recognised as icons only those adhering to the old canons, and had gone on commissioning them from craftsmen-painters who existed quite separately from the world of high art. Malevich places the head of his peasant in imitation of that most popular of Russian icon types, invented in Russia and expressing a Russian need for informality and sweetness, the *Virgin of Vladimir*, who inclines her head to that of the Christ child and to us and offers herself as mother and intercessor. It was a miracle-working icon, then to be seen in one of the Kremlin churches but familiar everywhere through an infinity of copies.

Later Malevich was to designate his *Black Square* an icon and to display it as an icon in his section of the 'Zero-Ten' exhibition in Petrograd (1915–16). He saw this milestone painting as a symbolic object, standing between our world and the world of the spirit, and he implied that that spiritual world, into which he wished his art to lead mankind, was of an essentially religious nature. His mystical bent is clear also from his writings. What needs stressing is that mysticism, Christian or otherwise, was widespread among his contemporaries, including those of the left. Lenin's repeated assaults on it is evidence of its strength. Mysticism was central to Russian Symbolism and had found its finest and most influential expression in the poetry, lectures and books of Vladimir Soloviev, who had died in 1900; it was fuelled by western and oriental influences among which Theosophy is now the best known. Mysticism was of the left, Marxist, associated with new theories in physics and in mathematics as well as with utopian visions of space travel and a deathless human race possessing the universe. It was equally of the right, the radical right that sought to clear Christian thought of the sophistication of centuries and return to a primitive belief capable of uniting the world.

It was, probably in this second form, the mental habitat of Alexei Yavlensky (Jawlensky), born into the military nobility and himself a graduate of a military academy. In 1896 he left the army with the rank of captain and moved to Munich to devote himself wholly to painting. There he got to know Kandinsky, who had made the same move in the same year. Yavlensky's painting of a head nicknamed *Black Mouth* was done in 1917. Having to leave Germany at the start of the war, Yavlensky had gone to Switzerland, and in 1917 he was

Kasimir Malevich, Head of a Peasant 1910/11
gouache on cardboard 46 x 46 cm

Alexej Jawlensky, Black Mouth 1917
oil on board 40 x 30 cm

in Zurich. There he began his long series of heads, starting from simplified portraits and developing into more or less abstract images for contemplation and meditation, some of them titled 'heads of saints' and even 'heads of the Saviour'. 1917 saw his turning from the earthly focus to the mystical, the moment when the painter recognized and accepted the transcendental direction of his vision.

Both paintings, the Malevich and the Yavlensky, exhibit the underlying geometry and the dematerialization that mark the icon tradition. Yavlensky's historical association with Expressionism, principally because of where he worked, has tended to obscure this fact. Colour used non-descriptively does inevitably take on expressive force, and colour determined neither by appearances nor by a system of representation can be said to reveal the painter's emotion or vision. But neither Yavlensky in Germany and Switzerland, nor Malevich in Russia (nor, for that matter Kandinsky in Munich, Moscow, Weimar or Paris) should be seen as concerned primarily or prominently with emotional self-revelation nor with revealing the world as an individual experience. Tolstoy, in *What is Art?* appears to have given the directive for their art:

> To evoke in oneself a feeling one has experienced, and having evoked it, then by means of movement, lines, colours, sounds or forms expressed in word, so to transmit that feeling that others experience the same feeling – this is the activity of art.

That too may sound like a recipe for Expressionism, but Tolstoy's text taken as a whole is unambiguous: the feeling he refers to is a perception of the spiritual life of the time, not a private emotion, let alone a mood. The function of art is to unite mankind on the spiritual plane; individuality counts because personal conviction has an affective power that results in the 'infectiousness' which Tolstoy sees as the essential characteristic of true art. He associated this with the charged realism he found in the work of the Wanderers, that break-away group from the academies whose art became prominent during the 1880s and 1890s; one of them, Nikolai Ghe (Gay) was a particularly close and valued disciple. Malevich and Yavlensky, like Kandinsky, rejected Tolstoy's identification of realism as the only method of effective communication, but they consciously or unconsciously accepted the position taken by the great novelist-prophet.

Comparison of the two paintings reveals significant similarities in addition to the common debt to icon painting. But also differences, among which the most obvious could be seen as a difference in class reference: Malevich's head is that of a peasant, whereas Yavlensky's, not allocated in the title (which refers only to the black brushstroke representing the lips), suggests a woman of some elegance and thus perhaps *une bourgeoise*. Certainly Yavlensky's series springs from studies of women of his acquaintance. But this head, and others, suggest a reference also to exotic models, seen or imagined, and this head could be the head of, say, an Indian woman and an ordinary, peasant, woman at that, thus losing every class connotation. Style, as folk traditions everywhere demonstrate, is not the privilege of the privileged. Seen as an informal assembly of clear geometrical forms, the Yavlensky head is strikingly similar to Brancusi's head sculptures from about 1912 on, 'muses' and *Mlle Pogany*, and these certainly embody references to the Orient. In any case, it is incontrovertably the case that Malevich, Yavlensky and Kandinsky, and those who can be categorized as their disciples, looked inward in order to reach a reality that is transpersonal and superpersonal and reaches far beyond the egotism that is the source of Expressionist art.

German Expressionism too deserves more delicate, distinguishing enquiry than it has met with so far, but falls outside the scope of this essay. This being so, any reference to Klee's painting *Voice from Space* may seem

Paul Klee, Voice from Space 1939
oil and tempera on paper 50.5 x 38 cm
By courtesy of the Board of Trustees of the Victoria and Albert Museum, London

extravagant, though Klee's diversity has protected him against too absolute and readymade classifying. The picture's title itself asks us to consider it in the context of Malevich; it could be rendered 'voice from the ether' and thus have a stronger sense of the mystery of space. Klee's additional inscription, 'und du sollst dich satt essen' (and you shall eat your fill), sounds Biblical and remains mysterious though the thought also arises, this being Klee, that he may be playing with the gaunt and anxious face he has conjured up out of oil and tempera on the paper, and punning on those Ss on the right. The letter 'S' is said in German as much as in English – 'es' – and its plural could well be 'essen', which also means 'eat'. Pivoting art between humour and distress is a Klee speciality, as characteristic of him as his magical way of creating a telling image out of minimal resources. Heads are fairly common among his vast output. Some of them are specific, many of these starting from his own face. Some are types. Like Picasso, Klee knew that almost anything can become a face: any outline almost, containing forms that, however distantly, can be taken to hint at eyes, nose and mouth, placed almost anywhere within the outline, will be read as a face. This one is an image made of fat, coarse brushstrokes, like many of Klee's last years. Here, the vertical stroke on the left suggests that Klee did not set out to construct a face but that a face arose and ended by imposing itself, in spite of that unfacial element. We almost ignore it; the moment we begin to question the aptness of Klee's marks as components of a face the entire image threatens to disintegrate before our eyes. No part of it seems capable of securing the whole. Instead, the parts dissociate themselves the moment we focus on them, and start suggesting other possible images, a bowl, a boat, a landscape. In its way, this makes Klee's face as all embracing as Yavlensky's. 'For me,' wrote Yavlensky, 'the face is not just a face but the whole universe'. Klee spoke of his own work's coolness, its lack of 'passionate humanity'. It is the means of art, and 'the making visible that which could not be seen without the effort of making visible', that draw his commitment and the ever-growing range of his unblinkered vision.

★ ★ ★

Tatlin's name is to this day associated with that faction within Modernism which sought to embrace technology and the machine in expectation of a dynamic steel-and-glass utopia. Having visited Picasso in Paris and seen his new constructions, Tatlin – we are told – foreswore painting and devoted himself to constructing abstract reliefs referring to nothing but the materials of which they are made, and then going on to inventing that great impossible monument and Comintern centre, the Tatlin Tower of 1919–1920. When Soviet cultural policy turned against experimental art, he returned to painting of a more or less realistic sort.

In fact, we know of three paintings produced by Tatlin during 1916–17, major works that contribute to his development, are by no means by-products, and serve to illuminate his position as a leading figure – soon, *the* leading figure – in Russian art. John Milner, in his *Vladimir Tatlin and the Russian Avant-Garde* (Yale University Press, 1983), reproduces and discusses two of them. A third one is presented here for the first time. All three are paintings on wood, and are what is known as abstract: clusters of painted planes apparently in front of the support. The painting he named *Board No. 1* (Milner plate 136) is given the date 1917. Lettering on it names the street in which Tatlin was living and working then. The second is known merely as *Composition* (Milner colour plate III) and is assigned to 1916–17. Two words are painted on it: 'MAY' and 'MONTH'. The third has no lettering, but I shall suggest that it does incorporate outward references. In all three cases, we are made very conscious of the painting as a physical object: a substantial board plus paint. In the case of *Composition* the panel would seem to have been a found piece, presumably part of a piece of furniture. Much of its surface is left unpainted so that we can see the grain of the wood and also the marks left on it by its previous existence. Tatlin probably trimmed three of its corners, enhancing its character as an object. It is the smallest of the three paintings, 52×39 centimetres. *Board No. 1* is the largest, at 105×57 centimetres nearly three times the area of the former. Also, its format is more emphatically vertical. The third painting comes between the others in size but has precisely the same format as *Board No. 1*, the proportions of both coming out at 1.8:1. This is a format familiar in icon painting. In other respects too both these tall paintings manifest a more markedly iconic character than the squarer *Composition*. In both the ground is light in tone, a fine, luminous ivory colour frequently found in those icons that do not have a gold ground.

Tatlin was trained in the traditions of icon painting and stressed his indebtedness to them. These facts usually lead on to the comment that it was the physical character of icons, as objects of wood and paint, with gilding and often also with a cladding of silver or another metal and precious stones, that reinforced his concern for *faktura*, with the handling of materials and also with their visual and ethical role in the work. But, like Malevich and many another artist of his time and place, Tatlin was also responsive to the power of icons as images, and especially as images of an uplifting, exalting sort. The disposition of the planes and other forms in these paintings of 1916–17 is as much in the tradition of icon painting as of Cubism, and this is

Vladimir Tatlin, Untitled c.1916/17 tempera on wood 75.5 x 41.5 cm particularly so in the case of the third painting, which is dominated by slanting forms which fan out upwards. The tallest element in the cluster is a quotation from his *Painterly Relief* of 1913–14, formerly in the collection of Ivan Puni, known to us from old photographs and from Martyn Chalk's reconstruction. In the relief a crafted bar of wood with brass fittings rises steeply at something like 15° from the vertical to project beyond the top edge of the base board. Much the same, in painted form, occurs in the painting where this element becomes very prominent near the top and on the centre line of the composition. Much lower down, on the right, we see a painted ocular form similar to one in the *Painterly Relief* of the same date (and known to us in the same way), that which once belonged to Alexandra Exter. Another circular and part-shaded motif appears in the upper left-hand area of the cluster. One hesitates to associate this with an eye, yet there is about the sum of the elements a marked resemblance to the pose, gestures and silhouette of a type of icon

Martyn Chalk, reconstruction 1980 of Vladimir Tatlin's 'Painting Relief' 1913–14 wood, paper, pencil, gouache, wallpaper, etc. 60.5 x 29.2 x 6.6 cm

Martyn Chalk, reconstruction 1980/81 of Vladimir Tatlin's 'Painting Relief' 1913–14 wood, paper, gouache, oilpaint, card, etc. 70 x 40 x 6 cm

showing St John the Baptist as Forerunner (Podromos), i.e. as the winged messenger or herald of the coming Christ, prominent in Russian icon imagery and here shown in outline. I shall be stating and justifying elsewhere my belief that the image of the Baptist, a figure especially honoured in the Russian Church, recurs in Tatlin's work of the Revolutionary period. Whether or not this painting was done before, during or after the 'October' Revolution of 1917, it could well signify the expected termination of one age or dispensation and the opening of another. Change, as already said, was expected. Tatlin's mentor and friend, the poet Velimir Khlebnikov, had already prophecied the ending of an empire in 1917 and everyone knew which empire he meant. The *Podromos* is the hinge figure between the Old and the New Testament. Embodied in Tatlin's Tower, he announces the New Jerusalem of World Communism, to be achieved through the work of the Communist International, formed by Lenin in defiance of White and foreign attacks on the young Soviet state. In the painting, dating perhaps from the months leading up to the key events of the Revolution, he could be announcing the first steps in that global transformation, the redemption of Russia.

Simplified drawing of St. John Podromos icon 17th Century

It helps us to clarify his relationship to other artists of what was soon to be known as the 'left' sort (meaning Futurists and a range of other avant-garde artists). The 'Zero-Ten' exhibition held in Petersburg in December 1915 to January 1916 brought Malevich's Suprematism and Tatlin's nameless constructivist art into confrontation. At that time several of the other artists in the exhibition were making reliefs: Puni, Kliun, Rosanova, Popova, etc. Some of these reliefs were figurative; some included references to the visible world in a Cubist context of fragmentation; some were, as far as we can tell, wholly abstract. There was a Dadaist vein in some of them, a mocking of art and its privileged status – or so it seems to western eyes. It may be that this is an illusion that fuller information would remove; perhaps they are emblematic in a way which we do not as yet know how to read. If they are indeed Dadaistic, then they can be associated with the nihilistic vein in Russian Futurism, most evident in the miscellanies of verse, prose and images published in Moscow and St Petersburg particularly during 1912–14. If they were done in a Dadaist spirit, then it is remarkable how quickly it disappeared – as though the exhibition, its full title being 'Zero-Ten: Last Futurist Exhibition', was intended literally to allow this negative, sardonic aspect of Futurism its last swing. There is no sign of it in anybody's work in 1916 or after. It was never evident in Tatlin, though it gave every support to the idea of experimenting with a variety of materials, and it was wholly remote from Malevich's new revelatory art, though there were pointers towards it in his paintings with collaged elements of 1914, notably the *Soldier of the First Division* with its stuck-on thermometer.

Kliun's powerful untitled relief of 1916 shows the danger of assuming that the legendary clash between Malevich and Tatlin over and at the 'Zero-Ten' exhibition divided their friends and followers into distinct camps. Kliun was personally close to Malevich, yet he was also prominent among the relief makers who in 1915–16 formed around Tatlin. His 1916 relief confirms the latter allegiance, or at least his allegiance to Tatlin's succinct way with found materials, and Tatlin invited

Ivan Kliun, Untitled 1916 wood relief and collage 58.4 x 36.5 x 6.2 cm him to exhibit at the Moscow 'Magasin' exhibition that March. This was the exhibition; shown in a disused shop, at which Malevich showed nothing but pre-Suprematist works, for reasons that are not given but everyone guesses at. Nevertheless, in 1916 Kliun is also an active member of the circle around Malevich, developing the Suprematist idiom and preparing the first number of a group magazine to be entitled *Supremus* and to appear in early 1917 (it never did). Art historians looking for ways of explaining the blows exchanged by Malevich and Tatlin in December 1915 and Malevich's refusal (if that is what it was) to show Suprematist paintings in Tatlin's exhibition of 1916, have focused on the hint that Tatlin berated Malevich for the unprofessional character of his art. This is taken to imply that for Tatlin painting itself could no longer be offered as a progressive form of art, and perhaps also that Malevich's intentionally plain, even clumsy way of painting offended him. That Tatlin himself was producing significant paintings during 1916–17 would seem to deny the first part of this; their delicacy could be taken to support the second. At the same time, the modest forms used by Kliun could be thought to echo Suprematism as forms, though not as bits of matter. In other words, the evidence is that there were no clear party lines to be followed in the wake of Malevich and Tatlin. Kliun's associates in the Suprematist circle, the *Supremus* group, included such prominent makers of reliefs as Puni, Popova and Rosanova.

The group did not include Rodchenko. He emerged with the 'Magasin' exhibition as a Tatlin protégé, showing there sub-Cubist collages and works based on linear constructions formed with ruler and compasses. The dating of Rodchenko's work of these first years awaits scrutiny. German Karginov, in his Rodchenko monograph (Thames & Hudson, 1979) illustrates a number of paintings that combine the artist's enquiry into what can be formed with ruler and compasses plus added colour with something of Tatlin's mode of assembling forms on a surface; Karginov dates these 1916–18 following Rodchenko's own inscribed dates though at least some of these were added later. He also illustrates, as belonging to the years 1917–20, paintings that appear to echo Malevich's venture into cosmic dimensions. But it should also be noticed that Rodchenko, capable of complete plainness of manner when he wants it, in all these works demonstrates a concern with *faktura* that is evidence of Tatlin's influence at a profound level. Malevich the Suprematist used paint as a material with hue and density but no other qualities. Tatlin and Rodchenko allow paint its full character as a fluent and a friable medium, responsive to many modes of application, capable of changes of hue and tone, and thus apt to show the influence of light, space and adjacent forms. The principle of *faktura* demands that paint be used so as to make its contribution as paint to the presence and meaning of the work. Malevich uses it as an inert, opaque membrane, without modulation, in order to veto any possibility of that traditional signal of taste and virtuoso performance, *facture*. It is likely that he was led to this by a desire to emulate the quintessential icon whose very existence once saved image-making from the attacks of the iconoclasts, the famous icon of *The Saviour Not Made With Hands*, available to him in an ancient, honoured, copy in the Tretyakov Gallery. If Malevich's work was intended to suggest parthenogenesis, Tatlin's spoke of the rights of the materials to a full and characteristic share and the artist's role as organizer. His works are images of collaboration without loss of individuality. Consciously or unconsciously they reflect the visions of the new society offered by Aleksandr Bogdanov and other prominent Marxists of the time. Malevich's paintings, for all their radicalism, function as windows and thus can be said to adhere to a tradition that goes back at least to Alberti and the fifteenth century in Florence. On Tatlin's side, radicalism does not exclude what some would decry as an illusionistic use of paint and form, as when some of his planes (for instance one prominent in his third painted composition) pretend to be transparent and thus resemble glass elements in his constructions; in several Rodchenkos we see planes changing colour abruptly as they pass over other planes. Moreover, Malevich's forms, even when they multiply and appear to move freely in deep space, remain anonymous areas of paint, whereas Rodchenko's, following Tatlin's echoes of reliefs, often ask to be read as two-dimensional models for constructions, for large scale assemblages of steel and other materials.

Curved planes, toned sometimes to seem metallic, had been prominent in Malevich's work of 1912–14. It is remarkable that he abandoned them so decisively in 1915 with his turn to Suprematism. Why he did so may become clear in considering his astonishing *Suprematist Composition* of c.1917, with its single black form on a white ground. Suprematism had started with a succinct, black form on a white ground, the *Black Square*, as concentrated an assertion as could be imagined. He called it his 'zero'. It was the initiating and justifying image of the new art, which then went on to multiply its forms and compositional strategies. With the sweeping black form of the *Suprematist Composition* shown here we are back with the single form in black on a white field. But, as with almost every painting he did from 'zero' on, there is an essentially different relationship of form to ground. The square within a square is immobile and wellnigh spaceless; whether it is an inert image or a dynamic one, tensed in a visual field defined by its outer edges, will become clear only when we can see the original. Almost at once, Malevich opened the lense of his art to take in wider swathes of cosmic space. The forms

Kasimir Malevich, Suprematist Composition c.1917 oil on canvas 65.6 × 48.2 cm become things, visitors from outer space, a foretaste of worlds to be discovered when mankind, as foretold by the influential scholar-philosopher Nikolai Fedorov, ends internecine enmities to engage in the 'common task' of overcoming death and voyaging into space. Fedorov's vision was alive to Russian minds in 1917 and the succeeding years as part of the promise of a convivial, omnipotent global society formed by Communism. Malevich, like Mayakovsky, Khlebnikov, Tatlin and many another prominent person in education and the arts, expected the Revolution to effect a spiritual rebirth.

One black form on a white ground, that is all, yet it eludes any verbal description which is not at the same time interpretative. To start with we have no name for the shape. A horn-shape? No cornucopeia, certainly: too austere, too flat, not showering gifts. But is it a still shape or a dynamic one? We cannot avoid crediting it with motion, towards us or away from us, in any case swift motion. Going away from us it seems like a road to infinity, an invitation. Coming towards us it appears a messenger and a promise, perhaps the promise of which Lissitzky's *Story of Two Squares* will give a more detailed account. Black is the absence of light and of colour, but it is also the sum of all colours, maximal as well as minimal. And the shape can be said to be spiralling, a double spiral springing from one point, forming a broad and spreading band. Lenin, following Hegel, said that the progress of knowledge was like a spiral. Ehrenburg was to see the spiral as the expression *par excellence* of revolutionary dynamism; he was speaking of Tatlin's Tower. The spiral had traditionally been read as a symbol of natural growth and development, of destruction as well as creation, of power and the breath of the spirit. Susan Compton, in her Malevich thesis (University of London, 1982), has suggested that other Maleviches of this time, including the composition now in the Tate Gallery, employ alchemical symbols and thus tap ancient traditions of symbolism. Vyacheslav Ivanov, philosopher and poet, and most prominent theorist among the later Symbolists, maintained that it is through the use of symbolism that art becomes religious and thus achieves spiritual significance.

It is tempting to confront Tatlin's icon with Malevich's and to note the assembled, collaborative character of the first as against the absolute testimony offered by the second. Tatlin's image seems more earthly, more approachable; Malevich's more wholly visionary. Tatlin's speaks of cooperation; Malevich's of authority. Tatlin's things; Malevich's power. Yet these differences, expressive of personality, should not obscure the essential unison represented by these works: they are didactic images intended to elevate minds to the priorities of the world whose dawning they announce.

Romantic as this sounds, it is the essential base for understanding the impulse that gave Russia, around the time of the Revolution, the most potent art of this century. Since August 1914 Russia had been cut off from the West. She was thrown on her own resources. This isolation gave great additional force to what late nineteenth-century revivalism and then Russian Futurism had initiated, a systematic but also passionate investigation of Russia's own cultural character as distinct from the West's. Old Russia was Holy Russia, the only country and nation that never sanctified itself ('Holy Land' refers only to an area, not

Alexander Rodchenko, Untitled 1918
watercolour on paper 22.5 × 12 cm

to a country and people). The theme of Holy Russia's messianic role is heard again, stimulated by late nineteenth-century religious philosophy with its vision, powerfully expressed by Soloviev, of a great, global, Christian union under Russia's leadership. But now great new things were afoot, new but not wholly different. The pains and injustices of millennia were about to be ended. Man would be like God. Marxists, atheists denouncing religion as a distraction from social needs, announced that revolution plus technology would arm mankind with Godlike powers. Lunacharsky, who became Commissar of Enlightenment (minister of education and culture) at the end of 1917, had long taught that socialism was a new kind of religion destined to lift mankind to higher planes of existence. He regretted that Skryabin had died before the Revolution because his ritualistic, transcendental music could have given the new society its transnational voice. Long disliked in Soviet Russia for its mystical character, this music has ever since Gagarin's first great voyage been the accompaniment to Soviet cosmonauts' ventures into space and triumphant returns to earth. Aleksandr Blok, a poet close in age to Malevich, neither a socialist nor a theosophist but a sympathetic witness to the events of 1917, saw the chaos of everyday Petrograd and could not but fear that the values he had lived by would be destroyed by the whirlwind of change. Yet his perception too was optimistic. 'The moment', he wrote to his mother in March 1917, '. . . is a perilous one, but all is overcome by the awareness that a miracle has taken place and, therefore, we may expect more miracles.' And to his wife, two months later: 'the whole content of life has become World Revolution, at the head of which stands Russia'. (Avril Pyman, *The Life of Aleksandr Blok*, Oxford University Press, 1980, vol. 2, pp. 243 and 258.)

The fact is that the artistic expression of the Russian Revolution surfaced when Russia was without the cultural supply lines running to Berlin, Dresden, Munich, Zurich and above all, Paris. It is charged with indigenous motives and motifs. It is a growth out of western Modernism in that it was stimulated by aspects of Post-Impressionism and western Symbolism, and owed specific methods to Cubism and to Italian Futurism. But Russian eyes, coming away from the (western) realism that was the mode of the Wanderers, and opened by what was being discovered of Russia's older traditions of church and folk art, saw these western things in their own terms. They saw Cubism not as related to reality, as Gleizes and Metzinger claimed, but as a way of breaking out of reality into spiritual and speculative realms. And when Marinetti came to meet and harangue the avant-garde poets and painters who he assumed were his followers, he was appalled by their endless burrowing in the Slav and Russian past. It did not occur to him that the past, in Italy a burden and a parade ground, for Russia was rediscovered identity and roots. What was Marinetti's talk of racing automobiles and marching crowds compared with the Russian expectation of a great leap forward in human mental as well as physical capabilities, promised by Marx and implicit in Darwin?

It was this conviction of standing at the beginning of a new and glorious era that enabled Suprematism to be the visual language of the Soviet state for a time, filling halls and streets with its rhetoric of geometric shapes and strong colours, and also gave such an impact to the model and idea of Tatlin's Tower. Below the surface these things had little to do with Cubism, and much more with the Book of Revelation. There was also the need to address a vast public in terms that it would understand. That meant religious modes, new icons, processions in celebration of new feast days. A simplified model of the Tower was paraded through the streets like an image of the Madonna and Child.

The unison found in Malevich and Tatlin provides the basis for Rodchenko's untitled watercolour of 1918, delicate yet assertive, and for Popova's powerful *Architectonic Composition* of the same year. In many ways the Rodchenko is close to Tatlin's third painting. It has the same proportions and ground, and a similar disposition of forms. Popova's squarish canvas is one of a series of at least twelve paintings done that year, all deploying forcefully represented planes interacting in a pictorial space made, and then also unmade, by light and shade. During 1913–15 Popova had been associated with Tatlin. In 1916–17 she was close to Malevich and prominent in the Supremus group. By 1918 she was one of the teachers in Moscow's new State Free Art Studios. Until 1918 neither texture nor

Liubov Popova, Pictorial Architectonic 1918
oil on canvas 45 x 53 cm

light appeared in her *Architectonic Compositions*, painted in the manner of Malevich. Now *faktura* becomes all-important, and with it a sense of construction, of material planes interlocked. Strong colour is characteristic of the 1918 series, but few of them have the energy of this confrontation of blue and orange, nor the full tonal range from white to black. Those contrasts are echoed in the angling of the forms, inclined this way or that affirmatively. We must not overlook the subtlety of Popova's methods. The pictorial depth proposed by those contrasts is effectively countermanded by the location of the strongest notes. For example, the highlight on the large blue plane appearing to the right of the orange plane checks the spatial command of both the glowing orange and the darkening blue. And the highlit edge of the orange plane actually penetrates the bottom edge of that blue plane, pushing dark blue to the foremost position in the complex. Again, the top edge of the prominent orange plane is tucked behind an edge of black and dark blue. At the bottom of the painting we see light breaking through between the planes, lifting the arrangement free of the command of gravity. That was the key message of Malevich's and Tatlin's work, a response to the thought of Fedorov, Uspensky and others: that the minds of mankind were no longer earthbound and soon their bodies would follow. The arts turned to representing a new world without the classical teleology of beginning, middle, end, top and bottom, and hieratic orders.

A notable celebrant of this new multi-dimensional world emerged from under the wing of Malevich but was soon to enter fields of activity that Malevich (though not Tatlin) regarded as alien. El Lissitzky had studied architecture in Germany and had travelled in the West. Back in Russia he worked on architecture and also on illustrating Jewish books. He contributed to art exhibitions and in 1918 joined Tatlin and others as members of Lunacharsky's art organisation under the Commissariat. It was as architect and graphic artist that he went to teach under Chagall at the New Vitebsk art school in May 1919. Malevich arrived there soon after, bringing the idealism and methods of Suprematism and wresting the leadership of the school away from Chagall. By the end of that year Lissitzky had started work on the pictorial constructions he called *PROUN*, an acronym meaning either 'for the new school of art' or 'project for affirming the new'. How close he came to Tatlin's vision of and for the new international society is clearest from his set of lithographic images for *Victory over the Sun*, self-evidently a response to Tatlin's Tower and also to his attitude to materials. With that hindsight available to us we are able also to see Tatlin elements in the more obviously Suprematist world of his Prouns. Only one of the Maleviches shown in 'Zero-Ten', as far as we know, exhibited forms that implied mass. These forms were

El Lissitzky, Untitled c.1920/21
gouache on paper 15 x 15.5 cm

represented not by one-point perspective but by means of axonometric projection in which receding lines are plotted in parallel (i.e. meeting at infinity). Lissitzky's Prouns move Suprematism into the realm of three-dimensional objects. Axonometric projection was well known to him as architect, and his education may also have predisposed him towards in some senses a more realistic view of utopia. Suprematist planes often become things for him, and there is a suggestion that he used colour (and sometimes collage in lieu of colour) both symbolically and to indicate a range of materials of which those things might be made. He saw his Prouns as fusions of Suprematist and architectural thought but this makes sense only if we accept that such a fusion can happen only at a visionary level. In effect, his vision is more specific and to that degree more realistic than Malevich's, and this combination of the visionary with indications of the realisable is of course the ideal of Tatlin. Makeable objects hover in the infinite space of the Prouns. Their dimensions and sometimes their relative positioning is left ambiguous but their physicality is not. It is as though he were saying that the dream visions of Suprematism had become great expectations to be turned into facts tomorrow, thanks to the Revolution. His statements are made with a delicate touch akin to Tatlin's, a touch that values media and distinguishes between their contribution to the whole, and the dissemination of a set of his Proun images in the form of lithographs, published like the *Victory over the Sun* suite, in Hanover in 1923, gave his work immediate influence in Central Europe. He had come West in order to set up the First Russian Art Exhibition in Berlin and in Amsterdam. He remained in the West as a most potent influence.

★ ★ ★

In the West only the De Stijl movement offered a vision with anything like the same trans-cultural breadth and quasi-religious force, and even then on a much smaller scale and with much less preparation and support on the ideological level. What a century of progressive debate plus revolution achieved in Russia, war alone brought out in Holland. Whilst the armies of great nations struggled futilely over a few acres of Flanders mud, and whilst the Dadaists in Zurich celebrated their buffoonish requiem mass for civilization, the artists and designers of De Stijl stood up to propose a culture of harmonious relationships. They aimed at a radical reformation of western art and artistic thought, offering principles and purposes diametrically opposed to those that had become dominant in the last hundred years and which they saw continued even in the avant-garde of the pre-war years. They attacked the supposed psychological functions of art and thus also its entire value system.

Most obviously, and perhaps this is what hurt most, they denied art any autobiographical function and thus also all hero worship. Their art looked anonymous. It celebrated not individuals, real or fictional, nor specific human achievements, nor even God or God's work revealed in nature, but the structuring, ordering, transposing faculty of the human imagination. They removed art's representational function, and went on to up-end that function by proposing their compositions as model images for a new human environment. They agreed on a basic idiom that obviated the need for personal invention and thus placed every emphasis on development within its narrow confines. The idiom was evolved to carry every nuance of positive thought and to exclude every possibility of negative emotions being propagated. They offered to alter humanity's cultural diet overnight and promised an end to the global disease that had culminated in internecine war.

War helped them to be of one mind, but it was not long before fundamental differences between the three founders, Van Doesburg, Mondrian and Bart van der Leck, came out into the open. Van der Leck was really more concerned with universalizing the art of representation than with replacing it with a new art aimed at complementing rather than representing the visible world. His *Man and Woman* of 1920 shows how far he could go in using an unspecific system of notation to present a generalised but wholly legible image of an essentially classical sort. He asserts the abstract nature of the artist's means, yet allows us the traditional reward of recognition, emphasizing the heterogeneity of functions that the western tradition had prided itself on hiding. As though to demonstrate our perceptual powers, he assembles on his canvas marks that seem wholly inimical to illusionism yet give us a strong illusion of human presences. It is a paradoxical act, not truly related to the principles of De Stijl except in so far as it permits the use of primaries and simple geometric forms and excludes individualistic *facture*. The contrast with Mondrian's 'plus and minus' style of 1914–16 is instructive. 'Observing sea, sky and stars, I sought to indicate their plastic function through the multiplicity of crossing verticals'. The statement defines Mondrian's lifelong conception of painting as an art of relations, and helps to distinguish his use of abstract marks from van der Leck's. For one thing, the experiences offered by each are quite distinct. We see van der Leck's figures through the marks that indicate their presence, as in some Cubist paintings we glimpse the subject through and almost in spite of a shower of insubstantial planes. Van der Leck's marks are substantial, like bits from a building kit. Cunningly placed on the gamesboard of his almost square canvas, they precipitate rather than form or delineate an image, and do so with astonishing completeness. The two figures are nude; the man's right hand is on the woman's right shoulder; their left hands are together and come towards us. The formal pose implies a formal occasion – a modern version of a betrothal à la Arnolfini, and perhaps in terms of a mirror image, intended for the couple themselves? As with Egyptian statues, we feel in the presence of perfect yet

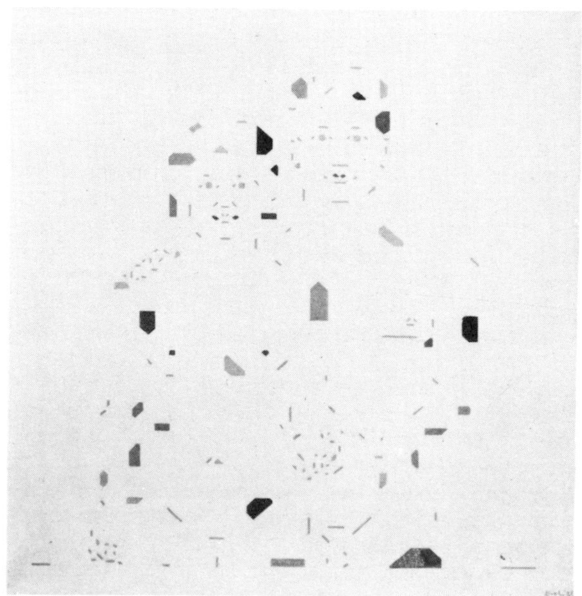

Bart van der Leck, Man en Vrouw 1926
oil on canvas 99.5 x 99 cm

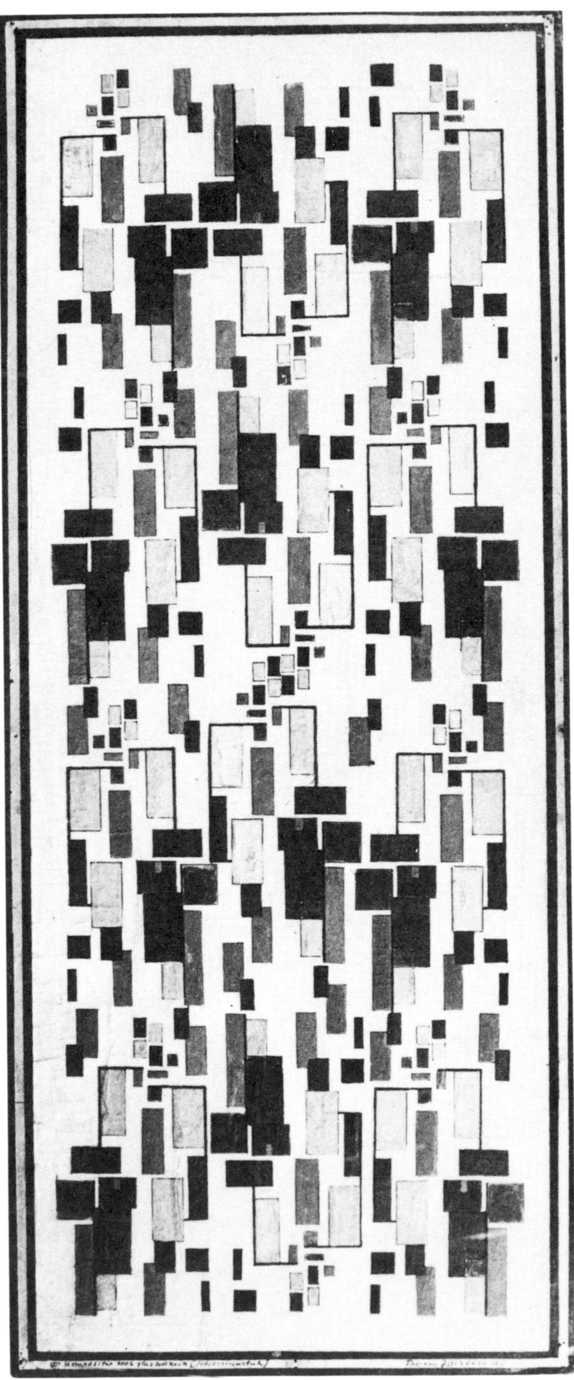

Theo van Doesburg, VI Composition for Glass Mosaic 1917
gouache on paper 74 x 30.5 cm

particular individuals, well-formed physically and psychologically. We are even tempted to read their faces in search of personalities and meaning. So involved are we in this socialising process that we scarcely notice that it requires us to un-see the bits in order to see the image.

In the Mondrian the marks are the image. They are the painter's response to a complex visual experience. They are also elements in a pictorial construction. Our attention may stay with them as that, noting their delicacy as well as their firmness and their free relationship to the charcoal lines already plotted on the canvas. Mondrian's sensibility rules the linear edifice; our sensibilities respond to the composition of marks but can, at the same time and without having to disconnect from that structure, receive from it the visual motif. This close identity of notation as structure and structure as motif suggests that Mondrian fully comprehended the processes and ambition of Cézanne, and proves his distance from Cubism.

During the immediately following years he evolved the complete Neoplasticist idiom, not so much a system as a resource, with which he proceeded to visible forms of energy with mankind's existence in space and light. Other De Stijl artists found stained glass a particularly effective medium. For Mondrian the painted surface was itself a light-engendering firmament. His dense building-up of paint as well as his dispositions results in an intensity which registers on the retina as light. This is not to say that light is in any sense the subject of Mondrian's mature art: it is rather the world in which we encounter his structures. His passion for light had always been apparent, for all the darkish tones encouraged by his The Hague School connections. He used Neo-Impressionism and then Fauvism as a way of producing light upon the canvas, and then adapted Cubism, for all its reliance on tonal shifts, into a means of assembling colour units, using light hues in some paintings, stronger ones in others. The 'plus and minus' series, with its black marks on a variety of off-white grounds, leads directly into those most subtle of pre-Neoplasticist paintings, the diamond canvases of 1918–19, with black or black and grey lines over a ground of muted white. Perhaps we should see those diamond paintings as the first fruits of Mondrian's maturity rather that the paintings of 1921. He himself signalled an arrival of sorts by inventing for them the all-important device of setting the canvas proud of its framing strips, so that the edge of the canvas is exhibited.

Mondrian's increasingly hermit-like activity, from June 1919 back in Paris and subsequently in London and New York, was brilliantly complemented by the organising and proselytising activity of Van Doesburg in Holland, France and Germany. His appetite for reforming art and design was unequalled, and it was supported by an income that enabled him to be mobile

Piet Mondrian, Composition Plus-Minus c.1916 oil and pencil on canvas 124.5 x 75 cm
coll. The National Museum of Modern Art, Kyoto

and by physical stamina that made mobility and waging cultural war on several fronts a positive pleasure. But his gifts as an *animateur* were matched by exceptional gifts as artist, as well as a talent for finding major collaborators such as the architect Cornelis van Eesteren. He was not an artist driven by one great concept, like Mondrian. That being so, he was more responsive to movements around him, willing to redirect his thought and even to work on what would sometimes seem contradictory principles. He was also more omnivorous in what he was willing to take on, from the interior decoration of a staircase and hallway to concrete poetry. The international life of De Stijl was wholly his creation.

The meeting of Russian and Dutch Modernism in post-war Germany produced something like an explosion in constructive art and a transformation of design work such as typography and lay-out, architecture and interior design. The Bauhaus tends to be seen as the protagonist in this drama, but was rather its beneficiary. Lissitzky and Van Doesburg were the prime movers. The Russian art exhibition in Berlin and the Congress of International Progressive Artists in Düsseldorf, both in 1922, were prominent events. Journals such as the revamped *De Stijl*, *Veshch*, *Mecano*, *G* and *ABC* disseminated theory and images. The Bauhaus absorbed the new methods and ideals directly and indirectly, through contact with Lissitzky and Van Doesburg at various levels, with Kandinsky and then also Moholy-Nagy (Lissitzky's most energetic yet unacknowledging disciple) on the Bauhaus faculty, and through its growing involvement with architecture via Gropius, Meyer and then Mies van der Rohe as successive directors. Until 1922 there was no hint at the Bauhaus of its Elementarist programme. Then suddenly Itten was asked to go, and soon after Moholy was taken on. Expressionism and spiritualism was exchanged for internationalism with a rationalist flavour.

Lazlo Moholy-Nagy, Konstruktionen 1923
one of a portfolio of 6 lithographs from the Kestnermappe 6 60.3 x 44.1 cm

Successive Annely Juda Fine Art exhibitions have represented aspects of this many-facetted development, by showing works by the artists already named as well as many others, well established (Baumeister, Schlemmer) as well as less well known outside the specialist world. Always there were stars, but this was quite particularly a period when others could contribute significantly and when collaboration thrived on principle as well as by chance. What is also becoming much clearer, thanks especially to the exhibition and catalogue *Dada – Constructivism* (1984), is the extent to which irrational, nihilistic and intentionally disruptive art served the aims of Elementarism. The conventionally stressed opposition between the two tendencies could obviously not be total, if only because of the number of significant individuals working in both, including Van Doesburg, Arp and Schwitters. The two tendencies shared a political social attitude. They also shared an internationalist view of the new culture, and stressed this in their polemics. It is convenient to see Dada as destructive, Elementarism as the constructive force, and their mutual roles as being those of clearing the decks and building anew. But they were more intimately united than that, concurrent rather than successive, complementary and interdependent campaigns rather than distinct developments that found common ground. Both are clearly heirs of Romanticism. Constructivism and Elementarism continue the Romantic aspiration of saving the world through art. Dadaism is the most extreme position yet attempted under the Romantic rubric that enjoined artists to be the 'legislators of mankind', here extended into the functions both of judge and hangman. Moreover, the political direction of both reminds us how little Expressionism and western Modernism in general had confronted social realities. War and war's aftermath helped. News from Russia stimulated activism. In Germany Dadaism and Elementarism were outspokenly socialist. Some of the protagonists became members of the German Communist Party in response to Weimar duplicities. One of the virtues of the 'Dada – Constructivism' show was that propaganda items were prominent in it among the works of 'pure' art that tend to represent this phase in the museums: they belong together and teach us to question the word 'pure'

It may not be easy for people used to the rich diet of exhibitions of the last ten years and to the catalogues, books and articles that have been appearing, to imagine the dearth of information behind which everything I have been referring to was hidden twenty five years ago. I started teaching the history of modern art in the mid-1950s. There was nothing on the Russians, nothing on Mondrian and De Stijl, other than generalising references in general accounts. Some of these limited enquiry rather than supporting it, and this applies especially to some of the Museum of Modern Art's books, for all their great value in other respects. Alfred H. Barr's *Cubism and Abstract Art* for example. That exciting and greatly valued book-catalogue, produced for the exhibition of 1936, was a tremendous help to anyone trying to grasp what happened and what it signified. But it also, in its title and argument, implied a cause-and-effect relationship that still tends to dominate accounts of modern art. The Museum of Modern Art's *Bauhaus 1919–1928*, first published in 1938 and edited by Herbert Bayer and Walter and Ilse Gropius, ubiquitous, authoritative in manner and long the only ready source of information on a subject of particular interest when art and design education were growing through a period of renewal, was incomplete and evasive to the point of mendaciousness. Italian Futurism was hardly ever mentioned until Reyner Banham's rousing *Theory and Design in the First Machine Age* appeared in 1960; vivid, unceremonious, full of quotations and references that tempted one to explore further, and to become critical in a field where solemn respect had been the norm. I do not mean to offer a chronological account of the gradual opening up of the field so much as to give some sense of the need we felt then for information and visual information. There was no Mondrian, no Malevich in a public collection in this country. When Seuphor's fat book on Mondrian came out in 1956, the first monograph, we

Willi Baumeister, Drei Gestaffelte Figuren mit Schwarz 1920
oil on canvas with relief 57.5 x 45.5 cm
coll. National Museum of Wales

Oskar Schlemmer, Zwei Freunde 1936
oil, tempera and pencil on paper laid on canvas
64 x 44 cm

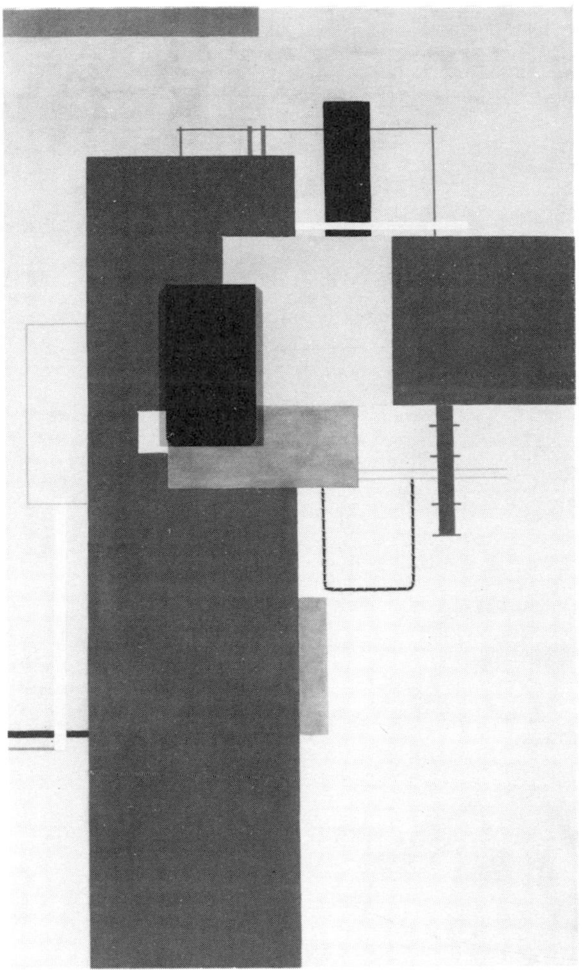

Friedrich Vordemberge-Gildewart, Grosse Konstruktion 1924
oil, wood and wire on canvas 175 x 105 cm

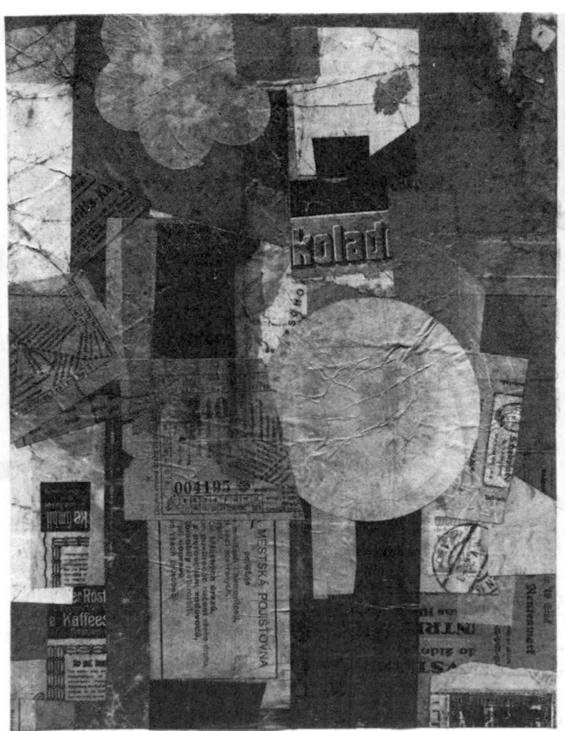

Kurt Schwitters, Dieser ist Friedel Vordemberges Drahtfrühling
1927 collage 29 x 22 cm

seized it and came away grateful for the illustrations but also cross with its often vacuous text. The library of Leeds College of Art consisted of a short and uncared-for run of this and that, fizzling out with Impressionism in black and white. I recall the excitement of the painter Trevor Bell over the Boeck and Sabartès *Picasso* monograph of 1953: he had left the College a year earlier, and he had not heard of Picasso, let alone been encouraged to look at his work.

Annely Juda's historical exhibitions have been a major – and, because of their continuity, enormously enriching, reinforcing – contribution to the widening of our awareness of modern art and modern art history. They were, and continue to be, occasions for meeting, enjoying, becoming intimate with, a host of examples of that bustling activity of especially the post-1918 years, when Paris waned and the interaction of Russia, Central Europe and the Netherlands peaked to provide outstanding examples of new art and design but also to publicise questions about the function and morality of art that concern us still. The present exhibition celebrates her achievement on a scale that can only hint at its fullness. This catalogue should also pay homage to its predecessors, for the visual and verbal information preserved in them. Their texts are often of major importance, documentary texts as well as essays by specialist scholars. I should like to end by paying tribute to one of these, a frequent contributor to Annely Juda Fine Art catalogues – Andrei Nakov. We await his Malevich monograph with impatience, but meanwhile honour him for his information and analyses. Long may the exhibitions and the catalogues continue . . . to remind us, amongst other things, that Modernism is not a closed subject.

Norbert Lynton
July 1985

Norbert Lynton is professor of the History of Art and dean of the School of European Studies at the University of Sussex. His interpretative account of Russian art and design of the Revolutionary period is being published by the Phaidon Press.

Masterpieces of the Avantgarde

Exhibition

Page

Antiquities

1 Sakizabad Sculpture *c.*2000 BC
in form of a horse
copper, Iran
9 x 12 cm
Exhibited: Annely Juda Fine Art, London
'Modern Images in Ancient Times' cat. no. 6
illus., 1969–70

2 Rhyton *c.*1000 BC
in form of a bull
grey clay, Ardibil, Azerbaijan
20.5 x 23.5 cm
Exhibited: Annely Juda Fine Art, London
'Modern Images in Ancient Times' cat. no. 4
illus., 1969–70

3 Axe *c.*1000 BC
with Human Head on both sides
bronze, Luristan
11.5 x 15.5 cm
Exhibited: Annely Juda Fine Art, London
'Modern Images in Ancient Times' cat. no. 16
illus., 1969–70

4 Sculpture *c.*1780
in form of a dog
iron, West Africa
8.3 x 18.5 cm
Exhibited: Annely Juda Fine Art, London
'Modern Images in Ancient Times' cat. no. 82
illus., 1969–70

3

1

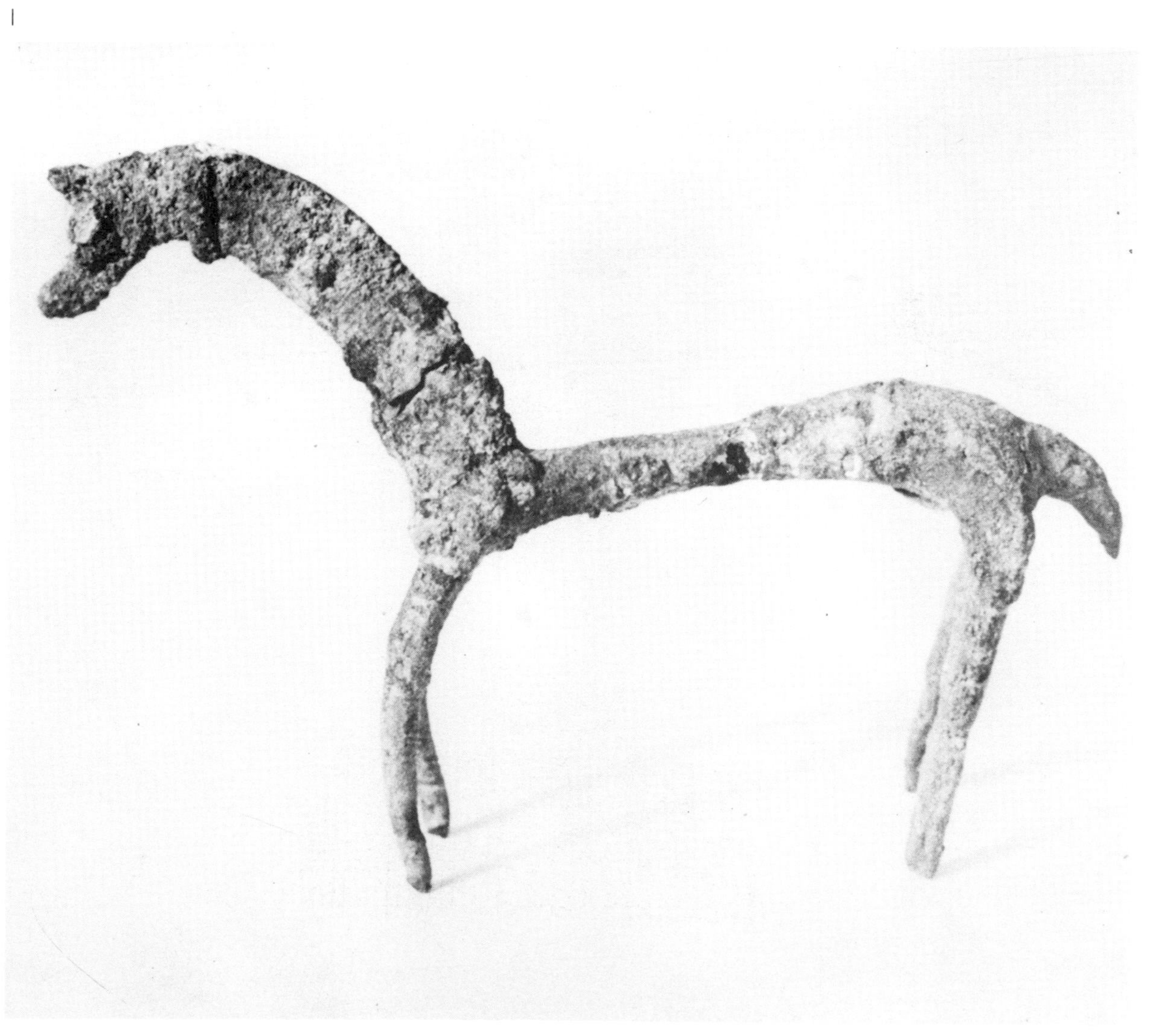

Jean Arp

5 Tête se réflètant dans un miroir, oeil,
nez, ride 1926
oil on board with cutouts
42 x 24.5 cm
Exhibited: Galerie Le Centaure, Brussels 'Arp' cat. no. 9, 1928. Mercury Gallery, New York 1939. New School for Social Research, New York 1941. Annely Juda Fine Art, London 'Dada-Constructivism' cat. no. 4 illus., 1984
Literature: Bernd Rau 'Jean Arp, Die Reliefs' cat. no. 94 illus. p.52 Hatje 1981

6 Untitled 1947
papier dechiré
49.5 x 32 cm
initialled on verso
This work was exchanged by Arp in 1947 in Meudon with Vordemberge-Gildewart for his Composition No. 105, 1936
Exhibited: Annely Juda Fine Art, London 'Vordemberge-Gildewart Remembered' cat. no. 16, 1974. 'Collages and Reliefs 1910–1945' cat. no. 9, Annely Juda Fine Art, London; La Boetie Inc., New York 1982

7 Relief Sculpture 1959
bronze, edition of 5
39 x 35 x 8.5 cm
Exhibited: Annely Juda Fine Art, London 'Vordemberge-Gildewart Remembered' cat. no. 20, 1974
Literature: Hans Arp Oeuvre cat. no. 193

5

6

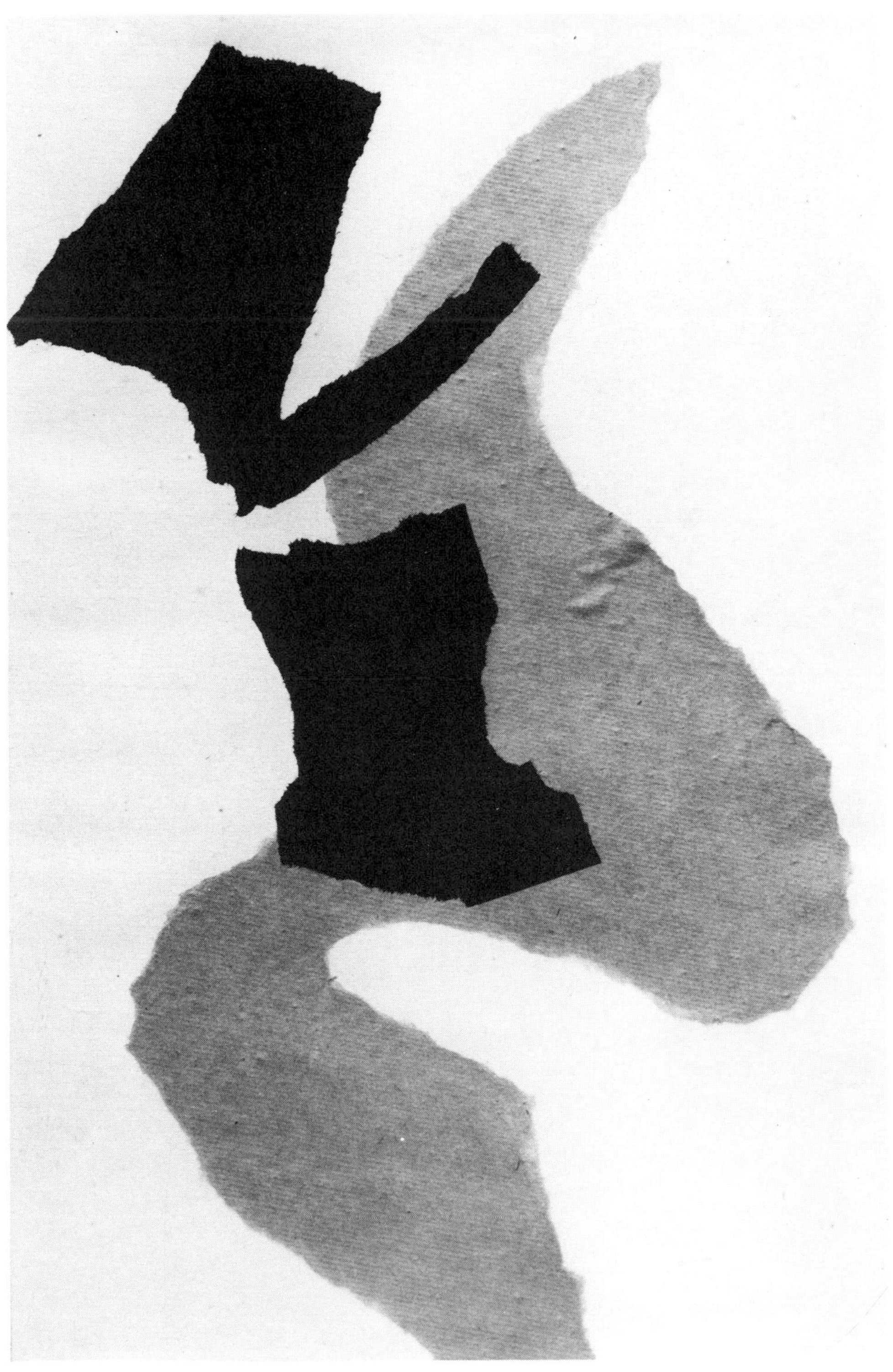

7

Balthus

8 Jeune Fille à sa Toilette 1948
oil on canvas
55.9 x 46.4 cm
initialled and dated upper left
Exhibited: Annely Juda Fine Art, London 'Balthus Drawings' 1968. The Tate Gallery, London 'Balthus' cat. no. 27 p. 63, 1968
Literature: Centre Georges Pompidou, Paris 'Balthus' illus. no. 87 p. 355, 1984

8

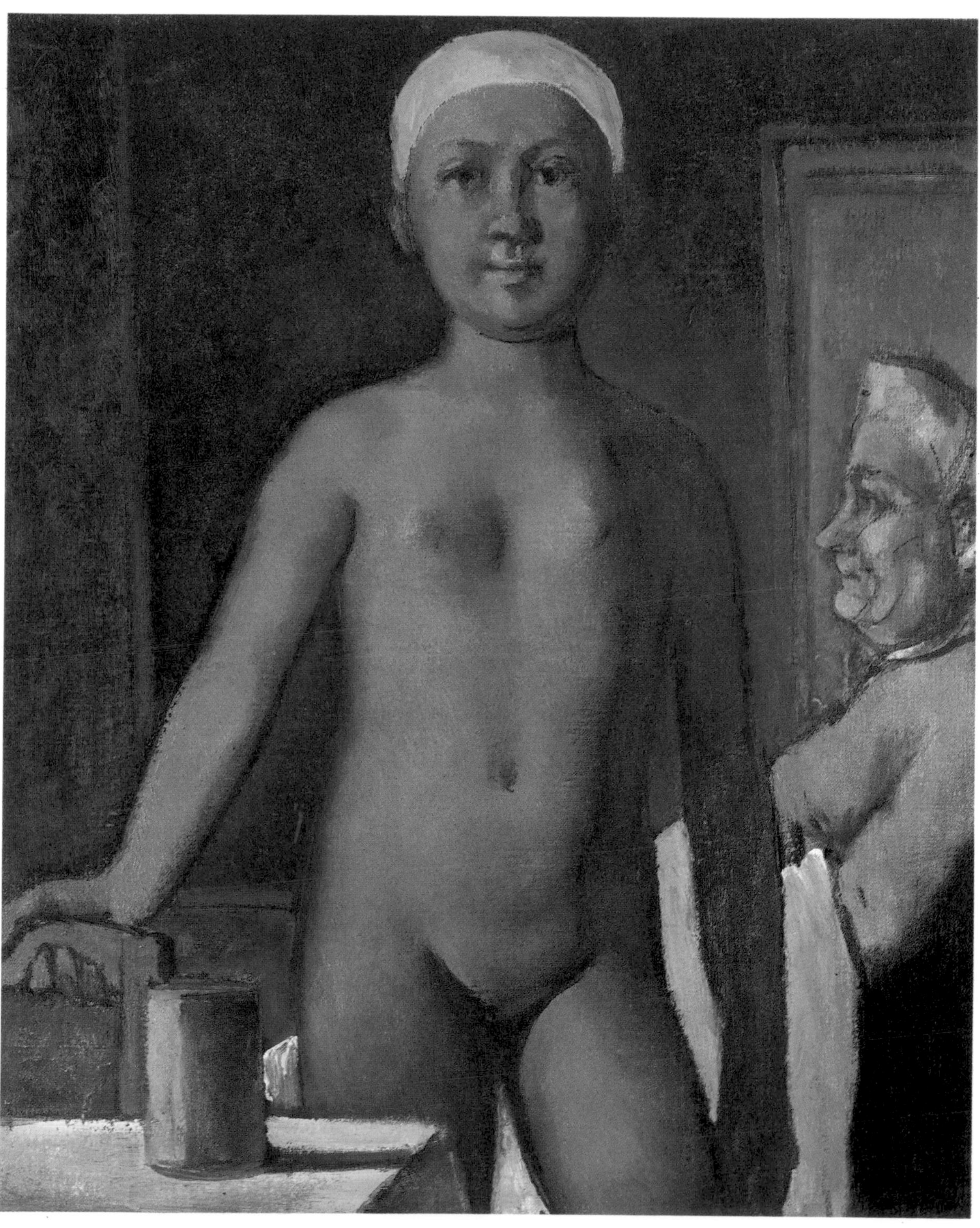

Ella Bergmann-Michel

9 Mit drei weissen Pfeilen (B 180) 1924
(Herta Wescher Spektrum)
indian ink and collage
75 x 60 cm
signed, dated and numbered lower centre
Exhibited: Kunstverein, Paderborn 'Ella Bergmann-Robert Michel Collagen' cat. no. EBM 11, 1970. Galerie Bargera, Köln 'Ella Bergmann-Michel + Robert Michel' cat. no. 7, 1974. Annely Juda Fine Art, London 'Ella Bergmann-Michel Collages and Drawings 1917–1931' cat. no. 22 illus., 1984

9

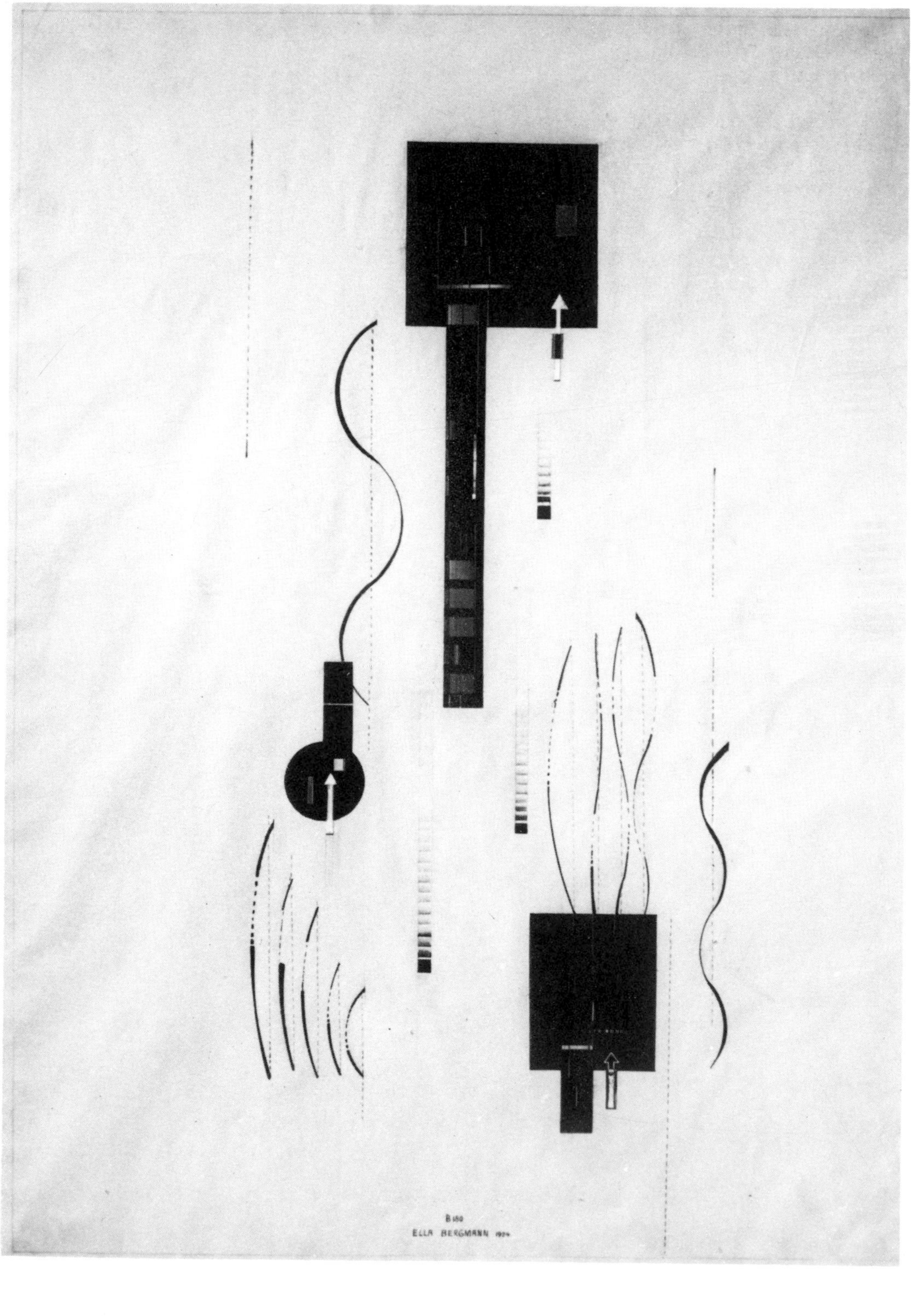

Cesar Domela

10 Composition néo-plastique No.5 F 1926
oil on canvas
105 x 81 cm
inscribed lower left
Literature: Alain Clairet 'Domela Catalogue raisonne de l'Oeuvre de Cesar Domela – Niewenhuis (peintures, reliefs, sculptures)' illus. no. 20 p.74, Editions Carmen Martinez, Paris 1978

10

Alberto Giacometti

11 Head
pencil
40.5 x 33 cm
signed lower right
Provenance: James Lord, Paris

12 Heads 1948
double drawing
each sheet 26 x 18.5 cm
one sheet signed lower left

12

11

Natalie Gontcharova

13 Baigneuse 1912
oil on canvas
139.5 x 95.5 cm
signed lower right; signed, titled, dated and inscribed '43 rue de Seine Paris 6' on verso
Exhibited: 'Russian Art of the Revolution' cat. no. 5, Andrew Dickson White Museum of Art; Cornell University, Ithica; Brooklyn Museum of Art, New York 1971. Leonard Hutton Galleries, New York 'Russian Avant-Garde: 1908–1922' cat. no. 27 illus., 1971. 'The Avant-Garde in Russia 1910–1930 New Perspectives' cat. no. 65, Los Angeles County Museum of Art; Hirshhorn Museum and Sculpture Garden, Washington 1980–81

13

Jean Gorin

14 Composition 1930
oil on canvas
46 x 38 cm
on canvas on verso 'Jean Gorin No.2 1930' and
'N 24', on stretcher 'Gorin 1930, Nort s/Erdre'
Exhibited: Annely Juda Fine Art, London
'Configuration 1910–1940' cat. no. 13
illus. p. 17, 1981

14

Vilmos Huszar

15 Untitled 1924
painted wood relief
26.5 x 31.5 x 5.2 cm
monogrammed on verso 'VH'

16 Still-Life c.1925–30
oil on canvas
35.5 x 43.5 cm
signed lower right

16

15

Paul Klee

17 Dorf (Vorstadtartig) 1915
brush drawing with black watercolour
10.1 x 26 cm
titled lower right, dated and numbered lower left
Literature: Paul Klee oeuvre cat. no. 222

18 Flusslandschaft 1924
drawing with charcoal wash on thin vellum on card
23.6 x 28.5 cm
titled and dated 1924.55 on mount
Literature: 'Paul Klee Drawings' no. 29, ed. Grohman, publ. M. DuMont, Köln

17

18

Ivan Kliun

19 Untitled 1916
wood relief and collage
58.4 x 36.5 x 6.2 cm
initialled and dated top right, signed in Russian on verso
Private Collection
Exhibited: Annely Juda Fine Art, London 'Configuration 1910–1940' cat. no. 29 illus. p. 29 in colour, 1981
Literature: Andrei Nakov 'L'Avant-Garde Russe' illus. p. 40 in colour, Fernand Hazan, Paris 1984

20 Composition 1921
oil on canvas
64.5 x 46 cm
signed and dated lower left
Exhibited: Annely Juda Fine Art, London 'Configuration 1910–1940' cat. no. 36 illus. p. 33 in colour, 1981. Tokyo Gallery, Tokyo 'Annely Juda Fine Art at Tokyo Gallery – Russian Constructivism' cat. p. 26 illus. in colour, 1983. Annely Juda Fine Art, London 'Dada-Constructivism' cat. no. 79 illus., 1984
Literature: Andrei B. Nakov 'Abstrait/Concret Art Non-Objectif Russe et Polonais' illus. p. 216, Transédition, Paris 1981

21 Untitled 1922
wood relief
39 x 26 x 3 cm
signed and dated top left
Exhibited: Annely Juda Fine Art, London 'Collages and Reliefs 1910–1945' ex. cat., 1982. Tokyo Gallery, Tokyo 'Annely Juda Fine Art at Tokyo Gallery – Russian Constructivism' cat. p. 26 illus. in colour, 1983. Annely Juda Fine Art, London 'Dada-Constructivism' cat. no. 80 illus. in colour, 1984

19

20

Gustav Klucis

22 Architectural Study c.1920/25
gouache, indian ink and pencil on paper laid down on board
39.5 x 24.8 cm
Exhibited: 'The Non-Objective World 1914–1955' Annely Juda Fine Art, London; University Art Museum at Austin, Texas; Galerie Liatowitsch, Basel cat. no. 69 illus. p. 105, 1973–74. 'Russian Constructivism: Laboratory Period' Annely Juda Fine Art, London; Art Gallery of Ontario, Toronto cat. no. 7 illus. p. 7, 1975. National Gallery of West Berlin 'The 15th Council of Europe Exhibition: Trends of the Twenties' Section 1, p. 136 illus. no. 50, cat. no. 1/217, 1977. Scottish National Gallery of Modern Art, Edinburgh 'Liberated Colour and Form' cat. no. 18 illus. p. 25, 1978. Annely Juda Fine Art, London 'Dada-Constructivism' cat. no. 81 illus., 1984
Literature: John Milner 'Russian Revolutionary Art' illus. p. 80, publ. Oresko Books Ltd., 1979

23 Untitled 1920s
collage
18.8 x 14.7 cm
Exhibited: Annely Juda Fine Art, London 'Dada-Constructivism' cat. no. 82 illus. p. 44, 1984

23

Henri Laurens

24 Le Torse 1935
bronze cast no. 6/6
67 x 54 x 43 cm
monogrammed and numbered, stamped
'C. Valsuani Cire Perdue'
Exhibited: Grand Palais, Paris 'Henri Laurens, exposition de la donation aux Musees Nationaux' (another cast) cat. no. 46 illus., 1967
Literature: 'The Sculpture of Henri Laurens' illus. pp. 154 and 155, publ. Harry N. Abrams Inc., New York

24

Fernand Leger

25 Composition aux Deux Fruits 1938
oil on canvas
92 x 65 cm
signed and dated lower right; signed, titled and dated on verso

25

Lazar El Lissitzky

26 Proun – First Group 1919/20 (winter)
watercolour and pencil on thin cardboard
25.6 x 21 cm
Exhibited: Tokyo Gallery, Tokyo 'Annely Juda Fine Art at Tokyo Gallery – Russian Constructivism' cat. p. 24 illus. in colour, 1983. Annely Juda Fine Art, London 'Dada-Constructivism' cat. no. 90 illus., 1984. Galerie Maeght-Lelong, New York 'Classic Drawings' cat. no. 5, 1984–85

27 Worrier 1923
no.4 from 'Victory over the Sun' portfolio
colour lithograph, edition of 75
53.5 x 45 cm
signed
printed by Rob. Leunis and Chapman GmbH, Hanover
Literature: Sophie Lissitzky-Küppers 'El Lissitzky Life, Letters, Texts' Thames and Hudson 1968

27

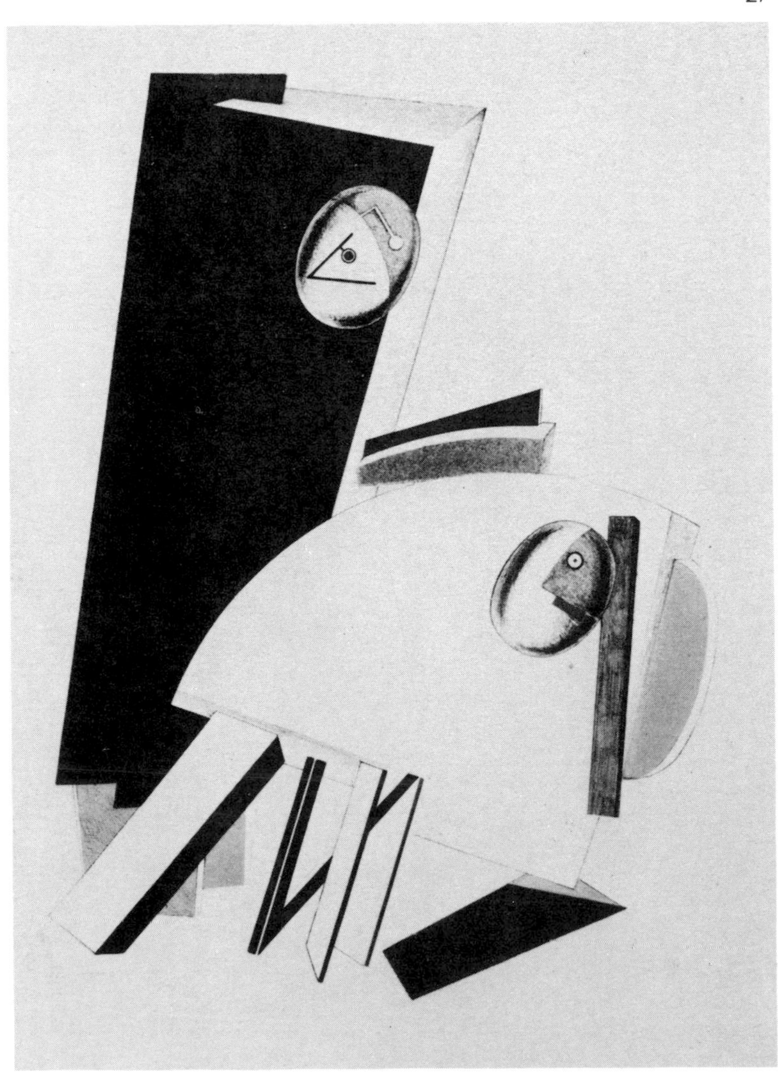

26

Kasimir Malevich

28 Head of a Peasant 1910–1911
gouache on cardboard
46 x 46 cm
initialled lower right 'km'
Private Collection
Exhibited: Annely Juda Fine Art, London 'Russian Pioneers: At the Origins of Non-Objective Art' cat. no. 22, 1976. Centre Georges Pompidou, Paris 'Malevitch' cat. no. 12 illus. p. 40, 1978. Annely Juda Fine Art, London 'The First Russian Show – A Commemoration' cat. no. 36 illus. p. 117 in colour, 1983
Literature: Troels Anderson 'Malevich' p. 85 no. 20 illus., publ. Stedelijk Museum, Amsterdam 1970. Jean-Claude Marcade, Centre Georges Pompidou 'Malevitch 1878–1978' illus. no. 50, publ. Cahiers l'Age d'Homme, Lausanne 1979

29 Suprematist Composition c.1916
pencil on paper
18.2 x 11 cm
Exhibited: Annely Juda Fine Art, London 'The Non-Objective World 1914–24' cat. no. 6 illus., 1970. Hayward Gallery, London 'Art in Revolution' 1971. 'Kunst in der Revolution' Frankfurter Kunstverein; Wurttembergischer Kunstverein, Stuttgart; Kunsthalle, Köln; cat. no. 44, 1972–73. Kettle's Yard Gallery, Cambridge 'Circle: International Survey of Constructive Art' cat. no. 18, 1982. Tokyo Gallery, Tokyo 'Annely Juda Fine Art at Tokyo Gallery – Russian Constructivism' cat. p. 20 illus., 1983. Annely Juda Fine Art, London 'The First Russian Show – A Commemoration' cat. no. 41, 1983. Staatliche Kunsthalle, Baden-Baden 'Kosmische Bilder in der Kunst des 20. Jahrhunderts' cat. no. 93 illus. no. 73, 1983–84

30 Suprematist Composition c.1916
pencil on paper
17 x 11.7 cm
Exhibited: Annely Juda Fine Art, London 'The Non-Objective World 1914–1924' cat. no. 9 illus., 1970. Hayward Gallery, London 'Art in Revolution' 1971. 'Kunst in der Revolution' Frankfurter Kunstverein; Wurtembergischer Kunstverein, Stuttgart; Kunsthalle, Köln; cat. no. 42, 1972–73. Kettle's Yard Gallery, Cambridge 'Circle: International Survey of Constructive Art' cat. no. 19 illus. p. 24, 1982. Tokyo Gallery, Tokyo 'Annely Juda Fine Art at Tokyo Gallery – Russian Constructivism' cat. p. 20 illus., 1983. Annely Juda Fine Art, London 'The First Russian Show – A Commemoration' cat. no. 42, 1983. Staatliche Kunsthalle, Baden-Baden 'Kosmische Bilder in der Kunst des 20. Jahrhunderts' cat. no. 94 illus. no. 75, 1983–84. Galerie Maeght-Lelong, New York 'Classic Drawings' cat. no. 10, 1984–85

31 Haymaking 1911/28
oil on canvas
57.4 x 44 cm
initialled and dated lower right
This painting was originally painted in 1911 but it was destroyed by fire in Kiev and Malevich re-painted it in 1928. The original painting is illustrated in Camilla Gray 'The Great Experiment: Russian Art 1863–1922' illus. no. 88, Thames and Hudson 1962

31

28

30

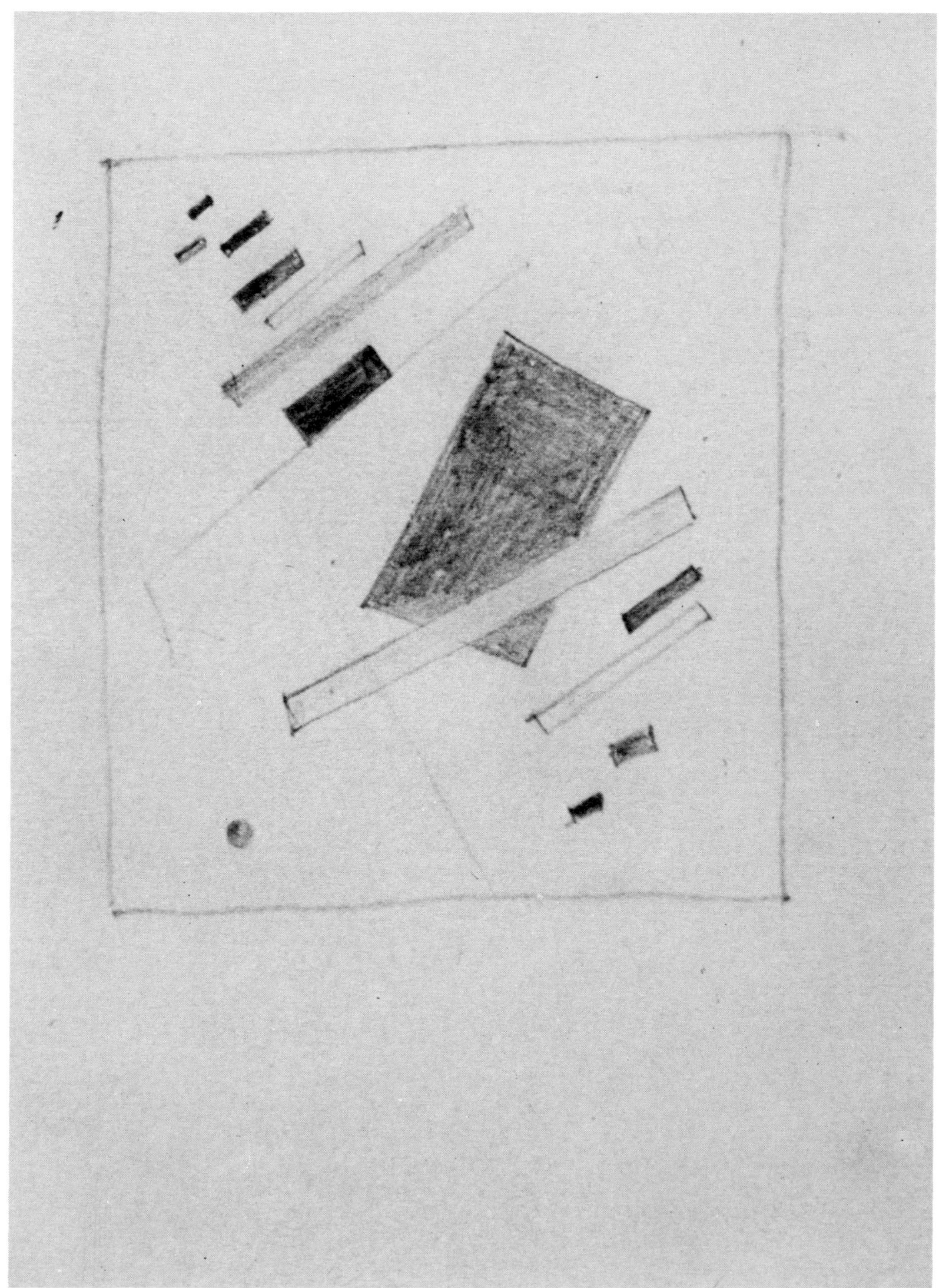

Robert Michel

32 Alu Paradies I 1930
(Col & Alu – Klebtechnik)
ink, wash and silver paint collaged on card
74 x 77 cm
titled top left, initialled and dated lower right; signed, titled and dated on verso
Exhibited: Schloss Morsbroich, Leverkusen 'Pioniere der Bildcollage Ella Bergmann und Robert Michel Werke von 1917 bis 1962' cat. no. 60, 1963. Kunstverein Paderborn 'Ella Bergmann-Robert Michel Collagen' cat. no. 44, 1970. Annely Juda Fine Art, London 'Ella Bergmann-Michel, Robert Michel Retrospective 1917–1966' cat. no. 35, 1972. Galerie Bargera, Köln 'Ella Bergmann-Michel + Robert Michel' cat. no. 16 illus., 1974. Barbara Mathes Gallery, New York 'Robert Michel Works on Paper 1918–1930' cat. no. 15, 1984

32

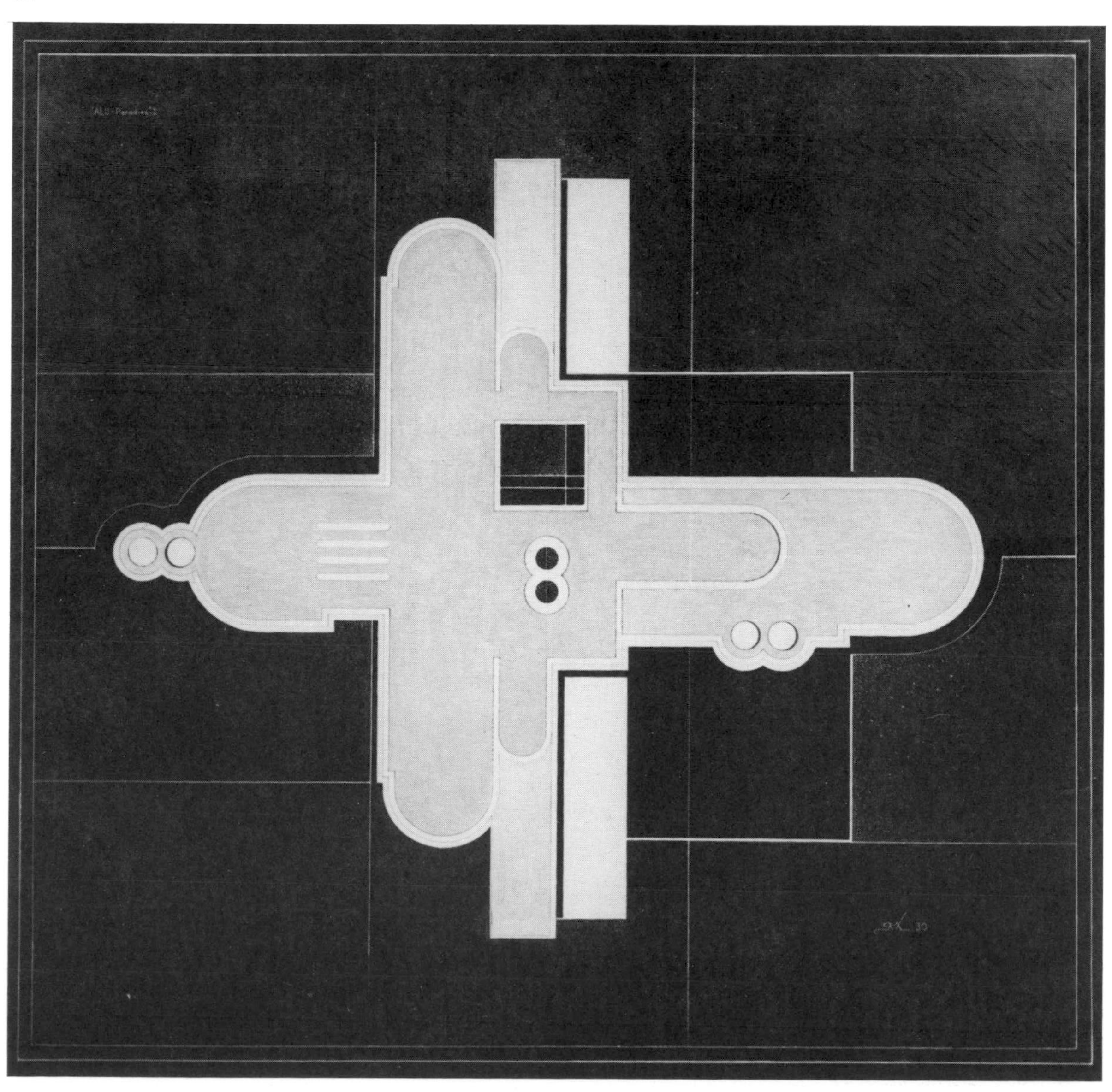

Lazlo Moholy-Nagy

33 CH-Beata 2 1939
oil on canvas
120 x 120 cm
signed, titled and dated on verso
Exhibited: Annely Juda Fine Art, London
'Dada-Constructivism' cat. no. 105 illus., 1984

34 Mills 4 1940
oil on canvas
77.5 x 66.5 cm signed, titled & dated on verso
This work was executed during the summer of 1940 while Moholy-Nagy was teaching at Mills College, Oakland, California
Exhibited: Annely Juda Fine Art, London
'Dada-Constructivism' cat. no. 106 illus., 1984

33

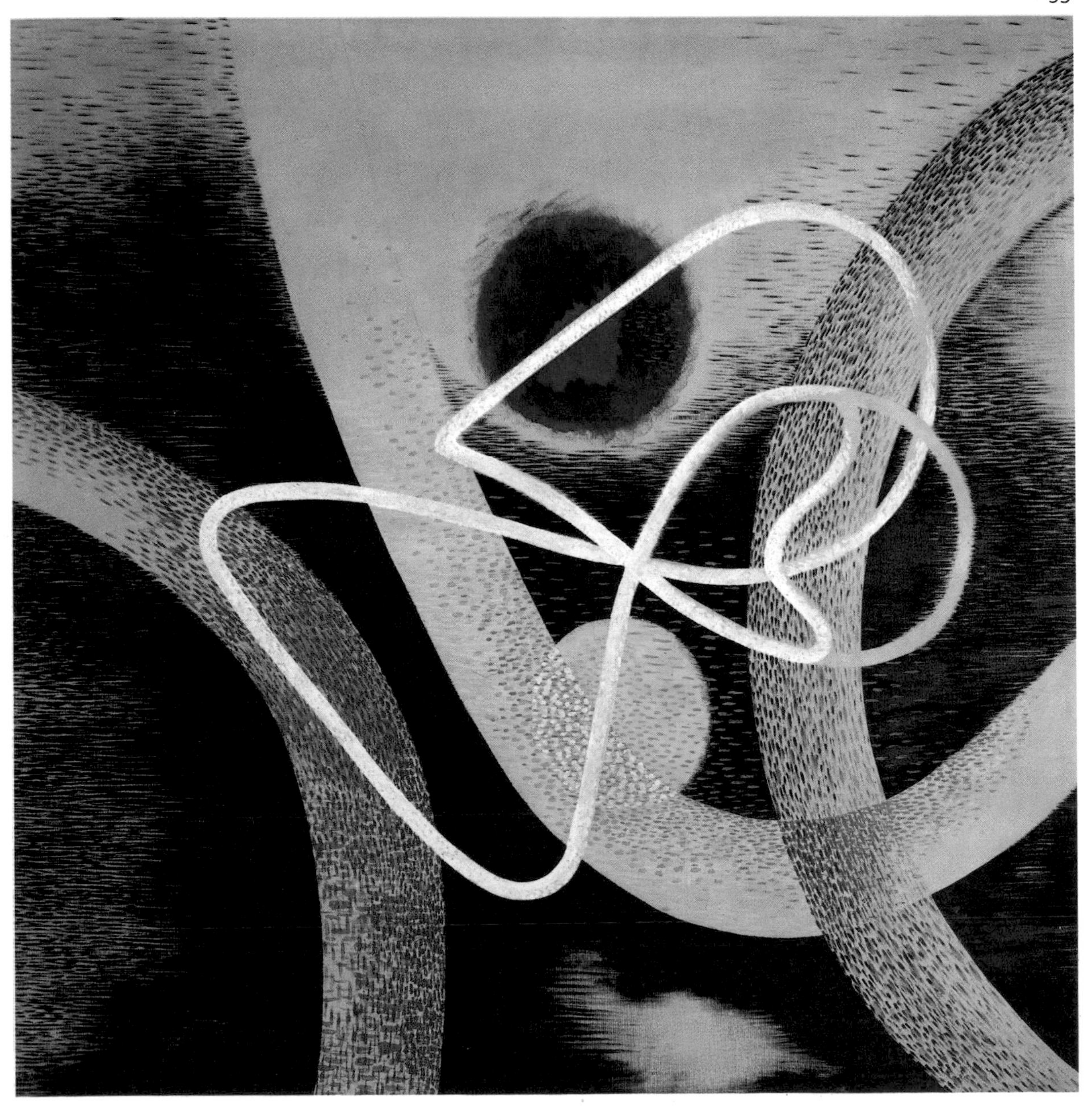

34

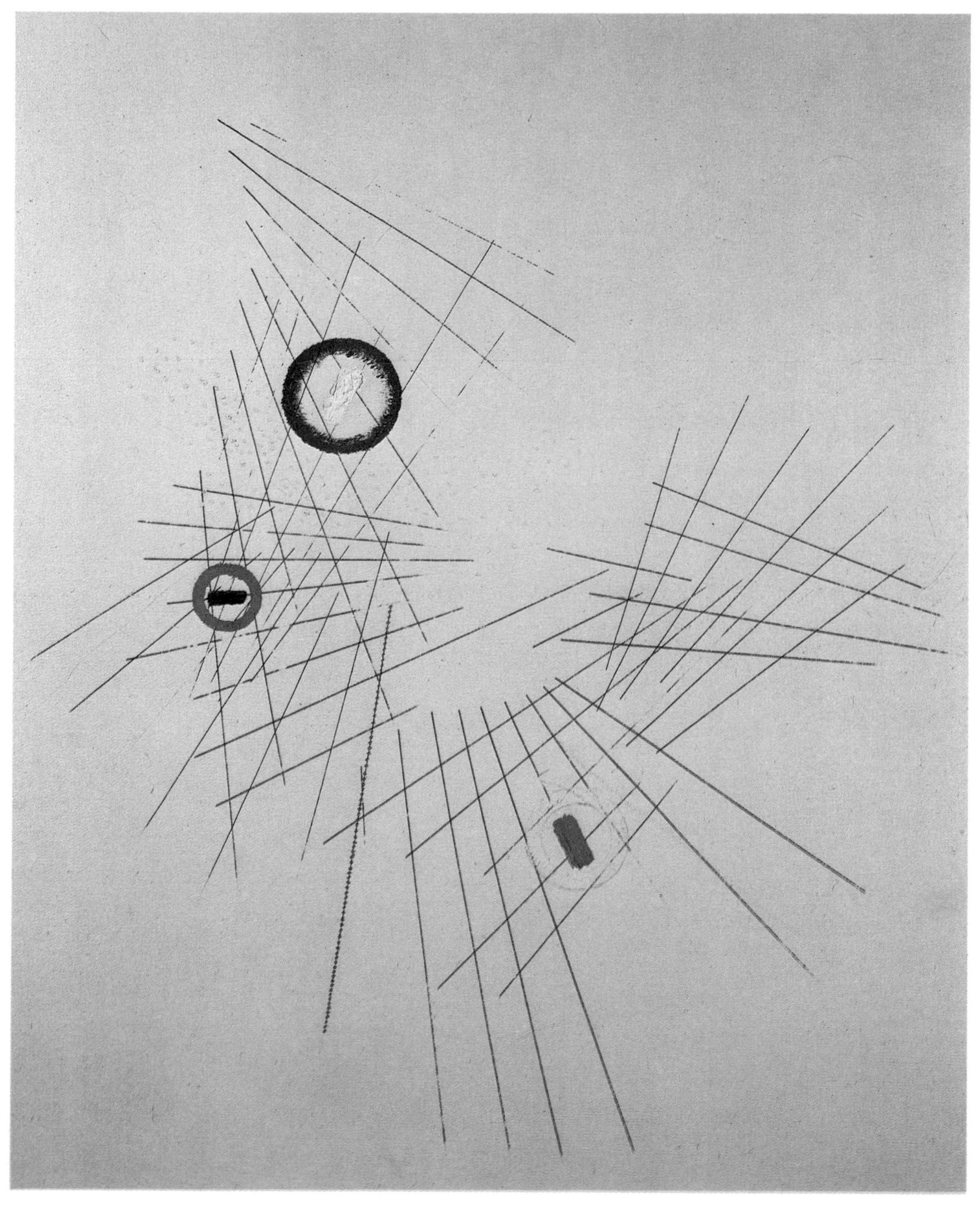

Piet Mondrian

35 Trees along the Gein (Weidenbäume)
c.1903 (1905?)
oil on canvas
38.1 x 24.8 cm
signed lower right
Exhibited: Solomon R. Guggenheim Museum, New York 'Centennial Exhibition-Mondrian Retrospective' cat. no. 13 illus. in colour p. 98, 1971. Kunstmuseum, Bern 'Mondrian' cat. no. 13 illus. in colour, 1972. Annely Juda Fine Art, London 'Configuration 1910–1940' cat. no. 49 illus. p. 50, 1981
Literature: Michel Seuphor 'Piet Mondrian' no. 105 p. 414, ed. Harry N. Abrams

35

Henry Moore

36 Ideas for Sculpture:
Draped Standing Figures 1942
chalk, indian ink and watercolour on laid paper
57.4 x 44.8 cm
signed and dated lower right, inscribed top centre
Provenance: Curt Valentin, New York
Exhibited: Art Gallery of Ontario, Toronto 'Henry Moore in Toronto Collections' cat. no. 35, 1967. Art Gallery of Ontario, Toronto 'An Exhibition Commemorating the Opening of the Henry Moore Sculpture Centre at the Art Gallery of Ontario' 1974. 'The Drawings of Henry Moore' cat. no. 196 p. 125 illus. p. 124 Tate Gallery, London; Art Gallery of Ontario, Toronto 1977–78
Literature: David Sylvester 'Henry Moore, Sculpture and Drawings 1921–1948' vol. 1, illus. p. 244, Lund Humphries, London 1957. Kenneth Clark 'Henry Moore Drawings' p. 139 illus. p. 144, London 1974

37 Mother and Child, Curved 1983
bronze ed. no. 9/9
height 58.5 cm
signed on base
Provenance: The Artist

36

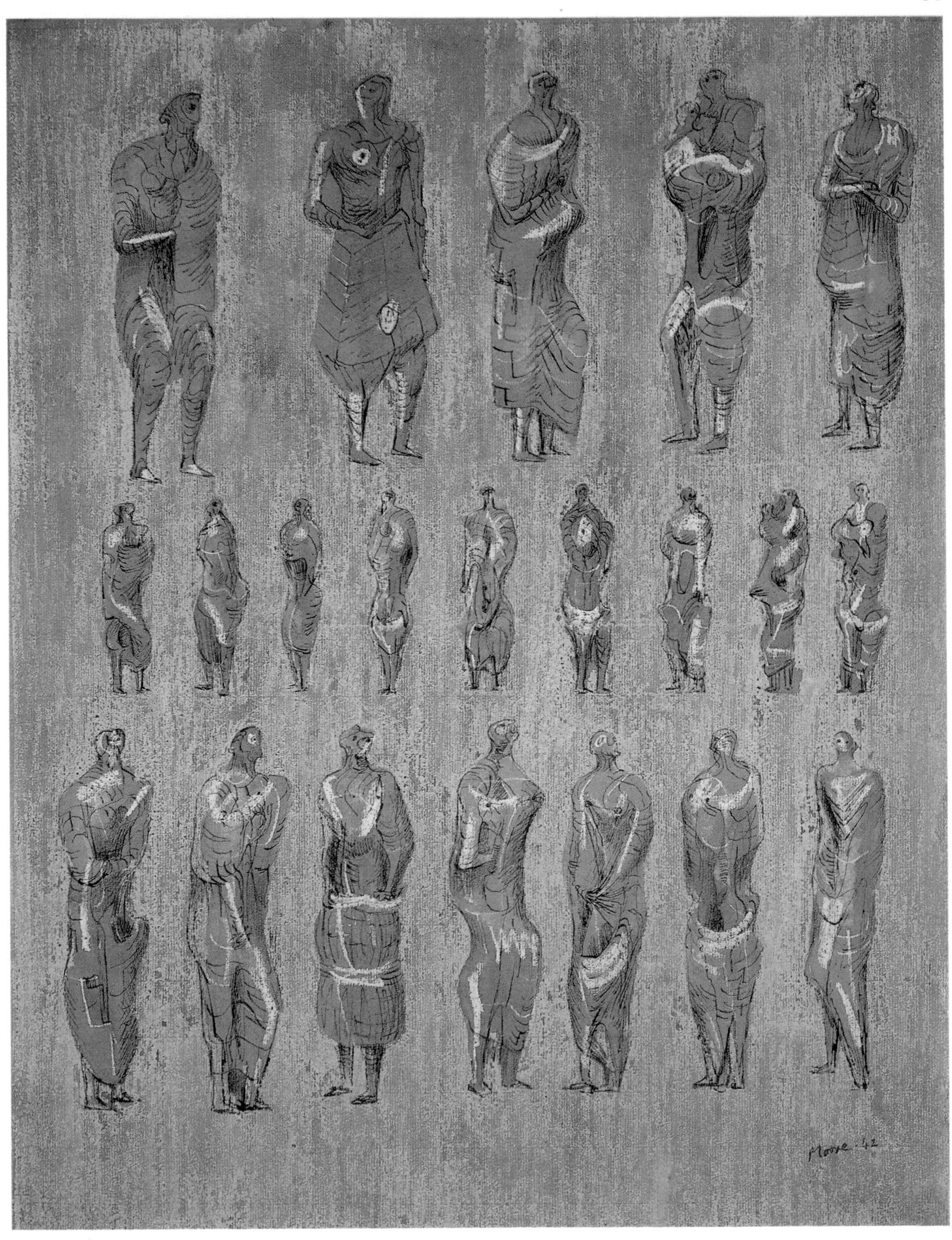

37

Pablo Picasso

38 Figure 28.1.37
pencil drawing
40.5 x 31.5 cm
signed and dated lower left
Exhibited: Annely Juda Fine Art, London 'Surrealist Drawings' cat. no. 48 illus., 1969
Literature: Christian Zervos 'Pablo Picasso' vol. 8 p. 150 illus. no. 323, publ. Cahiers d'Art, Paris

39 Les Pigeons Perches 25th February 1960
oil on canvas
130 x 162 cm
signed top right
Literature: Christian Zervos 'Pablo Picasso' vol. 19 p. 53 no. 198, publ. Cahiers d'Art, Paris

39

38

Liubov Popova

40 Pictorial Architectonic Composition 1918
oil on board
52 x 44.5 cm
numbered on verso $\frac{\text{N58}}{119}$

Private Collection
Exhibited: Scottish National Gallery of Modern Art 'Liberated Colour and Form Russian Non-Objective Art 1915–1922' cat. no. 49 illus. p. 29, 1978. The Tate Gallery, London 'Abstraction: Towards a New Art Painting 1910–20' cat. no. 337, 1980. 'The Avant-Garde in Russia, 1910–1930: New Perspectives' Los Angeles County Museum of Art; Hirshhorn Museum and Sculpture Garden, Washington D.C. cat. no. 248, 1980–81. Annely Juda Fine Art, London 'The First Russian Show – A Commemoration' cat. no. 52 illus. p. 121 in colour, 1983
Literature: Andrei Nakov 'L'Avant-Garde Russe' illus. p. 45 in colour, Fernand Hazan, Paris 1984

40

Alexander Rodchenko

41 Untitled 1915
ink and watercolour lacquered on paper
25 x 25 cm
signed and dated lower right

42 Untitled 1915
wood relief
21 x 13 cm
signed and dated lower right
Exhibited: Annely Juda Fine Art, London 'Dada-Constructivism' cat. no. 126 illus., 1984

43 Untitled 1919
oil on wood
39 x 21.5 cm
signed and dated lower right
Exhibited: 'Alexander Rodtschenko (1891–1956) und Warwara Stepanowa (1894–1958)' cat. no. 53 illus. p. 155 in colour, Wilhelm-Lehmbruck Museum, Duisburg; Staatliche Kunsthalle, Baden-Baden 1983. Tokyo Gallery, Tokyo 'Annely Juda Fine Art at Tokyo Gallery – Russian Constructivism' cat. p. 19 illus. in colour, 1983. Annely Juda Fine Art, London 'Dada-Constructivism' cat. no. 128 illus. in colour, 1984

43

42

41

Kurt Schwitters

44 Untitled 1936
collage
image: 16.2 x 13.2 cm
mount: 33 x 25 cm
signed on mount
Exhibited: Annely Juda Fine Art, London
'Dada-Constructivism' cat. no. 136, 1984

45 Fine c.1945–47
oil and collage on card
image: 14.6 x 10.7 cm
mount: 23 x 17 cm
signed, titled left on mount and inscribed
Exhibited: Annely Juda Fine Art, London
'Dada-Constructivism' cat. no. 139, 1984

44

45

Vladimir Tatlin

46 Untitled c.1916–17
tempera and oil on board
75.5 x 41.5 cm
Private Collection
Exhibited: Staatsgalerie Stuttgart, Opening Exhibition cat. addendum p. 19 illus., 1984

46

Georges Vantongerloo

47 Fonction de Lignes 1936
watercolour, gouache and indian ink on card
49.8 x 60 cm
signed and dated 'G. Vantongerloo, Paris 1936' on card on verso
This work is a study for 'Function' 1936, oil on plywood, 82 x 100 cm. cf. 'A travelling Retrospective Exhibition Georges Vantongerloo' cat. no. 92 illus., 1980
Exhibited: Annely Juda Fine Art, London 'Dada-Constructivism' cat. no. 146 illus. in colour, 1984

47

Friedrich Vordemberge-Gildewart

48 Composition No.77 1933
oil on canvas with mounted wood
35 x 35 cm
Exhibited: Städtische Kunsthalle, Mannheim 'Friedrich Vordemberge-Gildewart' cat. no. 77, 1970. Galerie Bargera, Köln 'Die Abstrakten Hannover' cat. no. 72, 1975. Ulmer Museum 'Friedrich Vordemberge-Gildewart' cat. no. 33, 1975. 'Friedrich Vordemberge-Gildewart' cat. no. 31 illus., Quadrat Bottrop; Kunstmuseum Hannover 1980. Annely Juda Fine Art, London 'Dada-Constructivism' cat. no. 153 illus., 1984
Literature: Hans L. C. Jaffe 'Vordemberge-Gildewart Mensch und Werk' oeuvre cat. no. 81 illus., DuMont 1971

49 Composition No.94 1935
oil on canvas
100 x 80 cm
Exhibited: Annely Juda Fine Art, London 'Friedrich Vordemberge-Gildewart Retrospective' cat. no. 17, 1972. Annely Juda Fine Art, London 'Vordemberge-Gildewart Remembered' cat. no. 6, 1974. Ulmer Museum 'Friedrich Vordemberge-Gildewart' cat. no. 44, 1975. 'Friedrich Vordemberge-Gildewart' cat. no. 34, Quadrat Bottrop; Kunstmuseum Hannover 1980. Kettle's Yard Gallery, Cambridge 'Circle: International Survey of Constructive Art' cat. no. 36 illus. p. 31, 1982. Annely Juda Fine Art, London 'Dada-Constructivism' cat. no. 154, 1984
Literature: Hans L. C. Jaffe 'Vordemberge-Gildewart Mensch und Werk' oeuvre cat. no. 98 illus., DuMont 1971. Willy Rotzler 'Vordemberge-Gildewart' no. 23 illus. p. 73, Erker, St Gallen 1979

48

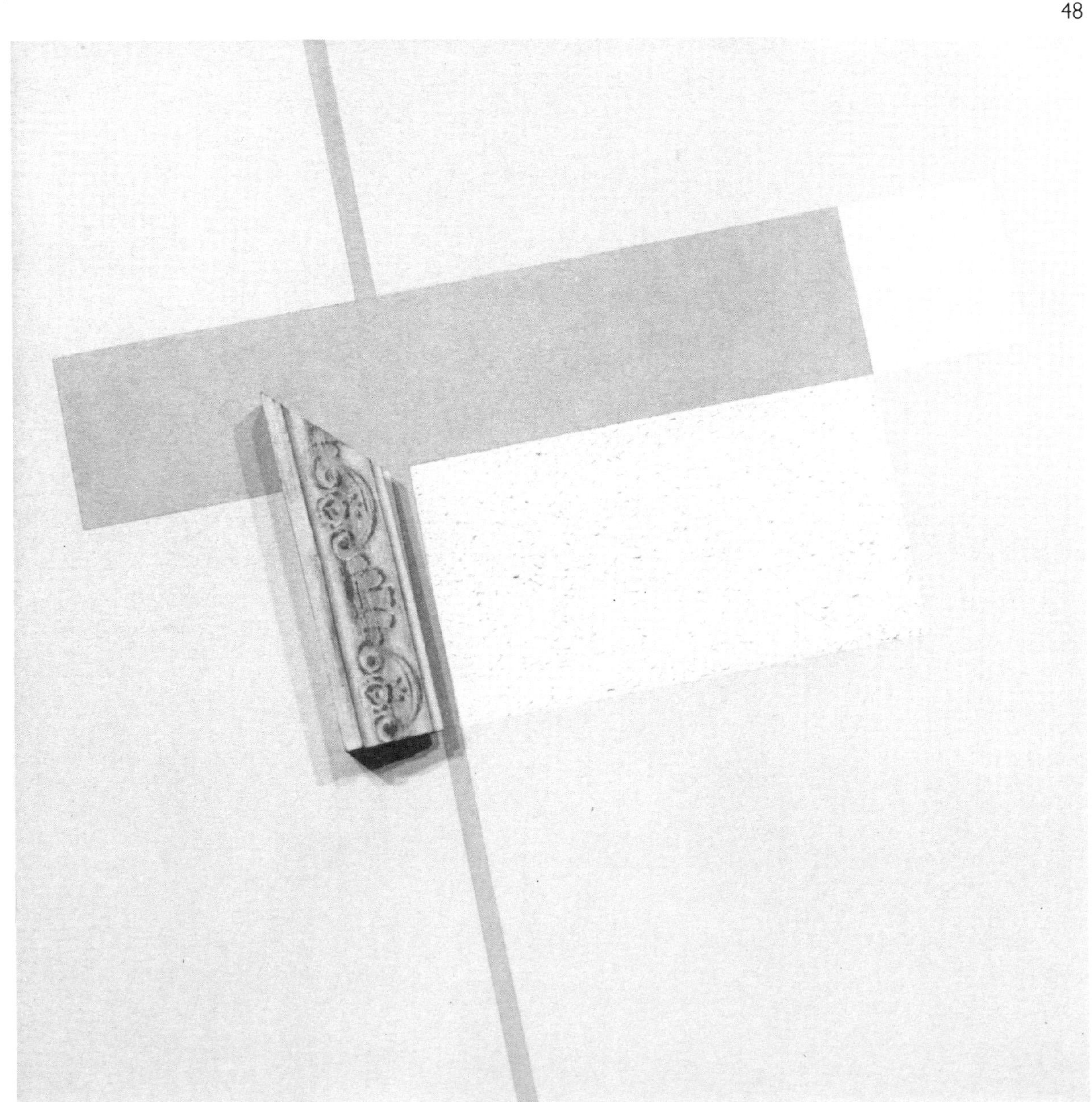

49

Three Decades of Contemporary Art

THE SIXTIES

The Sixties

It is impossible for me to record in a brief essay the historical evolution of the nineteen sixties, trace the roots of the general cultural explosion in England, for that is what it was, or describe in detail the extraordinary events in the art world of that era. All that I can do here is to offer a fragmented and abbreviated impression of the time. The main characteristics were optimism, openness and buoyancy. England was in a phase of unprecedented prosperity after the grey post-war times of austerity which lasted until the early fifties. The sense of security and comparative affluence of the sixties was doubtless based on specious national bookkeeping, but it was real enough for most of us to enjoy in our suddenly expanded daily lives. We travelled more, and London throughout the fifties had become increasingly international in its theatre, concerts, publications and exhibitions. We enjoyed ourselves tremendously.

Peter Daubeny's magnificent World Theatre series brought us Jean Vilar and Maria Casarés in the T.N.P., the Berliner Ensemble from Berlin and the Teatro Piccolo from Milan. We went to Ravi Shankar concerts and heard first performances of new works by Boulez, who became principal conductor of the BBC Symphony Orchestra under William Glock's brilliant direction of music at the BBC and we flocked to Stockhausen concerts; Merce Cuningham's dance company came to London, Kenneth MacMillan choreographed *Le Sacre du Printemps* with Nolan's great sets and costumes, Glen Tetley choreographed *Pierrot Lunaire* for Ballet Rambert, Callas sang *Traviata* at Covent Garden.

Bridget Riley and Ad Reinhardt began the Anglo-American exchange with *Poor Old Tired Horse*. We consulted the *I Ch'ing*, smoked a little pot, listened to Jimmy Hendrix, Aretha Franklin, Dionne Warwick, the Beatles and the Stones. We watched Delphine Seyrig float in a black wig through Alain Resnais' *L'Année Dernière à Marienbad* and Dirk Bogarde camp around doing a Snowdon take-off in rectangular bifocals in Losey's *Modesty Blaise*. Claude van Italie's *America Hurrah* and *Motel* appeared at the Royal Court and so did Albee's *Zoo Story*. We danced at the Ad Lib or at Wolf Mankiewicz's Pickwick Club, and in New York we danced the twist and the frug at Trudy Heller's, The Five Spot on St. Mark's Place, where I remember dancing with Judy Holliday, then married to Gerry Mulligan, while Larry Rivers played his trumpet with other musicians, and with Helen Frankenthaler at the old Apollo in Harlem – it was still just possible – where later, Jasper Johns, Tini Duchamp and myself watched, entranced, The Four Tops. There were summer visits to Lee Krasner at East Hampton, to David Smith at Bolton's Landing, Robert Motherwell at Provincetown and Edward Albee's annual pool party at Montauk. Warhol's silver-clad Factory was in full swing in New York with silk-screened portraits of Marilyn in production and some wild movies, notably *Blow Job*; Mark Rothko laboured with his large, sad paintings full of *pentimenti*, for the de Menil's chapel in Texas. I took Barnett Newman, and separately Mark Rothko to Coney Island to see the white whale, where Barney insisted on joining me on the parachute jump, to everyone's panic.

There was a constant exchange of visits among artists between London, New York and Los Angeles. We read Flannery O'Connor's stories and Ted Hughes' poetry. Peter Brook produced the *Marat/Sade* with Glenda Jackson playing Charlotte Corday and *Lear* and *Oedipus* with Schofield, Gielgud and Irene Worth. Antonioni made *Blow Up* in England; David Bailey and fashion photography boomed; the demarcation line between serious art and high style was blurred by the glossy magazines so that the serious inventions of Phillip King and Paul Huxley were mixed in with Mary Quant's mini skirts, and plastic shopping bags with Union Jacks: pop art had arrived and swinging London. Snowdon photographed everybody for *Private View*; a Jim Dine collage in the window of Robert Fraser's gallery caused the closure of the show by the police for obscenity. Innocent as always, I had purchased one of these collages for the Leicestershire Education Committee and testified to this effect to an unimpressed police court. Stewart Mason, our Education Officer, wrung his hands back in Leicestershire. Edward Bond's great and tragic play *Saved* arrived; the Lord Chamberlain's role was abolished after Bond's fantasy about Queen Victoria's lesbian relationship with Florence Nightingale, *Early Morning*, played at the Royal Court. Albee's edgy play *Who's Afraid of Virginia Woolf* was seen and Osborne's great diatribe *Inadmissable Evidence*. If the decade began with the dreamlike disruption of space and time in *L'année dernière à Marienbad* it ended with the exploitation of violence and bogus nostalgia of *Bonny and Clyde*. In between, Jeanne Moreau appeared in Truffaut's *Jules et Jim* celebrating obliquely the sexual liberation and ambiguities of the sixties and written by my friend, Henri-Pierre Roché, the collector and one-time secretary of the Maharajah who had commissioned, through Roché, three bronze Birds in Space by Brancusi for a pool by a shrine in India.

Early in the decade, Kennedy was assassinated. There were explosions of violence intermittently through the sixties among the black communities of Chicago, Los Angeles – the Watts district around Simon Rodia's fantastic tower – and New York. In Paris, the students made their protest in 1968, and in London there was a prolonged sit-in at Hornsey School of Art. Students increasingly refused to learn technical processes or to draw at life class. Surfeit and disbelief set in, and a revulsion against the financial excesses of some parts of the art world. In the background the war in Vietnam entered successive phases of atrocity.

In England, art thrived through the decade in a mood of vigorous confidence that began to ebb away or at least to be undermined by financial, social and political pressures towards the end of the decade. The confidence began in the art schools, with the *Young Contemporaries* shows in which Allen Jones, Patrick Caulfield, David Hockney, Paul Huxley, John Hoyland, Bridget Riley and practically all the liveliest artists first appeared – student exhibitions began to be visited by collectors and dealers in the late fifties. There were the *New Generation* shows at Whitechapel, with generous subvention from the Stuyvesant Foundation, and large retrospectives for Phillip King, Richard Smith, Anthony Caro, Ceri Richards, John Hoyland, Tim Scott, John Craxton, Bryan Kneale and others. At the Arts Council, Arnold Goodman's unflagging support for good policies was backed by Jenny Lee's financial wizardry as Minister for the Arts, an alliance in total contrast to the present-day régime. Pop art was created by Hamilton, Paolozzi and Peter Blake. Blake's record sleeve for *Sergeant Pepper* arrived. David Hockney flourished and delighted everybody. Bridget Riley participated in the *The Responsive Eye* show at the Museum of Modern Art in New York and discovered dress fabrics made from her painting – the demarcation line was indeed confused. Colour and transparency appeared in sculpture. King's *Genghis Khan*, Caro's miraculously floating sculpture *Prairie* and Tim Scott's series of great sculptural inventions, from *Peach Wheels* to *Quinquereme* were all created. It was a stirring and privileged time of true creativity and the very air seemed tonic. Moore, Hepworth, Nicholson, Burra and Bacon made some of their best work. Magazines and periodicals flourished, from the RCA publication *Ark* to *Metro* and the excellent *Studio International* under Peter Townsend. The space devoted to art in the popular press seems incredible now. When Sidney Nolan had his brilliant retrospective at the Whitechapel, two pages in *The Observer* celebrated the occasion. The public thronged to art exhibitions; at the Whitechapel, we had to ask for police help with the queues waiting to enter the gallery each morning for the great Rauschenberg exhibition. Public enthusiasm, in at least the first half of the sixties, was aroused by the freshness of colour and form in the painting of the period; the liberation of colour as content in certain other paintings of the time and the sheer imaginative clarity of the works by Riley, Huxley, Hoyland, Hockney and others. Of central importance was the way in which Caro had freed sculpture from the base and put it on the floor, so that it occupied our own space rather than a museum pedestal, and made open, constructed sculptures in steel in opposition to traditionally enclosed, solid, monolithic forms in bronze or wood. The dominant influences came from the U.S., largely stimulated by the Pollock show at the Whitechapel in 1958, the Tate Gallery show of American art in 1959 and large shows at the Whitechapel of work by Guston, Tobey, Johns, Rauschenberg, Rothko, Kline, Krasner, Louis, Motherwell and Frankenthaler in the late fifties and early sixties.

In all this activity, the galleries in London directed by Annely Juda and Alex Gregory-Hood played a vital part. Their backgrounds could not have been more different, and as they are very remarkable individuals I have recorded the outline of their life stories. This has been done at my own suggestion, I should add, and with the slightly embarrassed acquiescence of Annely and Alex.

Annely Juda was born on 23 September 1914 in Kassel, the elder of two daughters. Her younger sister, Eva, has lived in Israel since 1934. Annely's father, Kurt Brauer, and her mother, Margarete Goldmann, were both from Berlin, not orthodox Jews but liberal and emancipated, although they observed the Jewish holidays. They spoke no Hebrew; there were family lessons, but the language and literature seemed remote. Kurt Brauer was an experimental chemist who came to Kassel because he had discovered an exceptionally fine laboratory for sale, belonging originally to a friend of Goethe's. He found material tucked away in the laboratory – papers and notebooks – connected with Goethe's colour theory, compiled by friends and colleagues of Goethe's. Kurt Brauer made a good living by working in commercial experiments with washing powders, de-caffinated coffee, denicotinised cigarettes, dyes for foodstuffs and other synthetic products, but he was more of a pure scientist by nature than a practical man, his daughter remembers, and he was absorbed intermittently by the colour theory documents he found in his new workplace.

Margarete Brauer was a professional designer who had trained in Berlin at the Charlottenburg Art School and designed the typography and layout of large catalogues for department stores as well as working as a fashion designer. Annely remembers her mother's hair cut in a sharp Eton crop in the Twenties, her keen sympathy for the avantgarde in general and her father's support for this interest. The house was full of her mother's pictures and other paintings by friends; there was also a small Utrillo and a Vlaminck water-colour. But the museum at Kassel has an outstanding collection of paintings by Rembrandt, Rubens and van Dyck and these were the young Annely's introduction to art as well as the interior of her own house. Annely's paternal grandparents in Berlin were equally cultivated: her grandmother, formidable, red-haired, benignly alarming, ran a successful antique shop; her apartment contained a complete Biedermeier room in rosewood which Annely loved and slept in when she visited. In her own home in Kassel there was, naturally, antique furniture as well as the modern style that was so much part of her mother's life as a designer.

Among Annely's earliest memories of modern art is a van Gogh exhibition in Basle around 1920 when she was a small child, before she was a schoolgirl. In Basle there was also a splendid zoo and she remembers her own anxiety that the van Gogh show would usurp the time necessary for visiting the zoo before catching the train home. Later, at her grammar school, she was picked out by her art teacher among other promising students for extra art classes. She recalls being painted as a girl by her mother, who made many portraits of her family and friends.

At her grammar school, her teachers thought that Annely wanted to be an artist, but she really hankered after the design world of her mother: she loved clothes and, equally keen on style as a whole, she really wanted to be a clothes designer and decorator, much stimulated by her mother's example. At sixteen, there was a serious family crisis. Her father did not oppose Annely's choice of a career, but he insisted that his daughter sit for the equivalent of A-levels as a prelude to studying at university.

The prospect of studying art history persuaded Annely to accept this plan, but her studies were terminated when, at eighteen, she was forbidden as a Jewess to study at the university. The Nazis were in firm control in Kassel. She helped her father in the laboratory, but Kurt Brauer was an old-fashioned Socialist, with left wing sympathies and friendships and in 1933 he was imprisoned by the Nazis. Later in the year he was released and at once left for Palestine, via Switzerland. With a friend he established a modest factory in Jaffa, manufacturing foodstuffs. Annely joined her father in Palestine in July 1934; Annely's mother and sister Eva remained behind in Kassel until November to sell the laboratory. The family had already moved to a smaller apartment. The tension in the air of persecution and violence must have been terrible.

Annely's indomitable grandmother in Berlin refused to move: her husband had died and she had become a fatalist. Just before the war, the Nazis wanted to deport her to Theresienstadt. Alone and blind in Berlin, she committed suicide. Annely's other grandmother, on her mother's side, was moved to Theresienstadt, where she died in the camp. Some courageous souls among the thousands who were deported to Theresienstadt made watercolours and drawings of their daily lives undergoing slave labour in this final ghetto devised by the Nazis in a small rural town and these are preserved for us in Jerusalem, at the Yad Vashem Memorial to the six million Jews killed by the Nazis, so that we do not forget their fate. These watercolours and drawings are even more anguishing than the brutal photographic documentation of the holocaust elsewhere at Yad Vashem because of the patient efforts of the artists *to make something* of their drawings of what their everyday life had been reduced to: *this* blue wash here, *that* bit of horizon just sketched in *thus*.

Palestine in 1934 was a haven for Jewish refugees who could somehow get there, but it was still no picnic. It was hard for everyone and tough, in special ways, for educated people starting up all over again without much money. Life was lived in a rough frontier situation. Annely still wanted to design and attend university, but instead she had to work with her father at his factory.

And the whole family had to learn English or Hebrew, and Arabic, in order to survive. They spoke English only with difficulty. Annely learned some minimal Hebrew; her father swore he'd never learn, oppressed by its difficulties. Annely remembers a passing truck splashing mud over her father's white suit when they were present at an unloading near the docks in Jaffa, soon after her reunion with her father – and thinking forever afterwards that this incident was symbolic of the life they had to face. There was little to do except work and not much to amuse a girl between the ages of nineteen and twenty-three, which were the ages that Annely passed through in Israel. In the brief respites from the long hours of hard work there was beach life, cinema occasionally, books, sometimes dancing – but not the cosmopolitan life of Berlin, or even Kassel. Toscanini gave a concert; Annely met the violinist Huberman, through a boyfriend.

Annely remembers a joke about the tough time endured by the intelligentsia working in uncongenial jobs:

'If you called for a doctor near any building site, all the workmen descended . . . .' Or they worked as bus conductors. Her father survived with café life and gossip; the family had German friends. Annely was wretched and finally told her father that she had to leave. She wanted to try to push ahead somehow in her chosen path. The financial insecurity inseparable from this choice worried her parents, but her wishes prevailed.

Annely arrived in England in 1937 just in time for the Coronation of George VI, which she watched from the Marble Arch Corner House – after taking a ship to Bari and Naples with £25 from an aunt also in Israel. Goering was visiting Naples and speaking to the crowds: Annely left for Rome, then Paris. She arrived in Newhaven from Dieppe with £1, and after interrogation was allowed in when she produced evidence of friends in London. The mother of Hans Sachs, a trumpet player in the Israel Symphony Orchestra, ran a boarding house in Hampstead, already with its contingent of German refugees. Annely boarded with her in exchange for housework. Here also was another refugee family, the Judas, and Annely became friendly with their younger son, Paul.

Earning £1 a week, Annely was still determined to work as a designer and she began to study fashion design at the Reimann School, where Leonard Rosoman taught and held a life class and Alex Kroll, later of House and Garden, and Sal Dessau, who was later to marry Eric Estorick, were among her fellow students. At the end of 1938, Annely stopped work at the boarding house to study art every day. Paul Juda, who was studying law, paid for the lessons. In November 1939, Annely and Paul were married. The Reimann School split up soon after the outbreak of war; the students went home.

With the pressures and dispersals of the early years of the war, Paul Juda did not complete his law studies; he ran a sportswear and hairdressing business for Violet Cripps. He and Annely lived in Richmond and Annely – denied any possibility of working in the fashion or dress world by her husband – worked for the W.V.S. It is odd to think of the later stalwart champion of Malevich and Tatlin marooned among the felt hats and kilner jars of the W.V.S.

In 1942, Carol, Annely's first child was born. Annely was busy with being a wife and mother, but she saw exhibitions and visited the Tate, although she was not really conscious of contemporary English art until after the war. While the war lasted, there was family life, the W.V.S. and entertaining her husband's friends. Annely's parents and her sister had remained in Israel. At the end of the war, Kurt Brauer suffered a stroke. In 1948 he sold his factory in Jaffa, which had not been very successful, and he and Margarete came to England. Neither of them were very well. Kurt died in London in 1951, and Margarete returned to Israel, too unwell to make much of life in London.

In 1946, Annely's second child was born: David, who now runs the gallery so energetically with Annely – but in 1946, Annely still had a long way to go before finding her own path in art. In 1949, under the international process set up by the 'restitution of funds' scheme, Paul Juda sought to regain family property that had been confiscated by the Nazis in Cologne. He was persuaded by his family to return to Germany and to join his father's estate agency in Cologne. Annely was reluctant to return to Germany, but she went on the understanding that the move was not to be permanent.

The existence of a businessman's wife in post-war Germany, mostly in the country and not allowed to work by her husband, was not a congenial experience for Annely despite the comforts, a car and a chauffeur for example, of an apparently successful life created by her husband. The two children were sent to England to boarding school; a third child, Susan, was born in 1951. Annely bought a few pictures, visited some exhibitions, but was essentially in a different world far away from art.

In 1955, her husband's business ventures foundered and Annely's marriage came to an end. She returned to England with the three children. Susan was inhibited in English and attended Anna Freud's Kindergarten in Hampstead; her German nanny came to England: after 35 years she remains here to look after Annely and, occasionally, Susan's children. For Annely, this was a difficult period of re-establishing herself, but it was essentially, at the age of forty-one, her true beginning as an independent woman.

She found a job on the switchboard of the United Restitutions office and she returned to Mrs Sachs' boarding house, where she also worked on the telephone, doing two jobs to support herself and the children. To improve conditions, her mother returned from Israel for a spell to help.

While Annely was living in Germany, she had visited Portofino for a holiday with her husband and there she had met again Sal Dessau, last seen at the Reimann School, and now married to Eric Estorick, the well known collector of modern art. In 1956, Estorick, an American, was in London and looking for a secretary. Annely worked as a secretary for Eric Estorick from 1956 to 1958 administering his collection. She learned a great deal, with constant access to his excellent library of art books and catalogues and the Estorick collection, mostly of modern Italian art, but also containing fine paintings by Derain, Kandinsky, Modigliani and Utrillo in a large and generally rich collection. Part of her duties was to translate into English articles in French and German art periodicals.

Her professional sense had been aroused for the first time in the gallery and museum world one year previously, in 1955. Before returning from Germany to London with her children, Annely had visited the first

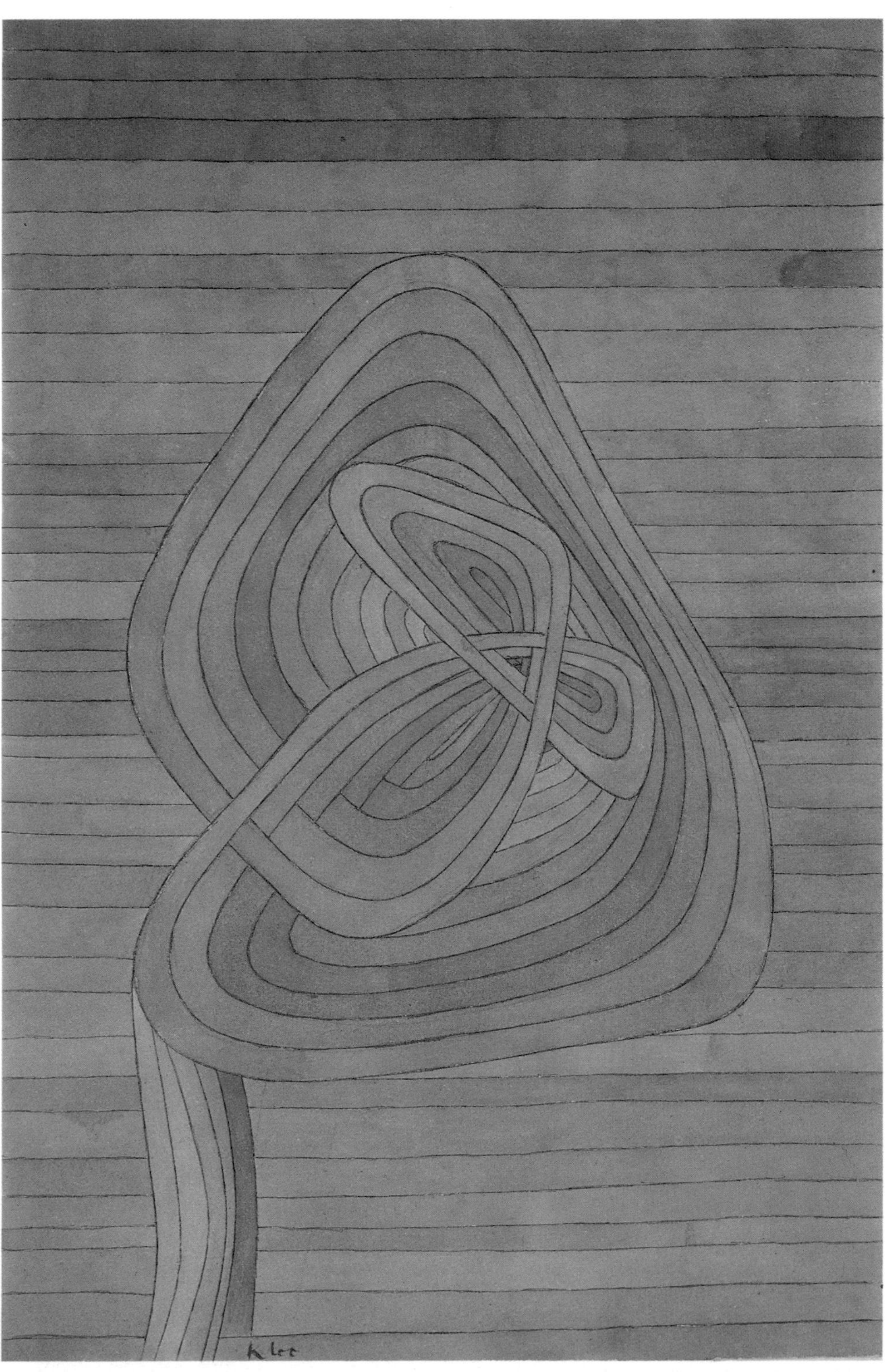

Paul Klee, Einsame Blüte 1934 watercolour on paper 48 x 32 cm

Dokumenta international exhibition of contemporary art in Kassel, her home town. A pre-war family friend, Arnold Bode, was the inventor of *Dokumenta* and its first selector and organiser. Annely took David, aged nine, to watch the installation of the huge exhibition.

As a young girl, Annely had been conscious of the work and troubled presence in Germany of the so-called 'forbidden' artists like Nolde, Beckmann and Jawlensky whose work was proscribed by the Nazis. Arnold Bode had begun life as an artist; Annely's mother had attended his classes. Bode was not Jewish, but his work was considered degenerate by the Nazis and he was forbidden to paint. His wife was French. He had stayed in Germany with a non-combatant role in the army during the war. In 1955, his concern for architecture and his love for modern art were the great stimulants behind *Dokumenta*; He wanted to help bring Germany, so repressively insulated in the thirties and forties, back into the international art world. He succeeded, with a brilliant exhibition – which had a unique focus through Bode's concern for architecture.

The experience of *Dokumenta* in Kassel in 1955 must have had its own undercurrents for Annely, after the wretched events of 1933–34; but she learned much from the biggest post-war exhibition of modern art and this experience, combined with her time with Eric Estorick in 1956–58, gave an additional impetus to her always strong desire to work and to participate in some way in the art world. For practical reasons of training and age, she had relinquished by now her earlier ambition to work as a designer.

She was not yet much aware of contemporary English art when she worked for Estorick; but she occupied herself with learning all she could of the work of the main figures in 20th century art, including, of course, those represented in Estorick's strong and compendious modern Italian collection.

Another childhood family friend in Kassel, von Buttlar, was now the Head of the Academy in Berlin. Later, he worked closely with Bode and Schmalenbach in Kassel on *Dokumenta*. Through her friendship with von Buttlar, Annely was able to arrange a showing of the Estorick collection in Berlin in 1957. The exhibition was greatly honoured, and provided the first survey in Germany, after the decades of isolation, of the work of Severini, Balla, Carra, Soffici, de Chirico, Seroni, Casella, Rosati, Rosai and de Pisis. Annely established good contacts with German officials and museum and gallery personnel from many countries through her visits to Kassel and Berlin.

Back in London, Annely became friendly with Ewan Phillips, director of the Kaplan Gallery in Duke Street, St. James's and late in 1958 began to work there: her first gallery job. She helped with exhibitions of work by Tinguely and the surrealist painter Leonor Fini, among others, and began to sense the complexity of gallery life. A visitor, Mrs Stern, interested in Epstein and a collector, suggested that with her backing Annely might start her own gallery.

In 1960, Annely found premises two doors away from Gimpel Fils in South Molton Street, and the Molton Gallery opened. Arnold Bode designed the gallery as a present. Word had got about in 1959 that she was about to open her own gallery and artists began to visit her at the Kaplan Gallery: John Coplans, Colquhoun and MacBryde. Her awareness of contemporary English art began to expand; but her opening exhibition was a show of Emilio Pettoruti, an Argentinian, Juan Gris-inspired abstract artist and contemporary of Cubism living in Paris, whose wife was an art critic. They were helpful on Annely's visits to Paris and arranged visits to other artists. Annely became part of a closely knit group of friends in Paris which included Campigli's wife, Baram – an Israeli artist, Clemente and Key Sato. There was little interest in London among her Paris friends: Paris was in the trough of a prolonged phase of insularity. In London she also showed work by Borés and Zadkine, bought some pictures by the twenty-one year old Australian painter, Brett Whitely and showed paintings by Robyn Denny, Avinash Chandra, Gillian Ayres, Bernard Cohen, the Australian artist Tony Underhill, and sculpture by William Turnbull and Oliffe Richmond, Henry Moore's long-term but creatively independent assistant.

Essentially, in addition to her prompt championing of some of the more advanced abstract artists in England, Annely specialized from the beginning in rather grand and highly enterprising shows of work by distinguished foreign artists, many of them of crucial importance to modern art: sculpture, drawings and lithographs by Zadkine, an Ecole de Paris show of post-war paintings and a fine Paul Klee show, all in 1961; collaboration with Betty Parsons and her New York Gallery in 1962 to show four American abstract painters . . . you had the same agreeably cosmopolitan feeling on entering the Molton Gallery that you had on visiting Erica Brausen at the nearby Hanover Gallery, another pioneer gallery in London in providing us with information about the best post-war European art, except that Annely lacked Erica's disdain for English provincialism and her dislike of American art. Annely had high standards, but was more open minded; her gallery was always informal and easy in its atmosphere.

She was off to an excellent start and she has never looked back. Her short, swift figure walking across the gallery to greet you – darting back to check something with a secretary, her usual offer of coffee, impatience with fuss or affectation, eagerness for exact knowledge, humorous distaste for silliness and ignorance – of which there is always a fair amount in the art world – and her brisk amiability have become well known and greatly appreciated internationally.

Her particular balance between Continental and English art was safely established. She had advice and help in the launching of the Molton Gallery from Charles Gimpel, Freddy Mayor and Victor Waddington among others. The Molton Gallery lasted for three years, with a broadly varied programme, before Annely changed her premises and moved to St. George Street where she opened the Hamilton Galleries in July 1963 with a show of paintings by the Australian artist, Klaus Friedeberger. Lawrence Alloway, Herbert Read and Theo Schlicht were among her patrons and supporters. Nika Hulton, Joe Hirshhorn and Ted Power were also among the collectors who bought works of art from Annely at this time. Erica Brausen, in her gallery opposite, was helpful and friendly.

Annely's unparochial policy of presenting Continental and English art continued with shows of work by Tess Jaray, Michael Kenny and Nicholas Georgiadis, among others, until her final move in 1968 to her present premises in Tottenham Mews and her emergence with David, as Annely Juda Fine Art. While she was still at the Molton Gallery, she gave an exhibition in October-November 1960 to the Israeli artist, Baram, who had helped guide her to artists in Paris. Alex Gregory-Hood walked in, as a collector, and bought a collage. They chatted affably and remained on friendly terms, but neither could have had any notion that one day they would become partners in a jointly administered gallery.

In October 1960, Alex Gregory-Hood was forty-five, one year younger than Annely, and had just resigned his commission in the regular army. He had been with the Grenadier Guards for a quarter of a century, since 1935, when he joined the Regiment on leaving Sandhurst and he had ended his career, after a distinguished war record, by commanding the Grenadier Guards as Colonel. He was then nominated for the Imperial Defence College, which in due course would have made him an exceptionally young General, but Alex rebelled at the prospect of a staff job and separation from his men. Feeling that he had enjoyed the best part of his army career and losing interest in the army as a vocation, Alex had resigned his commission in 1960 and in October, when he wandered into the Molton Gallery, he was technically unemployed for six months.

Alex became interested in contemporary art long before he left the army. Soon after the end of the war, he had begun to visit shows of modern art; he recalls a Nolde exhibition in Hamburg in 1947 which aroused great excitement in him. His visits to museums and galleries were occasional, not directed by any conscious plan, and conditioned by the practical army circumstances of time and place. In 1950, he began to collect contemporary art.

In 1955, through a developing interest in English abstract art, stimulated and helped by conversations with Victor Waddington, who exhibited the work of several St. Ives artists, Alex visited St. Ives as a budding collector for the first time. He enjoyed the company of Roger Leigh, the sculptor and an assistant to Barbara Hepworth – Leigh's family lived in a house near Alex's aunt at Stow-on-the-Wold – and Denis Mitchell, the sculptor, also an assistant to Hepworth. Through Leigh, Alex met Terry Frost, Roger Hilton and other artists, living in or staying regularly in St. Ives and he bought paintings by Frost, Hilton and W. Barns-Graham. He visited the studios of Nicholson and Hepworth and was affected by the freshness and integrity of the general level of art produced in St. Ives at this time. Alex's innate sense of the fitness of things was subconsciously at ease with the way in which art, at a conspicuously virtuous phase of its existence in St. Ives, was an accepted part of the life and consciousness of the town and with an effect, in light and texture and colour, on the physical nature of the work made there. As a collector, Alex was encouraged by the example of his grandfather, the Hon. Marshall Brooks, who had built up a distinguished collection of Italian and Dutch art.

Alex's background was unusual for a patron of contemporary art. The landed gentry, from which he was descended, had often acquired art collections of variable, sometimes considerable interest, but in the first half of the 20th century the tradition was rarely carried through into any serious interest in contemporary art. Country houses containing decent paintings by minor or major old masters too often had nothing of the 20th century, or came to a full stop with a few indifferent landscapes or portraits by academicians without serious merit. It is possible that Alex's sense of the healthiness of an evolving rather than a static tradition stimulated his interest in contemporary art or at least deepened it – but he has no acquisitive instinct, except for plants and trees.

Alex was born on 18th July 1915 at Tarporley, Cheshire in his maternal grandfather's house. His father, Charles Gregory-Hood, had been in the army briefly, but in Alex's early childhood was working as a land agent for some relatives, the Heber-Percy family, in Yorkshire. His mother was Dorothy Brooks, whose father was a cotton merchant in Manchester and his brother, a banker, became Lord Crawshaw in the 19th century; her mother's brother, Lord Willingdon, became Viceroy of India.

The Gregory's were an old Warwickshire family of country gentlemen, not particularly good and not especially bad, according to Alex. His father had taken over the family estate at Styvechale, near Coventry, on the death of his own father – Alex's grandfather – but in 1927 had been obliged to pull down Styvechale Hall, the family house since 1760, because of its vast and impractical size. Alex's earliest years were spent at Loppington Hall, Shropshire. Then, after living for some years in the manor house at Styvechale, before the demolition of nearby Styvechale Hall, Alex and his family moved to Loxley Hall at Loxley near Stratford-on-Avon, in 1927 when Alex was twelve.

This is where Alex spent his youth, on holiday from school or on leave from the army; and where later he was to plan sites for contemporary sculpture by Rowan Gallery artists in the spacious gardens in 1975 and to change the sculptures on these sites regularly from this time on – and to entertain house parties of artists and their families, and other friends in the art world, from 1962 onward – after the opening of the Rowan Gallery.

Loxley Hall is a William and Mary stone house, built c. 1700, with a substantial red brick Victorian extension, a courtyard with outbuildings and barns and a series of large, enclosed gardens of varied aspect and character, well planted with trees, bounded by a stream which separates the house and its substantial grounds from the gently undulating Warwickshire landscape. Alex describes the Victorian additions to the house as hideous and believes that the house works only from the inside, looking out at the fine views. Few of his friends agree with this opinion.

The church of Loxley, with discreet decorations by Anthony Green, is inside the gates of Loxley Hall and here weekend visitors are invited to attend Sunday morning service in the Gregory-Hood family box-pew. Some do not, and mooch lazily around the garden. After the service, the vicar and his wife return to Loxley Hall, a few steps away, with Alex and his guests for Sunday lunch. It is a charming practice, with delicate undertones of Jane Austen's set pieces, notably in the mixture of generations represented by young artists with their families, country neighbours and until recently, Alex's mother, who lived nearby and who died in 1983 at ninety-three.

This delightful background of nominal country squire, busy at weekends with county neighbours and local affairs as well as guests, is unusual for a dealer in advanced forms of contemporary art; and experiences of weekends at Loxley hall for the past twenty-five years have been decidedly unusual for Alex's country friends and neighbours and the innumerable artists and members of the art world who have been brought together in ways determined impassively and unswervingly by Alex's liking for thoroughly mixed company and his belief, quite accurate, that artists, like country folk, mostly lead segregated lives and should therefore mix together once in a while. But descriptions of Loxley weekends might more properly recur later in this short chronicle.

To say that the Gregorys are an old Warwickshire family of country gentlemen requires clarification and so does the identity of the Hoods, Alex's family on the side of his father's family. The Gregorys have lived in Warwickshire since 1500; there are records of their residence in a Tudor manor house in Coventry – Alex's son, Peter, still owns land near Coventry. (According to Alex the family did nothing – or they were gamblers, like one of the Mr Gregory's who was a gambling friend of the Prince Regent.) But an earlier Gregory ancestor was Recorder at Stoneleigh Abbey in Warwickshire during the reign of Henry VIII and Alex still has a document of one of the earliest deeds to land in Warwickshire dated 1086.

The Hoods became known, indeed famous, in the 18th century. A Reverend Hood was the vicar of a village in Somerset. A naval sea captain's carriage broke down in the village and the vicar lodged him while he waited for the repairs. He told marvellous stories of the sea to the vicar's three sons and when he left told them that if they ever wanted to join the Navy they could write to him for support. The eldest boy joined and became Lord Hood, Admiral of the Blue. The second boy joined his brother and became Admiral of the Red, Lord Bridport. The youngest boy wanted to join his brothers, but remained at home and drowned in a flooded ditch when he fell off a horse. Both the naval brothers achieved fame, notably with Nelson, and one of the Galapagos Islands is called Hood Island after Sir Samuel Hood. Alex's combined ancestry does suggest, at the very least, the possibility of a venturesome streak and an ability to take risks, which was well demonstrated when he left the army and embarked upon his new career in the art world at the age of forty-five. Well trained in discipline and clarity of thought and action, nothing in his life up to that moment had prepared him for such a radical change.

After attending a preparatory school, St. Aubyn's at Rottingdean, Alex was at Winchester which he says he did not greatly enjoy apart from showing a flair for athletics; he was a good hurdler. In 1934 he entered Sandhurst Military Academy through lack of any opposing ambition. There were some family precedents. He enjoyed Sandhurst, kept two horses and liked the comparative freedom after Winchester. He avoided army commission as an officer and even refused to become a sergeant over the other cadets. In despair, he was made a corporal.

In 1935, Alex graduated from Sandhurst and joined the Grenadier Guards. Again, there was some precedent for this among the Hoods. From 1936 to 1937, he was in Egypt, based mainly in Alexandria with its Coptic, Italian and Greek communities. He admits that at this time he was much more concerned with enjoying himself than with military matters, whilst his Commanding Officer, who became General Sir

Frederick 'Boy' Browning was establishing the strategy for the North African war. Alex loved Egypt, explored very little and found himself gradually set in the pattern of a soldier's life. In England, on leave, he went hunting.

In 1939, Alex was stationed in London and early that year he was made Adjutant to a territorial battalion; the Green Howards, in Yorkshire. After they left for France, he was ordered back to his own battalion. From 1940-44, Alex was involved in training in different forms in England and in 1944, he commanded a squadron in the second armoured battalion of the Grenadier Guards in the allied invasion of Europe. He ended up near Bremen and, soon after the Armistice, with the Guards Brigade in Berlin. The exigencies of the army totally claimed him all through the war, in which he was awarded the MC and bar.

In 1951, Alex became Brigade Major in charge of all Household Troops taking part in the ceremonial duties at the time of the Coronation. In 1956 he commanded the third battalion of the Grenadiers when they were sent to Malta, at the time of Suez, and subsequently to Cyprus. In 1959, he took command of his regiment, as Colonel, and then resigned his commission and left the army with the feeling that the interest and excitement for him was over. Alex would also have keenly disliked the inevitable separation from his men which promotion to the staff job would have entailed.

His mounting post-war interest in contemporary art was stimulated by the visits to St. Ives, but it was most particularly sharpened through friendship with David Gibbs, an ex-Guards friend who was working in the late 'fifties as a dealer, first at Tooth's gallery and then alone, and enthusiastically bringing to England large canvases by Barnett Newman, Pollock, Morris Louis and Lee Krasner. Gibbs was advising, with others, E. J. Power, the head of Pye-Murphy, in the formation of his collection and Alex liked the straightforward approach to modern art shown by Ted Power, whose collection ranged across a broad spectrum of contemporary art.

In 1961, shortly after buying the Baram collage from Annely, Alex took the professional plunge. Through a mutual friend, he heard of Diana Kingsmill who was about to open a gallery in Lowndes Street, a site disclosed by acquaintance with David Hicks, the decorator. Her husband had been in the Grenadier Guards; she had a business background in running a dress shop and an antiques business. Alex had half planned to start a commercial venture with David Gibbs, but Gibbs went to live in America and Alex began a partnership with Diana Kingsmill.

'Wonky' Kingsmill, as she always insisted on being called, after a childhood nickname, was excellent on the financial side. A woman of great charm and warmth, she was also just as extraordinary an addition as Alex to the contemporary art world in 1962, when the Rowan Gallery opened – named after Diana Kingsmill's maiden name. Both would have appeared less conspicuous if they had made their first appearance in Agnews, so strong was the elegant county atmosphere which seemed at first to surround them. Wonky radiated the impression, wholly deceptive, of playing benign hostess at a grand but informal party, however pressurised by work; Alex gave out a distinct aura of tactically 'damning the torpedeos' in addition to his keen partiality for strongly individual talent. It was a disarming and very likeable combination.

Alex and Wonky rapidly won the support and friendship of the contemporary art world. They were a formidable pair, setting off for a business trip to the Continent in Alex's smart but faintly raffish Jensen car. Wonky rapidly got the drift of things. Arriving at Leo Castelli's gallery in New York with an appointment to see Leo, doubtless on behalf of a Rowan artist, Wonky was told that Leo was on the 'phone – his favourite place. She waited, and was told after some time that Leo had been summoned by another urgent 'phone call. This happened yet again, lengthily; and Wonky, smiling imperturbably, left the gallery, walked across Madison Avenue to the Carlisle Hotel, still dressed in her plastic leopard-skin raincoat – for this was the era of pop art – and rang him up. She had grasped the fact that this was how Leo worked best.

The Rowan Gallery opened in 1962 and quickly established its own niche. From the beginning, it was agreed that there would be no dealing in more highly priced English or foreign art; the gallery would have to survive on contemporary sales. Alex and Wonky agreed to subsidise the gallery for five years and then to reconsider the whole venture if business had not broken even. After five years, the gallery was just barely paying its way; it was an exceptional achievement.

It was also, of course, a time without precedent in art in this country, a time of exceptional vitality, confidence and contact with important developments abroad, which had built up steadily through the 1950's and sustained itself until the latter part of the sixties, when art began to shift into a minimalist phase and in other ways, by the end of the decade, to gradually lose confidence in straight painting and sculpture and to explore social issues, performance art, kinetic art and other themes. Painting and sculpture went ahead, of course, but the climate changed by 1967-70.

It says a lot for the dedication of the Rowan Gallery and its serious principles that this change had no effect on its shows or the atmosphere of the gallery throughout the decade. The artists whose work was shown in the first five years were, and remain, among the most remarkable English painters and sculptors of the post-war period. Among the earliest exhibitors were the painters Paul Huxley, Jeremy Moon, Brian Fielding, Antony Donaldson, John Edwards and Anthony Green and the sculptors Phillip King, Isaac Witkin, William Tucker, Garth Evans and Barry

Flanagan. Bridget Riley joined the gallery in 1967. Phillip King's great inventions *Genghis Khan*, *Rosebud* and *Twilight* were first shown at the Rowan, and so were Paul Huxley's first majestic excursions into a synthesis between colour-field painting and purely abstract forms.

Although the vitality of English sculpture was internationally recognised, following the impact of Moore and Caro, it was courageous to take on, in 1962, young sculptors like Tucker and King whose works were then imaginatively so far ahead of the taste of most English or even Continental collectors.

The gallery from its earliest days was much helped by officials. The Tate bought some of its first works by these young artists and the boom period of the sixties meant that the Stuyvesant Collection was formed, based initially on purchases from the 'New Generation' shows which it subsidised at the Whitechapel; and the Gulbenkian Collection made purchases. It was the Rowan's original plan to show young but not necessarily English artists. Excepting a Joe Goode show in 1967, a Warhol show in 1968 and Les Levine in 1969 every other show since the gallery's inception has in fact been English.

Great efforts were made at the gallery to find new English collectors, to build up a supportive domestic base. Alex succeeded in persuading many of his country friends to collect contemporary art for the first time and he worked hard to persuade his business acquaintances to start company collections. In 1966-67, Sebastian de Ferranti, Chairman of Ferranti, asked Alex to make within two years a contemporary collection for the new offices at Millbank Tower. The collection included paintings by Caulfield and Hoyland

Phillip King, Genghis Khan 1963 plastic and fibreglass 213 x 274 x 366 cm
coll. The Tate Gallery, London

as well as Rowan artists. Sadly, it was dispersed in the new economic climate of the seventies, but other collections have stayed the test of time.

Although the first support had to come from English collectors, critics and officials, there were determined and increasingly successful efforts to arrange shows abroad for the Rowan artists. Wonky first visited the States in 1963 and Alex in 1964; innumerable visits were made to the Continent to arrange participation in group shows, much helped by the British Council's lively policy of presenting our best art abroad, and then one-man shows – Jeremy Moon showed at Galerie Müller, Stuttgart in 1967, for instance. But Martin Friedman's show, based very broadly on the Whitechapel exhibitions, opened at the Walker Art Center, Minneapolis in 1965: *London: The New Scene*, containing work by several of the Rowan artists and this was helpful. In the same year Robert Melville and myself presented *The English Eye* exhibition at the Marlborough-Gerson Gallery, in New York, the largest show of modern English art seen there, with a very strong impact. In 1968, Phillip King and Bridget Riley represented Britain at the Venice Biennale, and this too, with subsequent long tours, was a useful event, obviously for the artists, but also for the Rowan.

The devotion of Alex and Wonky to their artists was exemplary and sometimes touching. Barry Flanagan was represented in the Paris Biennale in 1967 by a large soft, coloured sculpture stuffed with sand. When Flanagan arrived in Paris to set the work up, just before the official opening, the promised sand, to the artists' precise specification, was not there and an unsuitable variety of sand had been delivered on site. Flanagan was under pressure, aggravated by the fact that his wife was expecting a child back in London, and he scrapped the sculpture, substituting another work. In London, Alex was incensed: the sand sculpture, after all, was reproduced in the catalogue as an official entry. He rang round Europe to find the correct sand and he and Wonky flew to Paris, made their way to the exhibition space, personally shovelled the offending, incorrect sand away and painstakingly filled the large sculpture with the sand they had procured. The vision is a funny one, of course, but it is typical of Alex's punctilious behaviour. (I am indebted for this charming story to Celia Plunkett, who worked at the gallery as Alex's personal assistant from 1969 to 1981, and whose own efficient style and flair for good working relationships exactly matched those of her employers.)

The impression that Alex gave of a 'damn the torpedoes' approach to life when he first opened the gallery is broadly accurate. He is a brave man who keenly respects merit but is unimpressed by importance or rank: he is tenaciously loyal to his artists. They are with him for life, you feel, unless they strongly wish to be elsewhere. His temper only shows itself with a few well-educated people from his own background who have occasionally derided the contemporary art that he shows, and who ought, in his view, to know better. He has travelled round the world several times, exhaustively and exhaustingly, on behalf of Bridget Riley and Phillip King – but his energy is used for all the Rowan artists.

One of the best Rowan rituals is the long series of informal lunches held by Alex in the office at which critics, officials, collectors and others in the art world sit down to eat and drink and to discuss art world affairs. They provide a much enjoyed fulcrum for meetings and useful exchange of news. The weekends at Loxley for artists and their families and other friends in the art world, have a special charm because of the pleasures of a delightful house and garden; but they are also refreshingly unconventional affairs. Nobody is asked merely because they are important or useful or should be flattered in any way, and they seem to exist for their own sake, without any business motives. They have given deep pleasure to a formidable list of visitors for the past twenty-five years.

Wonky Kingsmill worked with Alex throughout the sixties – she thrived on the high spirits and the expansive possibilities of the decade – and, battling as always with poor health, retired from the partnership in 1972, on the death of her husband. In 1968, the Gallery moved to Bruton Place, to capacious premises on two floors designed elegantly by Timothy Rendle, the architect. With Kasmin's smaller Bond Street premises converted by Richard Burton, the Rowan was the best looking gallery in London, like a beautifully lit, calm and enticing indoor tennis court seen from above on arriving at the balcony-like entrance with its chic diagonal slit in the wall for moving big canvases through and into the gallery.

The character of the gallery did not change so much as flower at Bruton Place, with strong exhibitions of work by Bridget Riley, whose magnificent explorations of colour were first seen at the end of the sixties; the first exhibition, in 1969, of paintings by Michael Craig-Martin which linked the gallery to a new aspect of art in their play with illusion and the conventions of depicting objects in space – and several shows of paintings by Jeremy Moon, who exhibited first in 1963 in Lowndes Street and whose exhibition in 1968 opened the new premises in Bruton Place.

Jeremy Moon, an especially intelligent and gifted young abstract painter exploring colour and minimal shapes in not especially popular or easy ways, was presented by Alex with staunch enthusiasm throughout the decade until the artist's untimely death in a motorbike accident in 1973. Alex's support for Moon's work continued, in his efforts to raise money for the artist's family.

Loyalty to artists is one of Alex's characteristics shared by Annely and David Juda. It is not unique to them, of course: the Gimpels, Erica Brausen, Nicholas Logsdail and Leslie Waddington have equally distinctive policies, but the Rowan's faith in English art was a constant beacon in the sixties.

I should not stray beyond the time of the sixties, but it is hard for me to leave Alex and Annely suspended in the time and space of that one particular era and I cannot resist a brief coda.

When it was announced in 1982 that Alex, with his lease running out in Bruton Place, was moving to Tottenham Mews and merging with Annely, many artists from both galleries took to their beds under strong sedation with ice packs on their heads, several others were admitted to hospital in comparable stages of shock and anxiety. Nobody had anything but respect for both partners, but artists, it must be explained to readers outside the professional art world, look upon fellow artists from another gallery with the utmost condescension and scepticism, rather as the sophisticated girls of St. Pauls, for example, look upon the lost residents of the Cheltenham educational establishment, or for that matter the fortunate students of the Royal College of Art look upon the underprivileged and uncouth students of the Slade. Or *vice versa*. It is not exactly team spirit: artists have the utmost difficulty in accepting fellow artists linked to their own gallery, only conversing with them when fortified by strong drink. They also grumble frequently at the shortcomings of their own management; but finally a disparate *alma mater* attitude prevails, notably when their work sells well and management is heard to be making transcontinental 'phone calls on their behalf at hourly intervals.

It was felt also that Alex, with his wholly engaging manner of receiving visitors in his office as if he were the unexpectedly free-wheeling and irreverent occupant of a newly-built Government House, might find it hard to adjust to Annely and David's contrasting way of conducting office affairs at 11 Tottenham Mews with maximum *brio* and excitement in the slide area of the two galleries on the second floor, like the market scene in *A Night in Casablanca*, in full view and earshot of a frequently bemused public. Both the Rowan and Annely Juda's gallery were always conspicuous for their warm and friendly atmosphere, but the system was different.

In the event, the galleries merged happily, with each half maintaining its own identity: Alex continues his lunch parties and his work downstairs; upstairs coffee and general post still prevails with Annely and David and their ever-game assistants. The exhibiting space for all the artists is excellent, and larger on occasion than before the merger. And Alex and Annely both have very comparable qualities of strength, tenacity and directness. They each had to wait until they were over forty before they could begin to work in the art world; both of them had long and complex lives, demanding courage, humour and discipline, before they opened their galleries. David Juda was younger when he began to work at the gallery after a time spent in the Merchant Navy. His energy, affability and direct approach are like his mother's best qualities, but his awareness of art has its own expanding focus, beginning with Christo's sophisticated follies for a democratic capitalist age and extending to Nigel Hall's tersely eloquent sculpture and Al Held's powerfully composed paintings. It is to David Juda, who has the responsibility of steering the gallery into the future, that this essay is respectfully dedicated.

Bryan Robertson
August 1985

Bryan Robertson was born in 1925, educated at Battersea Grammar School and in short courses at the Sorbonne. He lived in Paris in 1947 and was Director of the Heffer Gallery in Cambridge from 1949-1952. From 1953-1969 he was Director of the Whitechapel Gallery, London, presenting exhibitions ranging from Phillip King, John Hoyland, Tim Scott, Prunella Clough to Poliakof, Rothko, Tobey, Pollock, de Stael, Rauschenberg, Guston, Johns, Motherwell, Stubbs, Turner, Malevich, Mondrian, among others. From 1970-1975, he was Director of the Neuberger Museum, State University of New York and is now Design Consultant for the Royal Opera House, a Governor of the London Contemporary Dance Theatre and a Councillor of the Royal College of Art. He was art critic for *The Spectator* 1965-1970 and has contributed to many periodicals in England and abroad. Author of *Sydney Nolan* 1959, *Jackson Pollock* 1960, and *Private View*, with Snowdon and Russell, 1965. In 1983, he presented the Dufy exhibition at the Hayward Gallery and in 1984 a survey of English painting and sculpture 1950-60 at Artcurial, Paris and subsequently at the Serpentine Gallery, London in 1985.

The Sixties

Exhibition

Page

Abbreviated artists' biographies are to be found in the initial decade their work appears.

Gillian Ayres

Born in London 1930. Studied at Camberwell School of Art 1946–50. Worked at the AIA Gallery 1951–59. Taught at Bath Academy of Art, Corsham 1959–65 and at St. Martin's School of Art 1966–78. First solo exhibition at Gallery One in 1956 and then at the Redfern Gallery in 1958. One-woman exhibitions at the Molton Gallery 1960/62 and Hamilton Galleries 1963. Other principal solo exhibitions include Kasmin Gallery 1965 and regularly since (after 1979 Knoedler Gallery); Hoya Gallery 1973; Kettles Yard, Cambridge 1978; Retrospective exhibition, Museum of Modern Art, Oxford and tour 1981; Serpentine Gallery and U.K. tour 1984. Principal group exhibitions include the Paris Biennale 1959; 'Situation', RBA Galleries 1960; VII Tokyo Biennale 1963 and 'British Painting in the Sixties', Whitechapel Art Gallery; 1967–69 'British Paintings: The New Generation', Museum of Modern Art, New York; 'British Painting '74', Hayward Gallery 1974; 'British Paintings in the 1960's', Tate Gallery 1977; Hayward Annual 1980; 'As of Now', Peter Moores Project 7, Walker Art Gallery, Liverpool 1983. Public collections include the Tate Gallery; Victoria and Albert Museum; Museum of Modern Art, New York; Art Gallery of South Australia, Adelaide and the Gulbenkian Foundation, Lisbon. Lives and works in North Wales.

50 Blimps 1961
acrylic on canvas
152 x 152 cm

Roy Ascott

Born 1934 in Bath. Studied at the Art Department, University of Newcastle-upon-Tyne, 1955–59. Taught at Ipswich, Wolverhampton and Slade Schools of Art 1961–71. Currently Head of School of Fine Art, Gwent College of Higher Education, Wales. First one-man exhibition at the Univision Gallery, Newcastle, 1960 and subsequently at the Artists International Association Gallery, London 1961, before showing at the Molton Gallery in 1963 and the Hamilton Galleries in 1965. Other solo exhibitions include the Ikon Gallery, Birmingham 1968; Angela Flowers Gallery London 1970; Centre Georges Pompidou, Paris 1985. Selected group exhibitions include the 'International Exhibition of Kinetic Art', Stedelijk Museum, Amsterdam 1961; 1964/65 'British Painters of Today', Kunsthalle Dusseldorf and tour; 1968 'Integration of the Arts', College of Architects, Barcelona. Public collections in which his work is represented include the Manchester City Art Gallery; Kunstverein, Dusseldorf and the Arts Council of Great Britain.

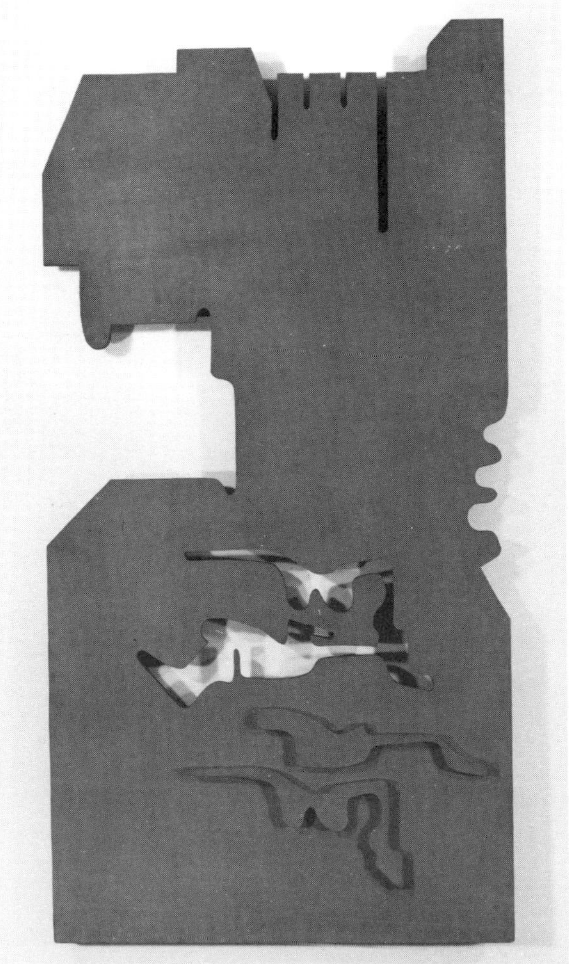

51 Reflex 1966
wood relief
155 x 79 cm

Antanas Brazdys

Born 1939 Lithuania. Studied at the Art Institute of Chicago and then at the Royal College of Art, London between 1962 and 1964. Taught at the Royal College of Art and at Cheltenham College of Art. In 1961 he was awarded the Edward L. Ryerson Foreign Travelling Fellowship, Art Institute of Chicago. In 1963 he won the Sainsbury Award and in 1968 the first prize in the Sunday Times sculpture competition. He has had one-man shows at the Hamilton Galleries, London in 1965; the Arnolfini Gallery, Bristol in 1966 and Annely Juda Fine Art, London in 1971. His group exhibitions include, 1960 Art Institute of Chicago; 1960–61 'New Horizons in Sculpture' Chicago; 1962 a two-man show at the University of Chicago; 1963 A.I.A. London; 1965 'Towards Art II' Arts Council of Great Britain; 1966 'Open Air Sculpture' Battersea Park, London; 1969 'Open Air Sculpture Exhibition' Blenheim Palace and 'Sculpture and Drawings' Annely Juda Fine Art, London; 1970 'Open Air Sculpture' Woburn Abbey; Salon de Mai, Paris; 1971 'Art Spectrum' Alexandra Palace, London. His work is in the collections of the Arts Council of Great Britain, Leicestershire Education Department and the British Steel Corporation.

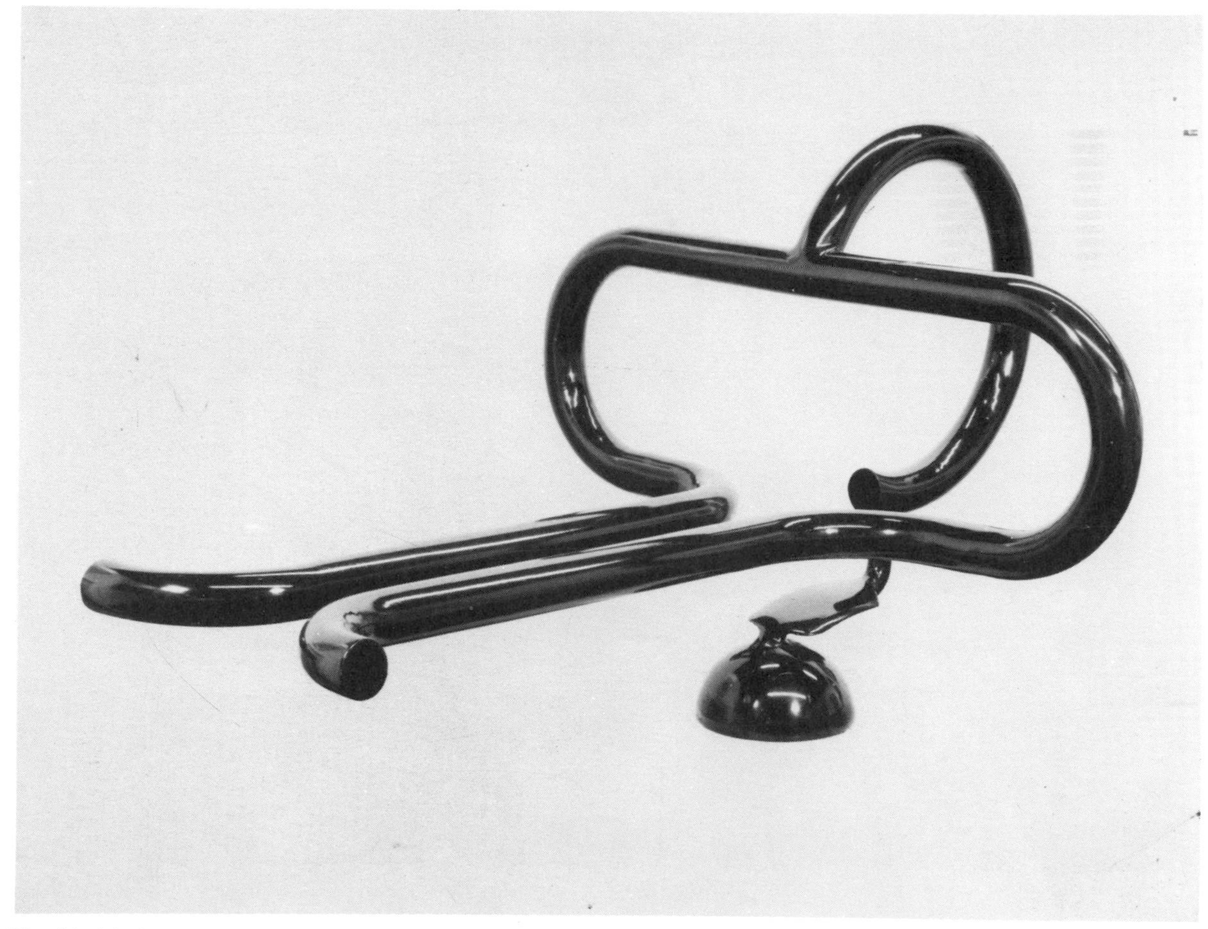

52 Untitled 1967
steel
61 × 80 × 114 cm

Bernard Cohen

Born in London in 1933. Began studies at S.W. Essex School of Art 1949–50. Went to St. Martin's School of Art 1950–51 and the Slade School 1951–54. Won scholarships to travel in Europe 1954–56. From 1961–77 he has held teaching posts at Ealing; St. Martin's and Chelsea School of Art; Slade School; University of New Mexico, Albuquerque; Minneapolis School of Art, Minnesota. He is currently the head of painting department at Wimbledon College of Art. His first one-man show was at Gimpel Fils in 1958 and subsequently in 1960. His solo exhibition at the Molton Gallery was in 1962, then at Kasmin Gallery in 1963; Betty Parsons Gallery, New York, 1967; Arnolfini Gallery, Bristol and Hayward Gallery, London (retrospective) 1972. He had regular exhibitions at Waddington Galleries, London from 1974–79. Amongst the important group exhibitions that have included his work are 'Situation', RBA Gallery, London, 1961; 'British Painting in the '60's', Whitechapel Gallery, London 1963; Documenta III, Kassel, 1964; 'London: The New Scene', Walker Art Center, Minneapolis and U.S. tour 1965; British Pavilion, 33rd Venice Biennale 1966; 'Marks on Canvas', Dortmund and European Tour 1969; 'British Painting and Sculpture 1960–70', National Gallery of Art, Washington, D.C. 1970; 'Arte Inglese Oggi', Milan 1976. His work is represented in several international museum collections including the Museum of Modern Art, New York; Walker Art Center, Minneapolis; Fogg Art Museum, Harvard University; Tate Gallery, London; Modern Museum, Dortmund and the Victoria and Albert Museum, London. He lives and works in London.

53 Ormand 1962
acrylic on canvas
101.5 x 127 cm

Avinash Chandra

Born 1931 in Simla, India. 1947–52 Studied painting at Delhi Polytechnic. 1953–56 joined staff Polytechnic, Delhi. 1954 awarded first prize, First National Exhibition of Art, New Delhi. 1956 came to live in London. 1962 won gold medal 'Prix Européenne' Ostend. 1964 represented in Documenta, Kassel. Has executed many commissions in U.K. and abroad for wall murals. Awarded John D. Rockefeller III Fund Fellowship 1965. His first one-man show was at Srinagar in 1951, followed by 1953–54, New Delhi; 1957 Imperial Institute, London; 1958 Ulster Museum, Belfast; Architectural Association, London; 1959 Queen's University, Belfast; 1960 Bear Lane Gallery, Oxford. He had a solo exhibition at the Molton Gallery, London in 1960 and 1962, and at the Hamilton Galleries in 1963, 1965 and 1967. Other one-man exhibitions include the Arnolfini Gallery, Bristol, 1961; Gulbenkian Museum of Oriental Art, Durham; Laing Art Gallery, Newcastle and York City Art Gallery, York, 1962; Graves Art Gallery, Sheffield 1963; Rose Fried Gallery, New York, 1968; Gallery Moos, Toronto, 1969; Kretschmer Gallery, New York 1971 and the October Gallery, London 1981. He was included in many group shows including several in India, and later 'Seven Indian Artists in Europe', Gallery One, London 1958; Gulbenkian Museum, Durham, 1962; 'Hamilton Painters and Sculptors', Hamilton Galleries, London and Edinburgh Festival, Indian Exhibition 1964; Arts Council of Great Britain 'Indian Painting Now', London and tour 1965. Among the many institutions that house his work are the Tate Gallery, London; Museum of Modern Art, Berlin; Ashmolean Museum, Oxford; Ulster Museum, Belfast; Museum of Modern Art, Haifa and the National Gallery of Modern Art, New Delhi.

54 Cityscape 1960
oil on canvas
76 x 101.6 cm

Antony Donaldson

Born 1939 in Surrey. 1958–62 Studied Slade School of Art. 1962 First Showed at Rowan Gallery and regularly to 1972. 1963 2nd prize John Moores Open Competition. 1966 Harkness Foundation Fellowship to U.S.A. 1966–68 Lived in Los Angeles. 1968 Nicholas Wilder Gallery, Los Angeles; 1970 Galerie von Loeper, Hamburg; 1971 Galerie Muller, Koln and Galerie de Luxembourg, Paris; 1973 Felicity Samuel Gallery, London; 1979 Rowan Gallery, London; 1983 Bonython Gallery, Adelaide and Hogarth Galleries, Sydney; 1984 Juda Rowan Gallery. Among many group exhibitions he took part in 1964 'The New Generation', Whitechapel Art Gallery, London; 1965 '4ieme Biennale des Jeunes', Musée d'Art Moderne, Paris; 1967 Carnegie Institute, Pittsburgh; 1969 Art Museum of Ateneum, Helsinki; 1974 'Premier Salon International d'Art Contemporain', Paris; 1985 Everard Read Gallery, Johannesburg. Among other public collections he is represented in Arts Council of Great Britain; Folkwang Museum, Essen; Government Art Collection; Gulbenkian Foundation; Olinda Museum, Brazil; Tate Gallery, London; Ulster Museum, Belfast.

'. . . the canvases are large, vivid and architectonic. Every aspect of the work – its scale, composition and lucent colour is commanding . . .'

Jane Livingstone, *Artforum*, May 1968

'. . . He operates at the lighter end of the spectrum, creating objects which hover between hedonism, nostalgia and that acrid realism which we associate with the penetrating light of California . . .'

Nigel Gosling, *The Observer*, 8 November 1970

55 For Jim Clark 1963
oil on canvas
152.5 x 152.5 cm

John Edwards

Born 1938 in London. Studied at Hornsey College of Art 1953–56 and 1958–60. In 1961 began teaching at Brighton College of Art, Chelsea and St. Martin's College of Art. First exhibited at the Rowan Gallery in 1967. Became artist in residence at Syracuse University, New York, 1976 and also had two other one-man exhibitions in the U.S.A. at the Osuna Gallery, Washington, D.C. in 1980 and Eaton/Shoen Gallery, San Francisco in 1981. He was included in the 'British Art Now' exhibition at the Guggenheim Museum, New York in 1980 and at the Royal Academy, London in 1981. The Newcastle-upon-Tyne Polytechnic organized a touring exhibition of his work in 1979 which travelled to Cambridge, Sheffield, Brighton and London. His work is represented in several public collections including the Arts Council of Great Britain; the British Council; Power Institute of Contemporary Art, Sydney and the Solomon R. Guggenheim Museum, New York. Since 1980 he has been Principal Lecturer at St. Martin's School of Art, and lives and works in London.

'. . . While many young abstract painters stay content with small academic exercises on a large scale, how refreshing to discover John Edwards (Rowan Gallery) an artist whose love of colour springs only from his senses and not from a colour-chart . . .'

Edwin Mullins, *Sunday Telegraph*, 12 February 1967

'. . . The swash-buckling John Edwards gets better and better. His latest show of paintings is brighter, bolder and more confident than ever before . . .'

Simon Vaughan Winter, *Evening News*, 4 May 1979

56 Temporal 1967
acrylic on canvas
122 x 122 cm

Garth Evans

Born 1934 in Cheshire. 1955–60 Studied at Manchester Regional College of Art and the Slade School of Fine Art, London. 1964 Gulbenkian Foundation Purchase Award. 1969 British Steel Corporation Fellowship, 1973 Visiting Professor of Art, Minneapolis College of Art and Design. 1975 Arts Council of Great Britain Major Award. 1981 Lives and works in New York. First showed at the Rowan Gallery in 1962 and regularly thereafter; 1979 'Garth sings Barry dances', Minneapolis Institute of Arts (with Barry Flanagan); 1983 Robert Elkon Gallery, New York; 1984 'Recent Wall Sculpture', Tibor de Nagy Gallery and 'Wall Works', H.F. Manes Gallery, New York. Among the many other group exhibitions that he took part in 1963 'Construction England', Arts Council Exhibition; 1966 'White on White', Kunsthalle Bern; 1967 'British Drawing, the New Generation', Museum of Modern Art, New York; 1972 'British Sculpture '72', Royal Academy, London; 1975 'The Condition of Sculpture', Hayward Gallery, London; 1979 'Hayward Annual', Hayward Gallery, London; 1982 'A Quadrille: Four sculptors by invitation', Robert Elkon Gallery, New York; 1983 'On an Intimate Dimension', Tibor de Nagy Gallery, New York; 1984 'Organic Abstractions', H.F. Manes Gallery, New York. Among the many other public collections that he is included in are The Arts Council of Great Britain; Hirshhorn Museum and Sculpture Garden, Washington, D.C.; Museum of Modern Art, New York; Museum of Modern Art, Rio de Janeiro; Metropolitan Museum of Art, New York; Power Institute of Contemporary Art, Sydney; Tate Gallery, London.

'. . . Cooler, cleaner – consciously elegant indeed – are a series of new sculptures in fibreglass by Garth Evans, which will shortly go on view. Evans is a very accomplished practitioner in the 'New Generation' idiom, and, it seems to me, a most intelligent manipulator of form . . .'

Edward Lucie-Smith, *Studio International*, September 1966

'. . . Garth Evans is showing some very accomplished sculptures at the Rowan Gallery – linear metal pieces which combine formal logic, sensibility and imagination . . .'

Nigel Gosling, *The Observer*, 20 February 1972

57 No. 25 Pink 1963
polyurethane on fibreglass
115.5 x 123 cm

Robyn Denny

Born 1930 Abinger, Surrey. Studied at St. Martin's College of Art and Royal College of Art 1951–57. 1965 and 1978 prizewinner John Moores Exhibition. 1958 First one-man exhibition Gimpel Fils, London and subsequently showed at the Molton Gallery in 1961. 1964–70 regular one-man exhibitions at Kasmin Gallery, London. 1965/67/71 Robert Elkon Gallery, New York. 1968 Galerie Renée Ziegler, Zurich. 1969 Waddington Galleries, London. 1970 Galerie Müller, Stuttgart and Cologne. 1973 Retrospective exhibition Tate Gallery, London and European tour. 1974 Marlborough Gallery, Rome. 1976 Galleria Morone, Milan. 1977 Waddington and Tooth Galleries, London. 1979/81/82 Bernard Jacobson, London and New York. 1985 Fine Arts Gallery, University of California at Irvine. Principal group exhibitions include 1959 Paris Biennale; 1961 'Art of Assemblage' Museum of Modern Art, New York; 1963 'British Painting in the 60's' Tate Gallery, London; 1970 'British Painting and Sculpture 1960–1970' National Gallery of Art, Washington D.C.; 1976 'Arte Inglese Oggi', Milan; 1977 Hayward Annual, London. Public collections include the Tate Gallery, London; Victoria and Albert Museum, London; Albright-Knox Art Gallery, Buffalo; Museum of Modern Art, New York and the Walker Art Center, Minneapolis. He lives and works in London.

58 Frontman 1961
oil on canvas
244 x 198 cm

Barry Flanagan

Born Prestatyn, Wales 1941. Studied at St. Martin's School of Art 1964–66. From 1967–71 he taught there and also at the Central School of Art. His first one-man exhibition was with the Rowan Gallery in 1966 where he showed regularly until he left the gallery in 1975. He has exhibited in many solo exhibitions internationally including the Fishbach Gallery, New York when he first visited the U.S.A. 1969; Galleria dell'Ariete, Milan 1968/74; Museum of Modern Art, New York and Oxford 1974, Art and Project, Amsterdam 1975/77; Van Abbemusuem, Eindhoven; and tour 1977; Serpentine Gallery, London and tour, 1978/79; Waddington Galleries, London 1980 and regularly since; Mostyn Art Gallery, Llandudno, Wales and tour 1981. He represented Britain at the XXXX Venice Biennale in 1982 which subsequently toured to Museum Haus Lange, Krefeld and Whitechapel Art Gallery, London. The Centre Pompidou, Paris, organized a retrospective exhibition of his work in 1983 when he also showed at the Pace Gallery, New York. In 1985 he has exhibited at the Richard Gray Gallery, Chicago and Waddington Galleries, London. His work is represented in many public collections internationally including the Tate Gallery, London; Kunsthaus, Zurich; Museum of Modern Art, New York; Stedelijk Museum, Amsterdam and the National Gallery of Canada, Ottawa. He lives and works in London.

59 Pdreeoo 1965
plaster, resin, ink and canvas
106.7 × 45.7 × 45.7 cm

Klaus Friedeberger

Born 1922 in Berlin. Australian Military Forces 1942–46. Studied painting in Sydney 1947–50. He won the Mosman Art Prize in 1949 and arrived in London in 1950. His first one-man show was at the Hamilton Galleries, London in 1963 and he has had two-man shows at the Bear Lane Gallery, Oxford in 1963 and the Clytie Jessop Gallery, London in 1967. Group exhibitions in which he has partcipated include the Commonwealth Jubilee Competition Exhibition at the National Gallery of New South Wales in 1951; 'Australian Artists', Imperial Institute, London in 1955 and 1956; Zwemmer Gallery, London 1960; 'Australian Painting and Sculpture in Europe Today' which travelled to the Städelsches Kunstinstitut, Frankfurt and other galleries in Germany and Holland in 1963; Ben Uri Gallery, London in 1964, 1966 and 1979; Hamilton Galleries, London 1964, 1965, 1966 and 1967; Europa Prize Exhibition, Ostend 1964 at which he was awarded a Gold Medal, and at which he again exhibited in 1966. In 1967 he was included in 'Personal Choice' at the Midland Group Gallery, Nottingham; 1968 Clytie Jessop Gallery, London; 1979 'Australian Artists of Fame and Promise' New South Wales House, London and in 1985 'The Joy of Paint, English Expressionism 1985' The Warwick Arts Trust, London. Klaus Friedeberger lives and works in London.

60 Children Playing (War Dance) 1963
oil on canvas
127 x 102 cm

Nicholas Georgiadis

Born in Athens in 1925. Trained as an architect in Athens and New York until 1952. Came to England in 1953 and studied at the Slade School, University College, London until 1955. He has designed stage sets for the Royal Opera House, Covent Garden; Metropolitain Opera, New York; the Old Vic; The Royal Court Theatre, London and the Vienna State Opera. His first one-man exhibition was at the Redfern Gallery, London in 1959, and subsequently in 1961. Other solo exhibitions include the Molton Gallery 1963; Galerie Merlin, Athens 1964; Hamilton Galleries and Galeria Naviglio, Milan, 1965; New Art Centre and Annely Juda Fine Art, London 1968. Principal group exhibitions include the Carnegie International, Pittsburgh 1955; John Moores Exhibition, Liverpool 1961 and 1965; Documenta III, Kassel 1964; Venice Biennale 1966; Whitechapel Art Gallery, London 1967; Theatre Designs Exhibition, Tubingen and sets for 'The Trojans', Victoria and Albert Museum, London 1969. Now only paints stage sets and theatre designs.

61 Project IX 1966
gouache on paper
55 x 57 cm

Anthony Green

Born 1939 in London. 1956–60 Studied at the Slade School of Fine Art. 1960 French Government Scholarship to Paris. 1967–69 Harkness Fellowship to U.S.A. In 1971 elected ARA. and in 1977 elected RA. 1962 First showed at Rowan Gallery and regularly thereafter. 1968 Lee Nordness Gallery, New York. 1971 Frans Hals Museum, Haarlem with tour. 1973/76/82 Galerie Dieter Brusberg, Hanover. 1975/77/81/84 Nishimura Gallery, Tokyo. 1975/79/83 Staempfli Gallery, New York. 1978 'Anthony Green Paintings' Rochdale Art Gallery and touring to museums in the United Kingdom. 1984 'One Day in the Life of a Picture' Scottish Arts Council exhibition touring museums in Scotland. Among many other group exhibitions he was included in 1965 'Figuration Narratiff' Galerie Creuze, Paris; 1966 Royal Academy and every subsequent year; 1973 'La peinture anglaise aujourd'hui' Musée d'Art Moderne, Paris; 1974 'British Painting '74' Hayward Gallery, London; 1979 'The British Art Show' touring museums in England; 1982 'Aspects of British Art Today' British Council exhibition touring Japan; 1984/85 'The Proper Study' British Council exhibition touring India. He is represented in many public collections including the Arts Council of Great Britain; The British Council; Frans Halsmuseum, Haarlem; National Museum of Wales, Cardiff; Olinda Museum, Brazil; Tate Gallery, London. He lives and works in London.

'. . . He has made painterly progress in the last two years, and turns the eccentrically shaped canvases now in vogue to odd personal use. If – as he mostly does – this 27 year old can keep pastiche-primitiveness at bay, he will be worth watching . . .'

Nigel Gosling, *The Observer*, 6 March, 1966

'. . . this is a highly sophisticated art that can be approached as story, symbol, and a complex working out of formal problems with an assimilated background of centuries of painting. It is a world worth both investigating and enjoying . . .'

Joseph Love, *Japan Times*, 30 March 1975

'. . . His formal invention and technical command, of surface, pattern, texture and extreme and distorted perspective, and outrageous asymmetry, are as astonishing as they are delightful . . .'

William Packer, *The Financial Times*, 14 July 1981

62 Mary's Garden 1966
oil on board
175.5 x 122 cm

Paul Huxley

Born 1938 in London. 1953–60 studied at the Harrow School of Art and the Royal Academy. First showed at the Rowan Gallery 1963. Won 1st prize in 'The New Generation' at the Whitchapel Art Gallery in 1964. Won a Harkness Fellowship to U.S.A. in 1965. Lived in New York 1965–67. Showed at the Kornblee Gallery, New York in 1967 and 1970; in the Galeria de Emenda, Lisbon, 1974 and the Forum Kunst, Rotweil, in 1975. In 1983 he won equal First Prize at the Tolly Cobbold/Eastern Arts 4th Annual Exhibition and in 1984 was commissioned to make a decorative design for King's Cross Station, London. He was included in, among many others, 1965 The Paris Biennale; 1968 'British Artists: Six Painters, Six Sculptors' at the Museum of Modern Art, New York and touring U.S.A. In 1969 'Marks on Canvas', Museum am Ostwall, Dortmund, and touring Germany; 1973 'Magic and Strong Medicine', Walker Art Gallery, Liverpool; 1976 'Arte Inglese Oggi', Palazzo Reale, Milan; 1980 'The British Art Show', Arts Council exhibition touring U.K.; 1984 'Pintura britanica contemporanea', Museo Municipal, Madrid. His work is represented in many public collections including Albright-Knox Gallery, Buffalo; Art Gallery of New South Wales, Sydney; Arts Council of Great Britain; Museum of Modern Art, New York; Tate Gallery, London.

'. . . As individual pictures go, I don't remember many more impressive, from a young artist, than the big new Paul Huxley at the Rowan Gallery . . .'

John Russell, *The Sunday Times*, December 1964

'. . . It is not easy to overstate the immediate impact of this exhibition, an impression at once of coolness and heat, of the utmost restraint brought to bear on a dazzling, wildly romantic exuberance . . .'

Hilary Spurling, *The Observer*, 5 September 1971

63 Untitled No. 48 1965
acrylic on canvas
172.5 x 172.5 cm

Michael Kenny

Born in Liverpool 1941. Studied at Liverpool College of Art and Slade School of Fine Art, London 1959–64. Is currently head of Sculpture Department Goldsmiths College of Art, where he has been teaching since 1966. His first one-man exhibition was at the Bear Lane Gallery, Oxford in 1964 and subsequently exhibited at Southampton University 1965 before his solo exhibition at the Hamilton Galleries in 1966. Other important one-man shows include the Serpentine Gallery 1977; Annely Juda Fine Art 1978 and regularly since then; Roundhouse Gallery 1979; U.K. touring exhibition organized by the Bluecoat Gallery, Liverpool 1981–82; Tokyo Gallery, Tokyo 1983 and 1985, and the Wilhelm-Lehmbruck-Museum, Duisburg 1984/85. Amongst the important group exhibitions that have included his work are the International Sculpture exhibition, Battersea Park, London 1966; 'Sculpture 60–66', Arts Council exhibition touring U.K. 1967/68; '16 Escultoros Britanicos', Buenos Aires 1969; 'Art into Landscape', Serpentine Gallery, London 1974; Documenta 6, Kassel 1977; 'Certain Traditions', touring Canada and U.K. 1978/79; 'European Dialogue', Third Sydney Biennale and Australian tour 1979–80 and in the same year 'The British Art Show', Mappin Art Gallery, Sheffield and U.K. tour; 'British Sculpture in the 20th Century', Whitechapel Art Gallery, London 1981–82; Hayward Annual 1982; 'The Sculpture Show', Hayward Gallery 1983; 'Sculptors' Drawings' British Council exhibition touring Japan and Korea 1984/85. His work is represented in several public collections including the Tate Gallery, London; Staatsgalerie, Stuttgart; Wilhelm-Lehmbruck-Museum, Duisburg; British Museum and Victoria and Albert Museum, London. He lives and works in London.

'. . . Michael Kenny's austere and mystical allegories – pale near-abstract ghosts of upright figures and Gothic towers – are shockingly original . . .'

Nigel Gosling, *The Observer*, 3 April 1966

'. . . Kenny is an overt romantic, and though it might be refined and abstracted to a degree, his work is always concerned with a human presence expressed through imagery, whether found, modified or made . . .'

William Packer, *The Financial Times*, 10 February 1981

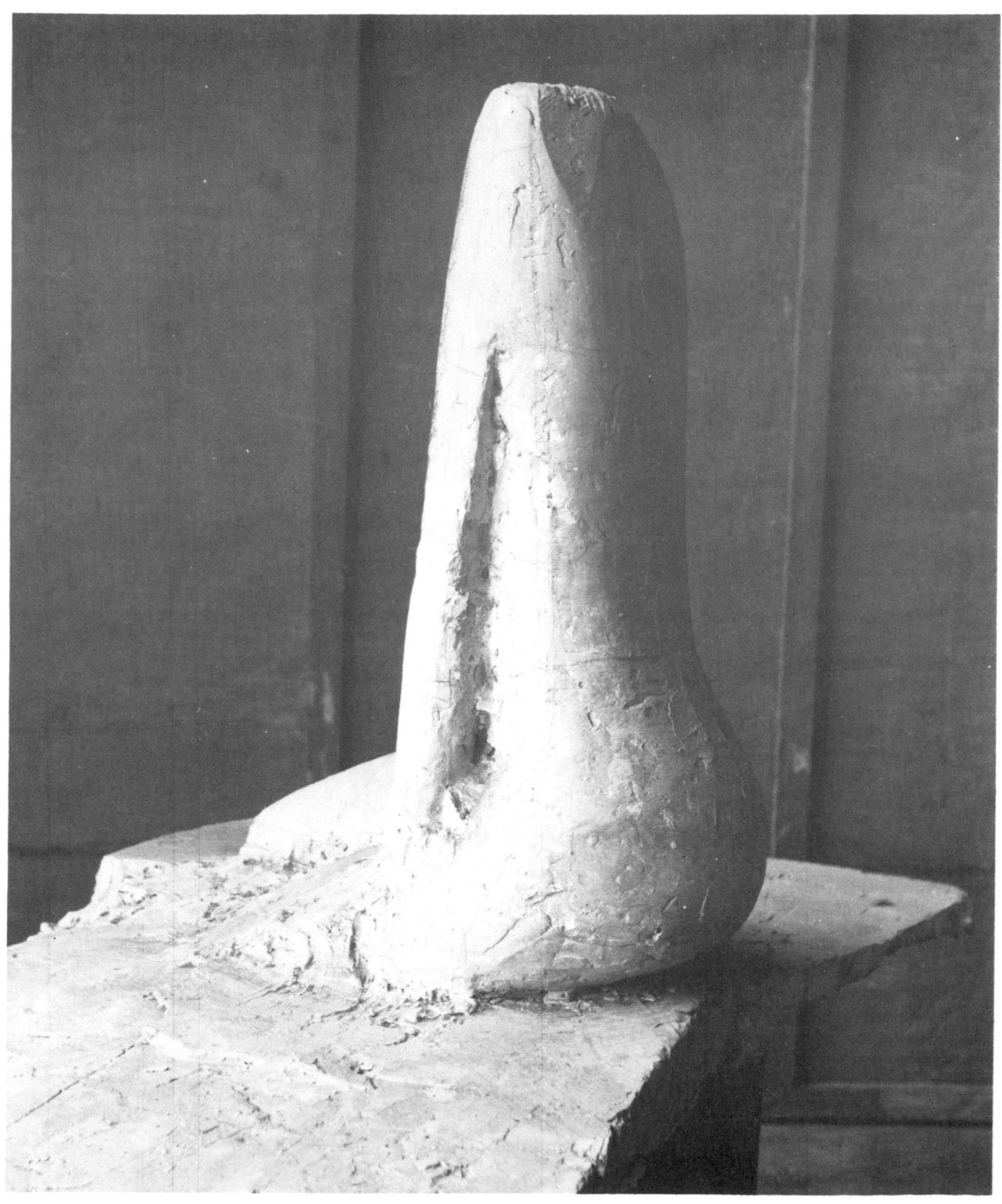

64 Die Lorelei 1964
painted plaster
78 x 139 x 74 cm

Michael Michaeledes

Born 1927. Studied art and architecture in England and Italy. 1954 won 'Philadelphios' panhellenic poetry prize, Athens. First one-man exhibition at the Leicester Galleries, 1959 and subsequently in 1962. Other solo exhibitions include Galleria Trastevere, Rome 1961; New Gallery, Belfast 1963 and 1967; Hamilton Galleries 1966; Arte Centro, Milan 1967; Galerie Swart, Amsterdam 1968; Annely Juda Fine Art 1972 and regularly since. Venice Biennale (Greek Pavilion) 1976; Painting Box Gallery, Zurich and Oliver Dowling Gallery, Dublin 1977. Amongst the group exhibitions that have included his work are the John Moores Exhibition, Liverpool 1967; Europe Prize for Painting, Ostende and AIA Gallery 1969; Europe Prize, Ostende and Palazzo Reale, Milan 1971; 2nd British Drawing Biennale, Middlesborough 1973; Contemporary Art Society, London 1975; Artists Market, London 1976–79; Contemporary Artists in Camden, Camden Arts Centre 1981. Public Collections include the Israel Museum, Jerusalem; Museo de arte Contemporaneo, Caracas; the Granada Foundation, Manchester; the McCrory Corporation, New York and the Arts Council of Great Britain. He lives and works in London.

'. . . *His method is peculiar to himself, unprimed cotton duck is stretched across a complex wooden support, tight against the sharp obtruding edges, and then moving away, curving and swelling towards the next point of tension, the form cast into high relief by the gentle raking light. Each work consists of several panels butted together that develop sequences of proportion or disposition, complicated and enriched by the fall of shadow and the variable reflection of light. The panels move out from the wall to invade floor and ceiling, lately becoming all but free-standing objects, unmistakeably sculptural (for the relief was always an ambiguous form)* . . .'

William Packer, *The Financial Times*, 29 July 1976

65 Earth and Sky I 1962
acrylic on linen
152.5 x 152.5 cm

Phillip King

Born 1934 in Kheredine, near Carthage. Read Modern Languages at Cambridge University 1954–57. Studied at St. Martin's College of Art 1957–58. Assistant to Henry Moore 1958–59. Began teaching at St. Martin's in 1959 and continued until 1980. Taught at Bennington College, Vermont, U.S.A. 1964. For two years he was a Trustee at the Tate Gallery (1967–69) and 1974 he received a C.B.E. During 1979–80 he was visiting professor at the Hochschule der Kunst in Berlin and artist in residence at the Alexander Mackie College, Sydney. He was appointed Professor of Sculpture at the Royal College of Art in 1980. 1964 First showed at Rowan Gallery and regularly thereafter. 1966 Richard Feigen Gallery, New York. 1968 Whitechapel Gallery, London and XXXIV Venice Biennale touring to Bochum and Rotterdam. 1974–75 Retrospective exhibition at Rijksmuseum Kröller-Müller, Otterlo and European Tour to Kunsthalle Dusseldorf, Kunsthalle Bern, Musée Galiera, Paris, Ulster Museum, Belfast; 1975–76 Arts Council Exhibition touring museums in Britain; 1981 Hayward Gallery, London. Among many other group shows in which he has participated are 1961 'British Sculpture', Jewish Museum, New York; 1964 Documenta III, Kassel; 1965 'London: The New Scene', Walker Art Center, Minneapolis and touring U.S.A.; 1966 'New Shapes of Colour', Stedelijk Museum, Amsterdam and touring; 1967 Pittsburgh International, Carnegie Institute and Fifth Guggenheim International Exhibition, New York; 1968 Documenta IV, Kassel; 1969 International Sculptors' Symposium, Osaka, Japan; 1970 'Contemporary British Art', Museum of Modern Art, Tokyo; 1971 'British Painting and Sculpture 1960–70', National Gallery of Art, Washington, D.C.; 1975 'The Condition of Sculpture', Hayward Art Gallery, London; 1976 'Arte Inglese Oggi', Palazzo Reale, Milan; 1977 Biennale de Paris, 'une anthologie: 1959–67', Paris; 1979 'The British Art Show', Arts Council exhibition touring museums in Britain; 1982 'Aspects of British Art Today', British Council exhibition touring Japan. Among many other public collections he is represented in those of the City of Rotterdam; Government Art Collection; Kröller-Müller National Museum, Otterlo; Los Angeles County Museum; Museum of Modern Art, New York; National Gallery of Australia, Canberra; Tate Gallery, London. He has also executed major commissions for C. & J. Clark Ltd., Street, Somerset; for the European Patent Office, Munich; for Romulus Construction Limited, London. He lives and works in London.

'. . . King, billed as one of the most amazing of the amazing young British sculptors, deserves his reputation. His wit and oblique viewpoint is backed up by a strong and serious formal sense . . .'

Lucy Lippard, *Art International*, 1966

'. . . Phillip King stood out, both as a man and an artist, from the moment of his first show at the Rowan Gallery in 1964. He stood out as a man by reason of his natural 'gravitas' and evident reasonableness; and he stood out as an artist by reason of the inventive fancy which seemed to start up all over again with each piece . . .'

John Russell, *The Times*, 12 July 1970

'. . . There is just no way for King not to be ranked as one of the best and most inventive of living sculptors. He has never made a dull piece, or one that has not an intelligent and original motivation somewhere in the back of it . . .'

John Russell, *The New York Times*, 28 June 1981

66 Twilight 1963
plastic, aluminium and wood
102 x 132 x 168 cm

Mark Lancaster

Born 1938 in Yorkshire. 1961–65 Studied at the Department of Fine Art, University of Newcastle. 1968–70 Artist in residence, King's College, Cambridge. 1972 Moved to New York. 1975 Designer for Merce Cunningham Dance Company. First showed at the Rowan Gallery in 1965 and regularly thereafter; 1970 School of Design, Harvard University; 1972/74 Betty Parsons Gallery, New York; 1973 Walker Art Gallery, Liverpool. Among many other group exhibitions he has taken part in 1966 'The New Generation', Whitechapel Gallery, London; 1966–67 'Aspects of New British Art' touring New Zealand and Australia; 1967 'British Drawing – The New Generation', Museum of Modern Art, New York; 1969 'Marks on Canvas', Museum am Ostwall, Dortmund and touring; 1970 'British Painting and Sculpture 1960–1970', National Gallery, Washington, D.C. and 'Contemporary British Art', National Museum of Modern Art, Tokyo; 1976 'Contemporary British Art', Cleveland Institute of Art; 1979 'The New American Painting', Janie C. Lee Gallery, Houston. Among many other Public Collections he is represented in the Art Gallery of South Australia; Arts Council of Great Britain; British Council; Museum of Modern Art, New York; Tate Gallery, London; Ulster Museum, Belfast; Victoria and Albert Museum; London.

'. . . Mark Lancaster, at the Rowan Gallery, is by contrast a young painter who proceeds with a certain stealthy elegance, making his points lightly and deftly, never lingering over any of them. He is above all an intelligent painter . . .'

John Russell, *The Sunday Times*, November 1965

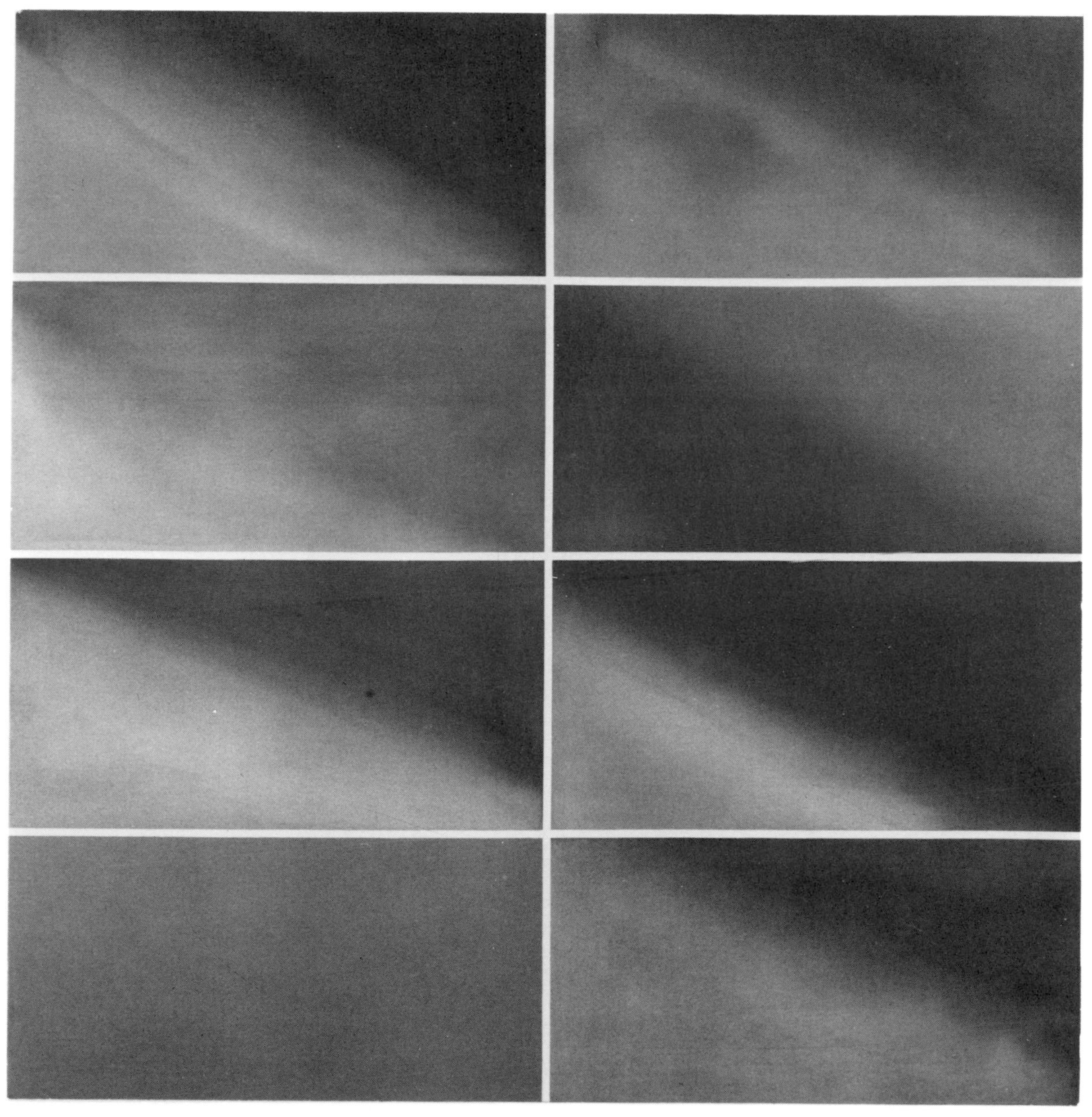

67 Cambridge Green 1968
liquitex on canvas
172.2 x 172.2 cm
coll. The Tate Gallery, London

Jeremy Moon

Born 1934 in Cheshire. 1954–57 Read law at Christ's College, Cambridge. 1961 Studied at Central School of Art. 1973 Killed in motorcycle accident. First showed at the Rowan Gallery in 1963 and regularly thereafter. 1967 Galerie Muller Stuttgart. Among many other group exhibitions he took part in 1965 'London–The New Scene', Walker Art Center, Minneapolis and touring; 1966 'London under Forty', Galerie Milano, Milan; 1967 5th Paris Biennale; 1968 'Britische Kunst Heute', Kunstverein, Hamburg; 1969 'Marks on Canvas', Museum am Ostwall, Dortmund and touring; 1974 'British Painting '74', Hayward Gallery, London; 1976 'Arte Inglese Oggi', Palazzo Reale, Milan; 1977 'Biennale de Paris, une anthologie 1959–1967', Paris. Among many other public collections he is represented in the Albright-Knox Gallery, Buffalo; Power Institute of Contemporary Art, Sydney; Scottish National Gallery of Contemporary Art, Edinburgh; Tate Gallery, London; Ulster Museum, Belfast; Walker Art Center, Minneapolis; Museum of Modern Art, Rio de Janeiro.

'. . . Jeremy Moon's work . . . is tight-lipped and demonstrative, the colours clean and flat, the statement on the canvas complete. The effect on the spectator may be one of energy or tranquility, but his role remains passive . . .'

Guy Brett, *The Guardian*, 2 September 1963

'. . . He is a very logical artist who explores the possibilities of a few favourite formal themes with exemplary patience and ingenuity . . .'

Nigel Gosling, *The Observer*, 6 May 1973

68 2/63 Cypher 1963
oil on canvas
147.5 x 132 cm

Bridget Riley

Born 1931 in London. 1949–55 Studied at Goldsmith's College of Art and the Royal College of Art. 1964 Peter Stuyvesant Foundation Travel Bursary to U.S.A. 1968 International Prize for Painting XXXIV Venice Biennale. 1969 with Peter Sedgeley pioneered the establishment of Space. 1972 awarded CBE. 1980–83 Colour project for Royal Liverpool Hospital. 1981 Appointed Trustee of the National Gallery. 1983 Collaborated with Ballet Rambert on 'Colour Moves'. 1961 first showed in London at Gallery One. 1967 joined Rowan Gallery and has exhibited there regularly since. Among her most important one-man shows were 1966 'Bridget Riley Drawings', Museum of Modern Art, New York and tour of U.S.A. 1968 XXXIV Venice Biennale and toured in Europe. 1970–71 European retrospective exhibition touring museums in Hanover, Dusseldorf, Basle, Bern, Turin, London and Prague. 1973 'Paintings and Drawings 1961–1973', Arts Council Touring Exhibition; 1975 Sidney Janis Gallery, New York and Galerie Beyeler, Basle; 1976 Coventry Gallery, Sydney; 1977 Minami Gallery, Tokyo; 1978–80 'Bridget Riley works 1959–78', a retrospective exhibition touring Buffalo, Dallas, Purchase, Perth, Sydney and Tokyo; 1983 'Bridget Riley paintings and drawings 1981–83', Nishimura Gallery, Tokyo; 1984–85 'Working with Colour', Arts Council touring exhibition. She has been included in a great number of group exhibitions all over the world including 1965 'London: the New Scene', Walker Art Center, Minneapolis and 'The Responsive Eye', Museum of Modern Art, New York; 1967 Pittsburgh International, Carnegie Institute; 1968 XXXIV Venice Biennale, and Documenta IV, Kassel; 1970 'Contemporary British Art', National Museum of Modern Art, Tokyo; 1973 'Fanfare for Europe', Christie's, London; 1974 'British Painting '74', Hayward Gallery, London; 1976 'Arte Inglese Oggi', Palazzo Reale, Milan; 1977 'Less is more', Sydney Janis Gallery, New York and Documenta VI, Kassel; 1977/78 'Recent British Art', British Council Exhibition touring Iran and Europe; 1982 'Aspects of British Art Today', Tokyo Metropolitan Art Museum and tour of Japanese Museums. Among many other public collections, she is included in the Tate Gallery, London; Chicago Institute of Art; Museum of Modern Art, New York; National Gallery of Australia, Canberra; Stedelijk Museum, Amsterdam; National Gallery, Berlin; National Museum of Modern Art, Tokyo. Lives and works in London, Cornwall and the South of France.

'. . . Her inventiveness is astounding. Those who accused her years ago of doing little more than enlarging optical illusion diagrams were confounded a while back. More important, the essential seriousness of her work becomes ever more apparent . . .'

Norbert Lynton, *The Guardian*, 29 July 1969

'. . . She is indeed one of the most consummate practitioners of that mode of abstract painting built on rigorous systems of pure color applied in patterns that alter the very way we perceive color. . .'

Hilton Kramer, *The New York Times*, 3 May 1975

'. . . Bridget Riley is one of the most distinguished of our abstract painters, from the moment of her national appearance in the early sixties a dominant figure in her generation and one of the few of our artists to enjoy a truly international reputation . . .'

William Packer, *The Financial Times*, 9 June 1981

69 Blaze 4 1963
emulsion on board
94.5 × 94.5 cm

William Turnbull

Born in Dundee, 1922. Worked as an illustrator before War Service. Studied 1946–48 at the Slade School. Spent two years in Paris before returning to London in 1950. Taught experimental design at the Central School of Art from 1952–61. Travelled extensively to the U.S.A. and the Far East. His first one-man exhibitions were held at the Hanover Gallery, London in 1950 and 1952 then at the I.C.A., London in 1957. Then showed at the Molton Gallery in 1960 and 1961. Amongst his other important one-man shows are those at the Marlborough-Gerson Gallery, New York 1963; Bennington College, Vermont 1965; IX Bienal, Sao Paulo 1967 and Waddington Galleries, London where he has exhibited regularly since. In 1968 the Hayward Gallery held a survey exhibition of his painting which was followed in 1973 at the Tate Gallery with a retrospective exhibition. Amongst the significant group exhibitions that have included his work are 'Abstract Art', Riverside Museum, New York 1951; British Pavilion Venice Biennale 1952; 'Situation', RBA Galleries, London 1960; 'Painting and Sculpture of a Decade', Tate Gallery, London 1964; Documenta 4, Kassel 1968; First International Exhibition of Modern Sculpture, Hakone Open Air Museum, Japan 1969; 'Arte Inglese Oggi', Milan 1976; Hayward Annual, Hayward Gallery, 1977 and 'British Sculpture in the 20th Century', Whitechapel Art Gallery, London 1982. His work is represented in several major public collections including the Albright-Knox Gallery, Buffalo; Hirshhorn Museum and Sculpture Garden and National Gallery of Art, Washington, D.C.; Tate Gallery, London; Städtisches Museum, Leverkusen and the Scottish National Gallery of Modern Art, Edinburgh. He lives and works in London.

70 Strange Object 1959
bronze on wood base ed. no. 2/4
39.4 x 25.5 x 24 cm

71 No. 9 1960
oil on canvas
178 × 178 cm

Patrick Scott

Born 1921 Kilbrittain, Ireland. Qualified as an architect but now paints full time. Governor of The National Gallery of Ireland, Director of Kilkenny Design Workshops and Trustee of the Irish Museums Trust. His first one-man exhibition was in 1944 at the White Stag Gallery, Dublin. Since 1961 he has shown regularly with the Dawson Gallery, Dublin. His other one-man shows include the XXX Biennale, Venice in 1960; Hamilton Galleries, London 1964; Taylor Galleries, Dublin 1977 and 1980; Oxford Gallery, Oxford 1978 and Annely Juda Fine Art, London in 1980. His work has been included in numerous group exhibitions amongst which are 'Recent Acquisitions', Museum of Modern Art, New York 1959; Guggenheim International, New York 1960; 'Goulding Collection' Municipal Gallery of Modern Art, Dublin 1961; 'Twelve Irish Painters' New York 1963; 'Paintings & Sculpture from Private Collections' Municipal Gallery, Dublin 1965; First International Exhibition of Drawings, Rijeka, Yugoslavia 1968; European tour of Modern Irish Painting 1969–1971; 'The Irish Imagination' touring Dublin, Boston, Philadelphia and Washington from 1971 to 1972; 'The Gordon Lambert Collection' Municipal Gallery of Modern Art, Dublin 1972; 'Artists Choice' Ulster Museum, Belfast 1973; Arts Council Gallery, Belfast 1974; 'Irish Directions in the Seventies', Dublin and North American tour in 1974 and 1975; 6th International Print Biennale, Bradford 1979; Roundhouse Gallery, London 1980. His work is in several international collections including the Museum of Modern Art, New York; Ulster Museum, Belfast; Municipal Gallery of Modern Art, Dublin; Contemporary Irish Art Society; Trinity College, Dublin; The Arts Council of Ireland; The Bank of Ireland, Dublin; Gulf Oil Corporation, Pittsburgh and the Joseph H. Hirshhorn Museum, Washington. Currently he lives and works in Dublin.

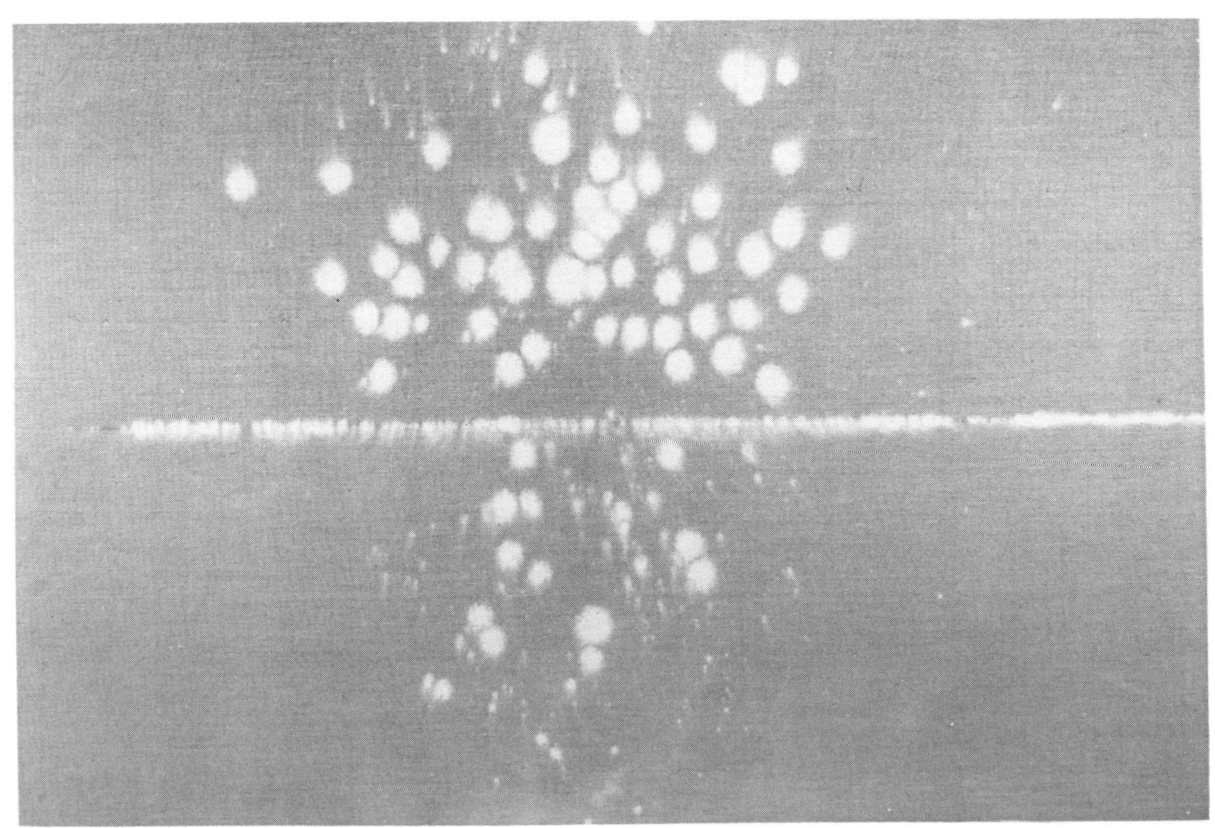

72 Through the Star Cloud (White Device) 1962
tempera on canvas
84 x 122 cm

Shinkichi Tajiri

Born 1923 Los Angeles. Studied sculpture in San Francisco 1941 and Art Institute of Chicago 1948–51. Visiting professor Minneapolis School of Art 1964–65. Exhibitions include Documenta II, Kassel 1959; Stedelijk Museum, Amsterdam 1960; 'Art of Assemblage', Museum of Modern Art, New York 1961; Geemente Museum, The Hague and Tokyo Biennale 1963; 1964 Documenta III, Kassel and Hamilton Galleries, London; Minneapolis Institute of Art 1965; Galerie Krikhaar, Amsterdam and Hamilton Galleries, London and Stedelijk Museum, Amsterdam 1967. Public collections include the Museum of Modern Art, New York; Boymans van Beuningen Museum, Rotterdam; Moderna Museet, Stockholm and the Stedelijk Museum, Amsterdam. Currently teaches in Berlin.

73 Warrior 1964
bronze
70 x 23.5 x 13 cm

William Tucker

Born in Cairo, 1935. Studied History, Oxford University, 1955–58. 1959–60 studied sculpture at St. Martin's School of Art. Taught at St. Martin's and Goldsmith's Schools of Art 1961–67. 1968 appointed Gregory Fellow at Leeds University. 1976 Lectureship University of Western Ontario. 1980/81 Guggenheim Fellow and currently teaches at Columbia University and the New York Studio School of Painting and Sculpture. First one-man exhibition at the Grabowski Gallery, London 1962 and then at the Rowan Gallery in 1963 and 1966. Other solo exhibitions include Kasmin Gallery 1967/69/77, Robert Elkon Gallery, New York 1968 and regularly until 1982; British Pavilion Venice Biennale 1972; Serpentine Gallery and Waddington Gallery, London 1973; Galerie Wintersberger, Cologne 1973/76; Galerie L'Isola, Rome 1981; Bernard Jacobson Gallery, London and Los Angeles 1982; David McKee Gallery, New York 1985. Principal group exhibitions include 'New Generation 1965', Whitechapel Art Gallery and 'London: The New Scene', Walker Art Center, Minneapolis and tour 1965; 'Primary Structures', Jewish Museum, New York 1966; Documenta IV, Kassel 1968; 'British Painting and Sculpture 1960–70', National Gallery of Art, Washington, D.C. 1971; 'The Condition of Sculpture', Hayward Gallery, London, 1975; 'Arte Inglese Oggi', Milan 1976; 'Contemporary Sculpture', Museum of Modern Art, New York 1979; 'The Sculpture Show', Serpentine Gallery, 1983. Public collections include the Tate Gallery; Museum of Modern Art, New York; Walker Art Center, Minneapolis; Victoria and Albert Museum, London and Guggenheim Museum, New York. Currently lives and works in New York.

74 Memphis 1965/66
plywood and fibreglass
76.2 x 142.3 x 165.1 cm
coll. The British Council

Tony Underhill

Born 1923 Sydney, Australia. Started painting when he was 18 at which age he joined the Australian Army. Studied with William Dobell whilst in the army. Discharged from the army in 1945 and moved to London in 1948 with periods of working and living in Italy, France, Spain and the U.S.A. He was head of post-graduate painting at Birmingham Polytechnic and died in London in 1978. In 1947 he had his first one-man show in Melbourne and subsequent exhibitions at Sydney, and Hobart, Tasmania. Between 1948 and 1957 he had several one-man shows in Italy, Spain, England and Australia. He showed at the Grabowski Gallery, London in 1960 and 1963 and at the Hamilton Galleries, London in 1964 and 1967; Rudy Komon Gallery, Sydney and Melbourne 1964; Demarco Gallery, Edinburgh, as well as Essex and Surrey Universities in 1967; University of Durham 1968; Museum at the University of Iowa, Des Moines and Feigen Gallery, Chicago 1970/71. From 1948 to 1960 he participated in numerous group exhibitions including London Group; Arts Council; and the Redfern, Mayor and Arthur Tooth Galleries, London. 1961–62 'Recent Australian Painting', Whitechapel Art Gallery, London and Arts Council tour; 1963 'Australian Painting and Sculpture in Europe Today' which toured Germany and Holland; 'Hamilton Artists 1966/67' Hamilton Galleries, London; Australian Representative at the Commonwealth Exhibition, Bristol City Art Gallery in 1968. In 1969 represented in a print show and in 1970 in 'Artists of the Gallery' at Annely Juda Fine Art, London. 1971 a two-man show at Coe College, University of Iowa and Cornell University; 1971–72 travelling exhibition, mid-West Museums, U.S.A. His work is represented in several public collections in Australia, Great Britain, U.S.A., etc.

75 Half Turned Figure 1967
oil on canvas
152.5 × 122 cm

Andy Warhol

Born 1930, Forest City, U.S.A. Studied at the Carnegie Institute of Technology, Pittsburgh 1945–49. Worked as an advertisement draughtsman in New York before his first one-man exhibition at the Hugo Gallery, New York 1952. By the early 1960's, his name was the most widely known in and outside America as the famous controversial 'Pop' artist of the decade. In 1965 he announced his retirement as an artist in order to devote himself to films, but nevertheless he continued unabated. Recent exhibitions of his work include the Albright-Knox Art Gallery, 1982 and the San Diego Museum of Art, 1983. He exhibited the 'most wanted men' series of paintings at the Rowan Gallery in 1968.

76 Marilyn Monroe 1967
screenprint on paper ed. no. 2a
93 x 93 cm

Michael Werner

Born 1912. Studied art in Paris. Guest tutor at Bath Academy of Art, 1959. 1964–68 lectured in sculpture at Bradford College of Art and from 1968 onwards has been a lecturer in fine art at Watford School of Art. His first one-man show was at Twenty Brook Street Gallery, London in 1949. He has had several one-man shows at the Beaux Arts Gallery, London in 1952, 1954 and 1955; the Obelisk Gallery, London in 1956 and 1959 and at Annely Juda Fine Art, London in 1975 and 1979. His other one-man shows include the Molton Gallery, London 1961; Hamilton Galleries, London 1964; a retrospective exhibition at the Bradford City Museum in 1965; Oxford Gallery, Oxford 1970; Walhall College, Watford 1973; 'Collages' I.C.A., London 1974; Camden Arts Centre, London 1978; Galerie Sudurgata, Reykyavik 1980; Galerie Alvensleben, Munich 1981. A retrospective exhibition of his sculpture, drawings and prints at the Round House Gallery, London marked his 70th Birthday in 1982. Among group shows in which he has participated are exhibitions at the Leicester Gallery; The Arts Council of Great Britain; The Royal Academy; Musée d'Art Moderne, Paris; Semiha Huber, Zurich; Gallery Richard Demarco, Edinburgh; Prospect Gallery, Glasgow; 'Giant Figure for Art Spectrum' Alexandra Palace, London and the Amnesty Sculpture Exhibitions in Bristol Cathedral, St. Paul's Cathedral and the Institute of Education, London. His commissions include a bust of G. B. Shaw for the Royal Court Theatre, London 1955; a mural of 18 panels for Foxford Comprehensive Secondary School, Coventry 1957 and a monumental figure of the Virgin for Bartram's Hostel, London in 1977. His work is in private collections as well as in the public collections of the Smithsonian Institute, Washington D.C.; County Museum of Modern Art, Los Angeles; Stellenbosch Museum, South Africa; New English Library, Oxford.

. . . Michael Werner at Annely Juda's is an interesting portrait sculptor, adept at conveying the look of people and animals. And his reclining rhinoceros, which looks like a stranded dinosaur, is hilariously disquieting. Cats, dogs, nudes, poets, scholars and old men are his subjects, handled with delicate finesse, showing that traditional modes, methods and idioms can be up-dated most satisfactorily; and there is certainly room for good portrait makers, a genre most sadly debased at the moment . . .'

Marina Vaizey, *The Sunday Times*, 26 January 1975

77 Column I 1964
aluminium and polyester
78.8 x 7.5 x 7.5 cm

Brian Young

Born 1934. Studied at St. Martin's and Central School of Art. Awarded British Council Scholarship to France and Italy 1960. Amongst the group exhibitions that have included his work are 'Six Young Contemporaries', Gimpel Fils 1958; 'Situation', R.B.A. Galleries 1960; New London Gallery 1961; Arts Council 'Situation' exhibition and tour 1962/63 and was first included at the Rowan Gallery in 'Five Young British Artists', 1962 and subsequently at the Whitechapel Art Gallery, 'British Paintings of the '60's', in 1963. Public collections include the Arts Council of Great Britain and the Gulbenkian Foundation, Lisbon. Lives and works in London.

78 Tilt 1961
oil on canvas
152.5 × 152.5 cm

THE SEVENTIES

The Seventies

In retrospect, the 1970s were, in Britain, a peculiarly bland time for the visual arts: surprising really, when we remember the 1960s. In 1960, the Arts Council had an exhibition of Picasso at the Tate; probably the first time a show of a modern master was attended by wall to wall people. Art became news in a way that was not always scandalous: contemporary art had for most of the century been treated in Britain with a combination of contempt, ridicule and amusement. The 1960s witnessed a change. This may have had something to do with the information, propaganda and exhibitions emerging from America, increased travel, and the slow emergence of European art after the war. But there was a new vitality, enormous activity, even energetic non-activity, from flower power to hippie-dom, to student protest and the rhetoric of student revolution. Paving stones had been hurled in Paris, shots fired at Kent State, and there was even a famous sit-in at Hornsey School of Art. Yet it was also the time, in England at least, of unprecedented affluence, the rise of pop, and affordable style.

Pop art and pop stars seemed to appear simultaneously, and in Britain at least, in the late 1960s and early 1970s the two intertwined. Pop stars had after all once been students at art schools – a pair of Beatles, Bryan Ferry, Ian Dury, Pete Townsend, to name but few. The artist Peter Blake has continued his involvement from the world famous record cover for the Beatles' 'Sergeant Pepper's Lonely Hearts Club Band' (1967) to the poster for Live Aid in 1985. In this atmosphere, art – even modern art became more accessible.

Glamour – of a kind – seemed to have infiltrated the contemporary British art world for the first time. Hockney, in the early 1960s, was photographed at the Royal College of Art, with brightly peroxided hair, and in a gold lamé suit. Yet it was gentle, genial, affectionate and agreeable: Hockney's heroes, as he portrayed himself and them in a 1961 print, were Mahatma Ghandi and Walt Whitman. Protest, on the part of many, was to come late in the decade.

Bryan Robertson, John Russell and Lord Snowdon compiled a vast book on the contemporary art scene called *Private View* (1965) a book that was, curiously, both cosy and expansive. In the main, British art remained personal, expressive, even at times endearing. Colour supplements were into life-styles; Conran had just arrived. There was an oddly beguiling, even lulling combination of sophistication and innocence. An interest in cooking was just beginning to take hold beyond the disciples of commonsensical and European Mrs Elizabeth David; kitchens were decorated with French onions on strings, sold to housewives in inner London by itinerant bicycling French peddlers, rusticity went hand in hand with urbanism and the rise of the middle class pressure groups (consumer associations, welfare groups, and a fervent belief that comprehensive education would cure all social ills) and the age of the blockbuster exhibition had just begun. In the 1960s it seemed at last in Britain as though art might again begin to matter. It had not mattered after all for a very long time. At the end of the 1960s, both Annely Juda and Alex Gregory-Hood had centrally located galleries, oases in the desert of jovial mediocrity that characterised much contemporary art dealing. These two were among the most important and active in just the handful of innovative galleries of

Christo, Wrapped Walk Ways (project for Loose Park, Kansas City) 1977 2-part collage 71 x 112 cm (overall)

the time. For what is deeply surprising, with hindsight, is the quite unusually small number of art galleries, let alone galleries devoted to 20th century, modern or contemporary art, there were anywhere in the country. The Tate, until nearly the end of the 1960s, was host to Arts Council exhibitions, or in the case of the influential 54–64 exhibition, those funded or sponsored by other organisations, in this case, the Gulbenkian. The Hayward Gallery did not open until 1968 – with, bravely indeed, Matisse. It is exceptionally difficult to remember with clarity the comparative paucity of exhibitions of contemporary art, even in the early 1970s, compared with now: and, even more, the very, very few galleries, commercial galleries, which were dealing. Only a very few places – the Whitechapel being one of the shining exceptions that proved the rule – had shown in the 1960s contemporary art on an international scale. *Arts Review* in 1970 had, for example, just over one and a half pages of listings for all London galleries, private and public; and less than a page for the whole country, outside London: well under three pages for the lot. In 1985, *Arts Review* listing – and no listings are now complete – is, with tighter spacing, seven pages; substantially more than double. It is against this background of relatively few exhibitions of any kind compared to now, far less public interest in the art market compared to now, and only a handful of galleries devoted to contemporary art, that we must evaluate the heroic, enlightening, enjoyable and important achievements of Annely Juda and Alex Gregory-Hood, and their fellow workers.

I began writing myself for a newspaper in 1970 – the *Financial Times*. I vividly remember my amazement and my delight at the unusually large space of the then Rowan, in Bruton Place, at that time one of the largest if not the largest spaces – long before warehouses, and warehouse studios and spaces became as usual as they are now. Equally, the smaller rooms at Tottenham Mews were conducive to the showing of art, often domestic in scale, but with large implications.

The art both galleries showed was very different one from the other, but with an emphasis in both instances on the abstract, rather than the figurative and representational (although the Rowan had showed Andy Warhol early on). With hindsight, the partnership of the 1980s seems natural, even inevitable. Rowan and Juda artists seem natural complements. At the time the emphases varied. Annely Juda's mews gallery was constructivist and international. Christo was given his first London show, in 1971, with an exceptionally exhilarating series of collages, photographs and mixed media works of 'Projects not Realised' – although in the intervening fourteen years several similar projects have been, such as the proposed wrapped walkways, realised in 1978 in Kansas City, with related collages and drawings shown here in 1979. Christo throughout the 1970s evolved some of the largest, most exuberant and memorable public art projects, involving in his work years of preparation and hundreds if not thousands of people. No public project has yet been carried out in England: our first hand knowledge of Christo, and his art, has come about through his involvement with the Judas. Christo is strikingly ambitious, in the real and not pejorative sense (curiously it is, I have often thought, only in England that ambition is a pejorative word, as is the phrase 'too clever by half'). Christo deals with the real world; he transforms it, in reality, dressing and undressing landscape and buildings, cloaking and uncloaking islands, streets and parks: Valley Curtain, Colorado; Running Fence, California are world famous. In this broadest sense of all, his work may be seen in part as an imaginative construction, carried out literally into the streets, packaging and unpackaging . . . Christo's ambitious, ironic and amazing proposals for wrapping Berlin's Reichstag were shown here in 1977.

Christo, born in Bulgaria, lives in New York and works internationally. A monumental artist, the American painter Al Held, has shown both in Europe and South America, but most extensively in North America, home too to several extensive public mural projects. His vertiginous paintings, black and white or, more recently, in brilliant fluorescent colour, turn the ideas of Renaissance perspective inside out and upside down, and then around again. Once more, his only private gallery showings in Britain have been at Annely Juda's. His art does not make news as Christo's does here: Christo has been shown in several public galleries. But, again, we have had our only British glimpse of Held's paintings in Britain at Tottenham Mews.

If, in part because of the pioneering historic exhibitions of non-objective art, suprematism, constructivism, abstraction, we associate contemporary work shown at Annely Juda's with geometric abstraction, this is a natural connection to make. But while the emphasis during the 1970s was on varying kinds of abstraction, on variants of the non-objective world in new guise in contemporary terms, the overall impression, as I look back was, perhaps surprisingly, of an unusual warmth and accessibility, of indeed a kind of lyrical, even freehand geometry, an art of architectonic values but always on a human scale.

Take, as it were, Michael Kenny. His sculptures, like tableaux, are a kind of freehand lyrical geometry, leaving plenty of room for the spectator to make up matching narratives and plots. That is, the artist's imagination works on the viewer in several ways: by

Al Held, D-C 1979 acrylic on canvas 244 x 426.8 cm coll. Dallas Museum of Fine Art

refinement and distillation, sensitising us to the extraordinary things to be found in the ordinary, and by suggesting almost with three dimensional pictograms, emotional crosscurrents between abstracted shapes which yet evoke human connotations. Kenny's sculpture can inhabit a room and, as I have seen, although the work is typically suggestive of a contained interior, it looks surprisingly at home out of doors, imposing its own framework with subtle discretion, inhabiting the cultivated garden and the contrived wilderness with as much ease as an indoor living room. These sculptures, constructed, contrived, are a lyrical geometry, which yet play off human connotations, exploring a creative tension between the objective and the subjective.

Michael Michaeledes is a Greek architect living in London, whose work – stretched unpainted, unprimed canvas, free standing or wall hanging reliefs, which was also the subject of an exhilarating exhibition at the Greek Pavillion at the Venice Biennale in 1976, explores with controlled exuberance the effect of light and shadow, glancing off shapes made of cloth on a wooden frame, which seemingly simple in concept turn out to be surprisingly complex in reality. Here with Michaeledes' work, shown in 1972 and 1975, we would seem to reach a pure abstraction. But again, everything is approachable, on a human scale, intensifying our apprehension of the cubes and boxes in which we live. White on white has a long ancestry in modernism, from Malevich on. Michaeledes' work recalls, perhaps, the Greek villages which look like shining sugar cubes scattered on a hillside, but just as much they remind us of the richness possible when a basic formal vocabulary is arranged and constructed in various permutations, all still related to the human scale.

Edwina Leapman's paintings – variegated white stripes on unprimed raw canvas, warm-toned, may remind us of endless horizon lines, but also, as her 1976 exhibition of paintings and drawings demonstrated, evocatively and provocatively explore yet another variation of Klee's famous dictum of taking a line for a walk.

In 1977, a group exhibition explored the work of the conscious inheritors in England of the continental constructivist tradition, looking at the work of Malcolm Hughes, Norman Dilworth, Peter Lowe and Jeffrey Steele. In the same year, the self-taught Frenchman, Francois Morellet, who had trained as an engineer, showed paintings, drawings and objects over a span of twenty years' worth of work. The basic form was again the line, arranged, however, so as to tease the eye with various perspectives in two dimensions, in paintings which made as much of empty white space as of strikingly dramatic criss-crossed blackness; and in metal with silvery grey, iridescent sheen.

Continental lyrical constructivists were shown extensively throughout the decade. There were Americans, such as Charmion von Wiegand, a self-taught painter who wrote the first American essay on

Michael Kenny, Black Blessed Virgin 1978/9 (foreground) Roundhouse Gallery, London 1979

Francois Morellet Paintings, Drawings and Objects 1954–77, 1977

Mondrian in 1943, an abstract artist herself, unafraid of boldly simple colours. She showed her work in 1974. In 1975, the Dutch sculptor, constructivist, and environmentalist, an artist who had often collaborated with architects on actual realised projects, Joost Baljeu, showed, reliefs, paintings and 'synthesist' constructions. The Swiss artist Gottfried Honegger also showed paintings and drawings in 1979, work built up in squares and rectangles of pure colour. The German artist Friedrich Vordemberge-Gildewart was shown extensively – a retrospective of forty years of work (1924–1962) in 1972, a key figure in the European scene, little-known in England, who showed at the very first Documenta, Kassel in 1955. He was at the centre of the European movement towards 'non-objectivity': typical of Annely Juda not only to show continental artists working in the styles, modes, idioms and theories of non-objectivity, but to remind us too of cultural and historical context and interconnections. The major historical shows which have taken place, afresh and freshly, each summer, until this, this jubilee year, have focussed on broad groupings, making the past live in the present. The shows devoted to a single person have stressed individuality, of course, but remembered here, and seen here, within the framework of the visual education provided summer after summer by the historical surveys. Other luminaries of the movement – the second generation as it were – were also the focus of special exhibitions such as Robert Michel and Ella Bergmann-Michel.

A fascinating rediscovery was the work of Alan Reynolds, who like several other British artists – Victor Pasmore being perhaps the best known example – have moved from a phase of outstandingly well received representational and figurative painting to a highly individual version of lyrical constructivism. Alan Reynolds' white-on-white and black and white paintings on wood, and black and white prints, are intuitively, not rigidly paced, producing a kind of natural proportion, the whole immaculate. The paintings are indeed shown in handmade frames made by the artist: each work is conceived as a whole, echoing the kind of concern evidenced by the earliest constructivists. An historical continuity has always been a salient feature in these exhibitions; there were several exhibitions in the early 1970s under the title of 'Modern Images in Ancient Times' a theme repeated rather grandiosely in the Museum of Modern Art, New York's blockbuster show of 1984 'Primitivism and 20th century art' and which surfaced in England as long ago as the late 1940s, with the ICA's 40,000 Years of Modern Art. But of course as we have seen in most instances the human presence in the work of the majority of artists who showed throughout the 1970s at Annely Juda's was conspicuous, even underlined, by its absence.

What was particularly evident was the extraordinary variety possible for an absolutely contemporary non-objective artist. The printmaker and painter Alan Green emerged during the 1970s as a major artist, first showing at Annely Juda's in 1970, and then throughout the decade in 1972, 1975, 1976 (etchings) and 1978. Now, with an international reputation, his immaculately crafted, sombre yet succulent paintings, drawings and prints are readily recognisable as a particular kind of intuitive, lyrical geometry, highly individual. Green's paintings are the product of painstaking effort, in which mixed media and layers and layers and layers of colour, so that black is never just black, blue never just blue, are soothed one onto the other. He is an artist whose work is almost impossible to reproduce. The paintings really are the art of the real, in which surface is all, what you see is what you see, and which make our awareness of the world expand. Green's art, so seemingly simple, reductive and minimal – a mere matter, we might think, of squares and rectangles, with an occasional flurry of line and scribble and thatching to add further flurries of surface incident – is a perfect example of less means more. In show after show throughout the decade – and he is working now as strongly as ever – he

Alan Reynolds Reliefs, 1978

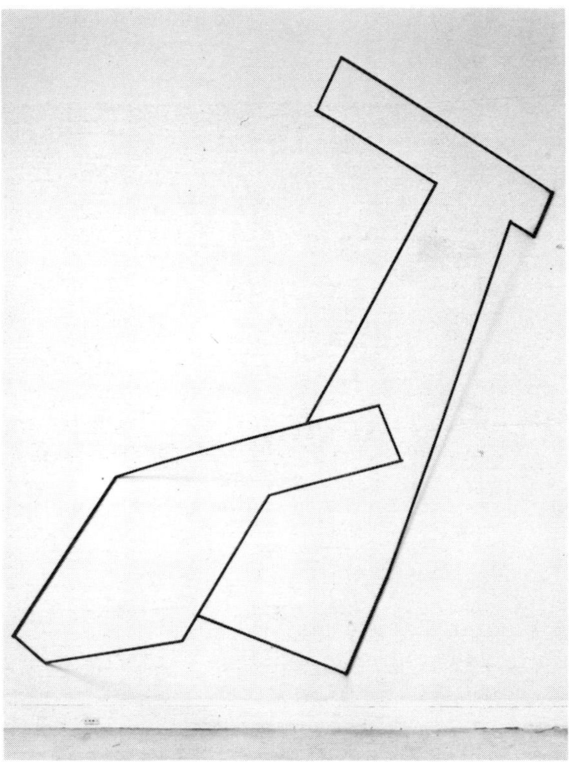

Nigel Hall, Borderline 1977
painted aluminium 267 x 262 x 78 cm
exh. Documenta VI, Kassel, 1977

emerged as a true original, who married continental constructivism with a highly English feel for nuance, colour, and surface texture. It is as though landscape had geometrized, but a geometry arrived at through the visual imagination without the aid of any scientific measure but the life of the emotions.

The sculptor Nigel Hall with painted wall hanging and extending aluminium rods also evoked, deliberately, wide open desert landscapes with another kind of intuitive geometry. His sculptures are drawings in space with elements painstakingly constructed and attached.

Thus, what emerged throughout the decade was the sheer liveliness of the intuitive geometry of non-objectivity, in which Continental theory was filtered through an English subjectivity, a restrained, reticent, yet fervent emotion, and Annely Juda's throughout the 1970s was a place where British and European art met, looking across the Channel not in the main to France, but to Holland, Germany and Switzerland. Above all these versions of intuitive geometry were enjoyable and exhilarating, various and eye opening.

Alex Gregory-Hood throughout the 1970s was committed, as he still is, to a remarkable group of British artists whom he nurtured and sustained. Again the emphasis was on abstraction but in the main a lyrical abstraction, based on a wonderfully hedonistic approach to colour and texture, to surprising shape, to interweavings of stripe, line, square.

Light and landscape, the changing atmosphere of English weather, are – it seems to me – at the heart of Bridget Riley's so-called 'optical' paintings, not so-called by the artist, but by others. The flow of her twisted, horizontal, vertical, wavy stripes of colour, which as it were mix in the eye, create quite overwhelming feelings of euphoria, the response we have to being aware of early morning, mid-morning, twilight. Paintings, gouaches, and prints were shown throughout the decade, and looking at a number of painters shown at the Rowan it is fascinating to see how the stripe, the line of colour, became a kind of motif put through various paces by various artists. Sean Scully, now living in New York, explored grids, superimposed stripes, and superimposed colours, often in shaped paintings. Jeremy Moon, who died tragically young in his late thirties, was an artist of exceptional gifts, exploring in all sorts of ways the shaped painting, and the grid and stripe floating in space. Paul Huxley made actors of geometric shapes, setting them in dialogue, here a crowd and there a space. Mark Lancaster, who went to America and has worked extensively with Merce Cunningham's dance company, also found a version of lyrical, expressive and painterly geometry. Michael Craig-Martin used his art, his sculpture to comment on art itself and illusion: mirrors teased, the world in Craig-Martin's art was not as it appeared, and once, with a glass of water – titled An Oak Tree – he actually took into the gallery world the debate concerning transubstantiation and consubstantiation. When does one substance become another? When is it an imitation, when the real thing, is

Jeremy Moon, No. 4/70 1970
acrylic on canvas 243.8 x 381 cm

Installation view of Paul Huxley's one-man show at the Galeria da Emenda, Lisbon, 1974

the artist someone who designates, points out, or someone who makes?

Sculpture was of great importance at the Rowan. Garth Evans used all sorts of substances, even paper and twisted wood to make sculptures which extended from relatively simple geometric shapes to floor hugging and floor covering carpets of strange substances, vital and curious.

Phillip King has become known world wide. His major exhibition at the Kröller-Müller, Otterlo, introduced a European public to a new British sculptor whose work extended through the decade from coloured plastics and neo-baroque idioms to painted metal, vast constructions with a myriad of interiors and exteriors, to the use of wood and slate and natural and organic materials. Again, all was to the human scale, and the strength and diversity of King's work was shown at a host of national and international exhibitions.

Martin Naylor works in an area between sculpture and painting, now with boxed constructions on the wall, suggesting strange and powerful narratives, now with free standing sculpture. Richard Kidd and Julian Hawkes also explored non-objective art, while Barry Flanagan, a kind of dandified joker, who has since turned to directly figurative bronze cast sculpture, actually made work out of rope, heaped up materials and other unexpected substances.

John Golding, also an art historian, moved from a kind of careful geometry into outbursts of succulent colour and wonderfully varied textures in paint and pastels, suggesting in both paintings and large works on paper the movement of light, changing light, as though pieces of sky had been made tangible and palpable. Colours softened from the boldest of reds and yellows to all the shades between, to blues and golds and pinks and sun yellows.

Installation view of Phillip King's one-man show at the Kröller-Müller Museum, Otterlo, 1974 foreground: Ascona 1972

Tim Head with slide installations and photographs actually dematerialised art, making tableaux of real objects which were then illusionistically produced in unexpected spaces in the gallery. Once the installation involved a real horse. The gallery, of course, as usual responded with efficient competence and remarkable good humour – as did the horse.

John Edwards is another lyrical abstractionist, who has explored the use of a single configuration – such as an X – putting it through various colorations, textures, backgrounds and foregrounds.

There are here too, several figurative artists. Antony Donaldson is much taken with the female form, stylised, painted, sculptured, enlarged and miniaturised. Anthony Green takes his own life, past, present, future, dream and nightmare, feelings strong, loving, tender, excited. He dreams himself as he would like to be, he reconstructs his past and that of his family, he paints homages to married love, he recalls in shaped canvas after shaped canvas the look of apartments, places, landscapes and trips where he and his own have been, have lived, have left, have stayed. It is an astonishing autobiography in paint, in which reality and fantasy creatively intermingle.

If Annely Juda's was in the 1970s a home to a special kind of lyrical constructivism, in which intuitive geometry married with the visual imagination, creating work which thoughtfully exercised both mind and eye, the direct impact of artists at the Rowan was perhaps more dramatic, more colourful, more overt: a lyrical abstraction in the main, toughened at times by the wilder shores of conceptualism, and danced through by the upfront life-in-paint of Anthony Green. Throughout, abstraction has been irradiated in the

Rowan Gallery Sculpture Garden at Loxley, 1978 left: Phillip King, Bali 1977 right: Garth Evans, 8 Cones Grey 1969

work of many an artist in both galleries by an unaffected love, understanding and observation of light and landscape, intelligently informed by a delight in form for its own sake. As Phillip King's sculptures so often suggest dwellings, spaces to inhabit, so John Golding and Bridget Riley suggest the firm reality of the light of imaginary landscapes, and Alan Green shows us the subtle textures and colours of a world always around us, but which he as an artist has refined, distilled and reduced to a graspable, seeable essential.

Throughout the 1970s, in Bruton Place and Tottenham Mews, home to many a good party and exuberant gathering, British art was sustained with a rare commitment. In a bland decade, here was sharpness, awareness, intelligence, above all a communicable gift not only of looking – but of seeing.

Throughout the 1970s, the exhausting if enjoyable task of showing British art abroad – and these British artists – took place in a variety of ways. The Judas are indefatigible art fair-ists, that new phenomenon, from Basle to Chicago, Paris to Cologne. If not always taking a stand, literally, visits would invariably be made. Internationalism is very hard work – and hard driving. But it has paid, certainly in prestige and also in sales. The British Council sponsored international exhibitions – Bridget Riley and Phillip King had major travelling shows in the 1970s – are obviously important, as are the links made with commercial galleries. Alex Gregory-Hood has had particularly strong connections with Australia and America; David Juda probably spends a third of the year on the road, out of the country, from airport to hired car and back again, and the Judas' strong links with Japan have been of course further confirmed with David Juda's marriage in Japan to a Japanese artist. There are Phillip Kings on major sites world-wide and the burgeoning list of exhibitions abroad for gallery artists is a reflection of all that solid work in the 1970s. In the mid 1980s a number of factors indicate that British artists might at last make the international breakthrough as a national group to be conjured with. Contemporary art has long been undervalued at home, but two decades after the initial post-war excitements, which really fructified in the 1960s – it is worth noting that Henry Moore only surged into international prominence from the late 1940s, and Bacon a decade and more after – it looks like launch time. If so, Annely Juda and Alex Gregory-Hood, with their substantial commitment and unswerving loyalty, deserve considerable credit.

Marina Vaizey
July 1985

Marina Vaizey has been the art critic for the *Sunday Times* since 1974. Before that she wrote on the visual arts for *The Financial Times* and *Arts Review*. She has served on the Arts Council and the Photography, Fine Art and Art History boards of the Council for National Academic rewards. Other committees include Paintings for Hospitals, the CAS and a period on the Advisory Committee of the Department of the Environment. Among her books are: *100 Masterpieces of Art* (1979), *Andrew Wyeth* (1980), *Artist as Photographer* (1982), *Peter Blake* (1985). Organised *'Critics Choice'* 1974 and chose the Arts Council touring exhibition (1982–1985) *'Painter as Photographer'*.

The Seventies

Exhibition

Page

Abbreviated artists' biographies are to be found in the initial decade their work appears.

Christo

Born Christo Javacheff, Gabrova, Bulgaria 1935. Studied at the Fine Arts Academy, Sofia 1952–56 and at the Burian Theatre, Prague in 1956. In 1957 he briefly worked at the Vienna Fine Arts Academy, before arriving in Paris the following year. His first projects in 1961 were for the 'Packaging of a Public Building', 'Stacked Oil Drums' and 'Dockside Packages', in Cologne harbour. Since then he has either proposed or completed projects in over twenty-five locations worldwide. Amongst those completed are '5,600 cubic metres Package' an Air Package for Documenta 4, 1968; 'Wrapped Coast, Little Bay, One Million Square Feet', Sydney, 1969; 'Valley Curtain, Grand Hogback, Rifle, Colorado', 1972; 'Wrapped Walkways, Loose Park, Kansas City' 1977–78; the 'Surrounded Islands, Biscayne Bay, Greater Miami', 1980–83; 'The Pont Neuf Wrapped', Paris 1985. His work in connection with these and other as yet unrealised projects has been exhibited worldwide. Among the most important of these exhibitions have been Galerie Haro Lauhus, Cologne 1961; Stedelijk van Abbemuseum, Eindhoven 1966; Museum of Modern Art, New York 1968; National Gallery of Victoria, Melbourne 1969; Kunsthalle, Dusseldorf 1973; Musée de Peinture et de Sculpture, Grenoble 1974; Minami Gallery, Tokyo and Annely Juda Fine Art, London, 1977; Rijksmuseum Kröller-Müller and Galerie Art in Progress, Munich 1978; ICA Boston, 1979; Museum Ludwig, Cologne, Juda Rowan Gallery and La Jolla Museum of Contemporary Art 1981; The Hara Museum of Contemporary Art, Tokyo 1982; Satani Gallery, Tokyo and Juda Rowan Gallery 1984. He lives and works in New York.

'. . . But Christo has made his name by taking the idea of the parcel further than anyone else, whenever possible making the idea a reality and working on an ever larger and more ambitious scale. There is a famous drawing by Henry Moore, made in 1942: 'Crowd Looking at a Tied-up Object', the tiny figures dwarfed by the sinister piece, waiting for it to be removed, to be unveiled, to surprise them in some way; but it was never, perhaps not intended, to be carried out . . .'

William Packer, *The Financial Times*, 22 November 1977

'. . . All the stretching and wrapping and surrounding have as much to do with philosophy as with aesthetics. Christo's art is executed to make people reconsider their thoughts; he wants to force them to think differently from their everyday ways of thinking . . .'

Ann Monroe *The Wall Street Journal*, 12 July 1984

79 Wrapped Monument (Project for Milan) 1970
pencil, charcoal, collage on board
101 × 73.6 cm

Michael Craig-Martin

Born in Dublin in 1941, he was resident in the U.S.A. from 1946–66. From 1961–66 he studied at Yale University and has been resident in Britain since 1966. He was an artist in residence at King's College, Cambridge 1970–72. His first one-man exhibition was at the Rowan Gallery in 1969 where he exhibited regularly until he left the gallery in 1981. Other solo exhibitions include the Arnolfini Gallery, Bristol, 1971; Galerie December, Munster 1974; Turnpike Gallery, Leigh and tour 1976/77; Institute of Modern Art, Brisbane and tour 1978; Galeria Foksal and Akumlatory, Poland 1979; Galerie Bama, Paris, 1980; Fifth Triennale, New Delhi, India 1982 and Waddington Galleries, London, where he has exhibited regularly since. Amongst the important group exhibitions that have included his work are Documenta VI, Kassel, 1977; 'Un Certain Art Anglais', Musée d'Art Moderne de la Ville de Paris, 1979; ROSC, Dublin 1980; 'British Sculpture in the 20th Century', Whitechapel Gallery, London 1981; 'Aspects of British Art Today', Tokyo Metropolitan Museum and tour of Japan, 1982; 'The British Art Show', Birmingham City Art Gallery and U.K. tour, 1984. His work is included in several major public collections including the Tate Gallery, London; Baltimore Museum of Art; Australian National Gallery, Canberra; Southampton Art Gallery and the Victoria and Albert Museum, London. He lives and works in London.

80 Untitled Painting No. 4 1976
oil paint and canvas
180.9 x 180.9 cm

John Davies

Born 1946 in Cheshire. 1963–67 studied at Hull and Manchester Colleges of Art. Slade School of Art 1968–70. Sainsbury Award 1970. His first one-man exhibition which was organised in collaboration with Annely Juda Fine Art was at the Whitechapel Gallery in 1972. He exhibited there again in 1975 and joined Marlborough Fine Art (London) Ltd. in 1980, where he has exhibited regularly since; 1981 Retrospective at the Kunstverein, Hamburg and tour; 1983 Ferens Art Gallery, Hull; 1985 Sainsbury Centre for Visual Arts, University of East Anglia, Norwich. Amongst the group exhibitions that have included his work are 1973 Biennale de Paris; 1974 'For the Last Time', Sammlung Ludwig, Neue Galerie Aachen; 1975 'Body and Soul', Peter Moores Project 3, Walker Art Gallery, Liverpool; 1977 Documenta VI, Kassel and 'Real Life', Peter Moores Project 4, Walker Art Gallery, Liverpool; 1978 4th Indian Triennale, New Delhi; 1979 3rd Biennale of Sydney, Art Gallery of New South Wales; 1981–82 'British Sculpture in the 20th Century', Whitechapel Art Gallery, London; 1983 'Aspects of British Art Today', Tokyo Metropolitan Museum and tour; 'British Art Show', Birmingham City Art Gallery and U.K. tour. His work is represented in several public collections including the Tate Gallery, London; Wilhelm-Lehmbruck-Museum, Duisburg; Museo de Bellas Artes, Caracas and the McCrory Corporation, New York. He lives and works in Kent.

81 Elderly Man 1971
mixed media
life size

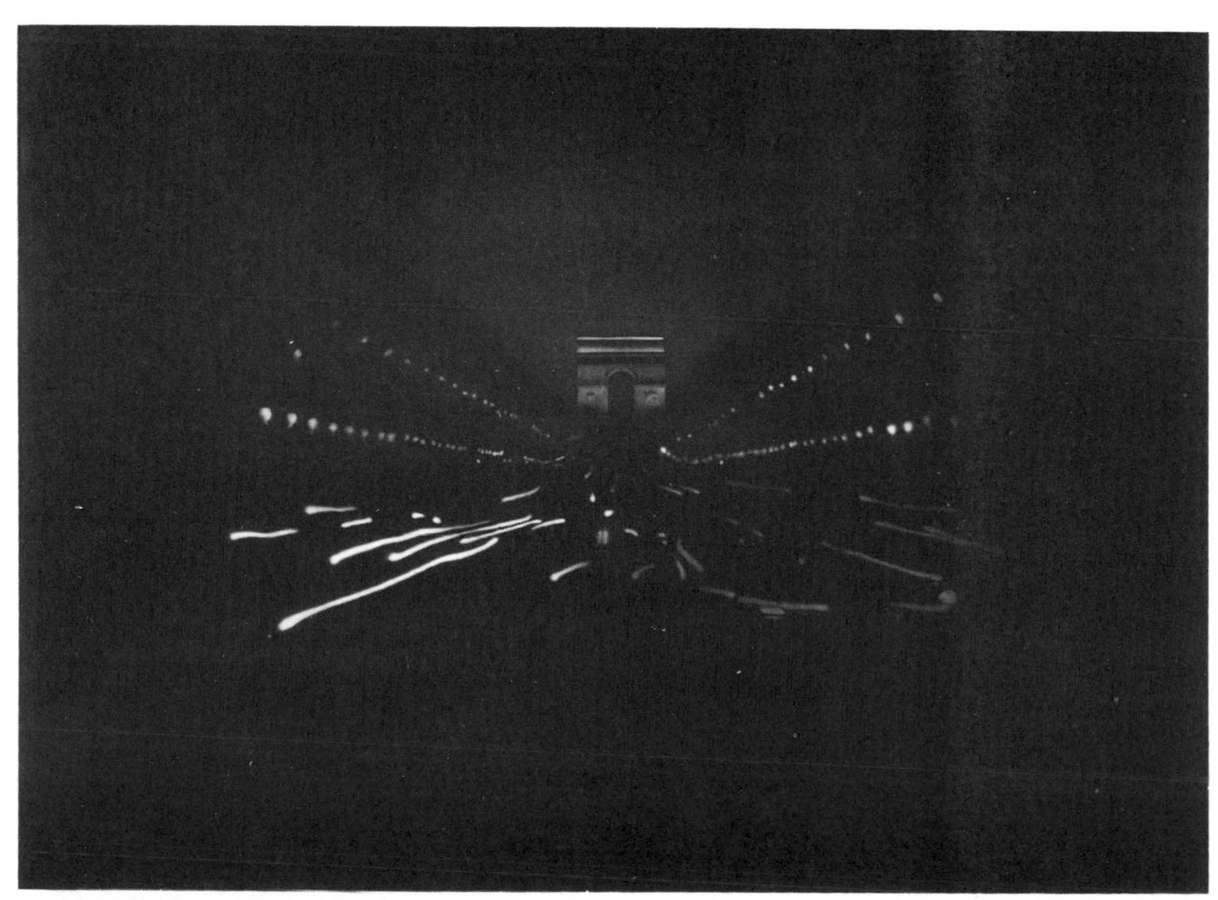

Anthony Donaldson

82 Paris by Night (L'Etoile) 1976
acrylic lacquer on beauty board
101.5 x 141.5 cm

Garth Evans

83 No. 46 (Spring) 1971
galvanised steel and paint
173.5 × 205.7 × 84.5 cm

John Edwards

84 Lap 1977/78
acrylic on canvas
182.9 x 169 cm

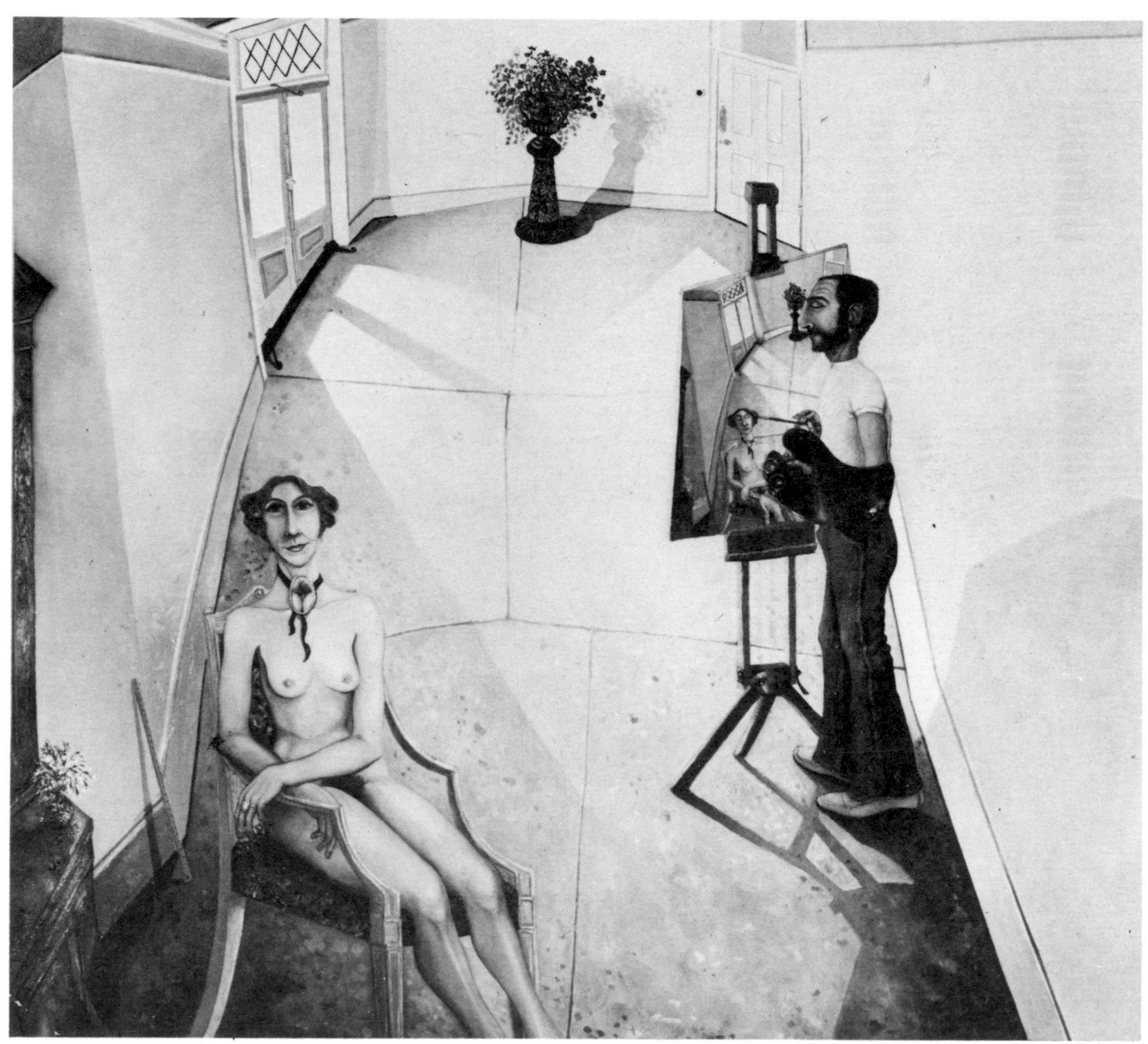

Anthony Green

85 The Life Painting 1972
oil on board
160 x 183 cm

John Golding

Born 1929 in Hastings. Educated in Mexico and Canada. 1959–81 Taught Courtauld Institute London, 1978–79 Slade Professor of Fine Art, Cambridge University. 1984 Trustee of the Tate Gallery, London. Over the last 25 years he has written a number of important books including 1959 *Cubism 1907–1914*, 1972 *Boccioni's Unique Forms of Continuity in Space*, 1978 *Matisse and Cubism*. He has also selected or co-selected exhibitions including 1981 'Picasso's Picassos' at the Hayward Gallery and 'Matisse's Drawings and Sculptures' at the Hayward and Museum of Modern Art, New York. First London exhibition 1962 Gallery One, first exhibition Rowan Gallery 1974 and has exhibited there regularly since. Other one-man shows include 1974 Holdsworth Gallery, Sydney; 1977 National Gallery of Modern Art, Edinburgh; 1982 'Drawings', Nishimura Gallery, Tokyo; 1984 Coventry Gallery, Sydney. Among many other group exhibitions he has participated in 1972 'Large paintings', Hayward Gallery, London; 1977 'British Painting 1952–71', Royal Academy, London and 'British Contemporary Art', Kunstlerhaus, Bregenz; 1984 Everard Read Gallery, Johannesburg. Public collections owning his work include Albright-Knox Gallery, Buffalo; Arts Council of Great Britain; British Council; Museum of Modern Art, New York; National Gallery of Australia, Canberra; Tate Gallery, London; Victoria and Albert Museum, London.

'. . . Golding has never engaged in the savage battle for success. He has managed to achieve, however, a mixture of sensibility and intellectual stature, and an ultimate seriousness, that few painters today in England can claim . . .'

Suzi Gablik, *Art in America*, March/April 1978

'. . . they are – simply – beautiful, a choreography of shimmering colour, vibrant and euphoric. With his every exhibition, the sheer pleasure to be found in Golding's orchestrating chords of colour splendidly increases . . .'

Marina Vaizey, *The Sunday Times*, 29 April 1984

86 G (RF) I 1977/78
acrylic on cotton duck
141.5 x 188 cm

Alan Green

Born in London 1932. Studied at Beckenham School of Art 1949–1953 and Royal College of Art 1955–58. From 1959–74 held teaching posts at Hornsey College of Art, Leeds Polytechnic and Ravensbourne College of Art. His first solo exhibition was at the AIA Gallery London in 1963 and he had his first one-man exhibition with Annely Juda Fine Art in 1970 and regularly since then. His work has been shown world-wide in one-man exhibitions including in the 1970's, Galerie Hervé Alexandre, Brussels 1974 and 1975; Art in Progress Munich 1974 and 1977; Galerie Klaus Lupke, Frankfurt 1976; Susan Caldwell Inc., New York; Nina Freudenheim, Buffalo and the Clark Gallery, Boston in 1978; Artline the Hague and Galerie Loyse Oppenheim, Nyon, Switzerland in 1979. A major retrospective exhibition of his work was organised by the Kunsthalle Bielefeld in 1979 which travelled to the Museum of Modern Art, Oxford. In the 1980's, Alan Green has exhibited extensively in Japan at the Kasahara Gallery, Osaka in 1981 and 1984, as well as in Europe including Gimpel Hanover and André Emmerich, Zurich in 1982/1984; Galerij S65, Aalst Belgium, in 1982/84 and Galerie Nicole Gonet Lausanne 1984 and at six galleries in West Germany including Galerie Heiner Hepper–Art in Progress, Dusseldorf 1980/82 and Galeries Klaus Lupke and Appel & Fertsch in Frankfurt in 1985. His work was included in the XII Biennale de Sao Paulo in 1973 and in Documenta VI, Kassel in 1977 as well as 'British Art Now' at the Guggenheim Museum, New York and tour 1980; Carnegie International, Pittsburgh and 'Aspects of British Art Today' which toured to five museums in Japan in 1982. He has won numerous international print prizes and his work is included in many important public collections including the Albright-Knox Gallery, Buffalo; Guggenheim Museum, New York; Kunstmuseums Dusseldorf, Hanover, Bielefeld and Zurich; Tate Gallery, London and the Tokyo Metropolitan Art Museum. He lives and works in London.

'. . . Green comes on as a four-square, honest craftsman. There's a straightforward frontality about Alan Green's new work, combined with a nice sense of scale and a steady, nuance-resisting command of colour, that builds up to an impressive body of work. Once or twice in the bigger ones – 'Four in the Morning' for instance – there is an echo of that archetypal English statement, James Ward's 'Gordale Scar.' Nothing finicky here, in any case: plain deeds and plain language all the way . . .'

John Russell, *The Sunday Times*, 18 March 1973

'. . . What I admire about this work is that it achieves maximum excitement through minimal means. It is always controlled, but never monkish . . .'

Waldemar Januszczak, *The Guardian*, 6 August 1985

87 Blocking Out 1972
acrylic on canvas
152.5 x 152.5 cm

Nigel Hall

Born in Bristol in 1943 and studied at the West of England College of Art, Bristol from 1960–64 and at the Royal College of Art, London, 1964–67. His first one-man exhibition was at the Galerie Givaudan, Paris 1967. In 1967/69 he won a Harkness Scholarship to work in the U.S.A. and exhibited at the Nicholas Wilder Gallery, Los Angeles, 1968 and again in 1972. His first one-man exhibition in London was at the Serpentine Gallery in 1970 and he subsequently showed with Felicity Samuel Gallery in 1972/74 and 1976. He first showed with Annely Juda Fine Art in 1978. Other important one-man shows include Robert Elkon Gallery, New York 1974/77/79 and 1983; University of Melbourne Art Gallery, Australia and tour 1978/79; Nishimura Gallery, Tokyo, 1980 and 1984; Warwick Arts Centre, London 1980; Staatliche Kunsthalle Baden-Baden 1982; Galerie Reckermann, Koln 1979/84 and Galerie Maeght Paris and Zurich 1981/82. Amongst the major group exhibitions that have included his work are 'New British Painting and Sculpture', UCLA Galleries, Los Angeles, and tour 1967–69; City Sculpture Project, Stuyvesant Foundation, 1972; 9th Paris Biennale, Museum of Modern Art Paris and 'The Condition of Sculpture', Hayward Gallery, London 1975; 'Arte Inglese Oggi', Milan 1976; Documenta VI, Kassel 1977; 'Constructivism and the Geometric Tradition', McCrory Corporation Collection and tour 1979–81; 'British Sculpture in the Twentieth Century', Whitechapel Art Gallery, London 1981–82 and 'Aspects of British Art Today', Tokyo Metropolitan Museum and tour 1982. His work is represented in several major international collections including the Australian National Gallery, Canberra; Art Gallery of New South Wales, Sydney; Dallas Museum of Fine Art; Scottish National Gallery of Modern Art, Edinburgh; Louisiana Museum, Denmark; Museum of Modern Art, New York; Musée National d'Art Moderne, Paris; Nationalgalerie, Berlin; Tate Gallery, London; National Museum of Art, Osaka, Japan; Tokyo Metropolitan Museum; Victoria and Albert Museum, London. He lives and works in London.

'. . . It says a lot therefore for Nigel Hall, already firmly and internationally established as one of the best of our younger artists, that his first exhibition with his new gallery, the Annely Juda, demonstrates an exciting development from his 1976 show at Felicity Samuel. Compared with his work of that time, in which his sculptural course appeared optional and his drawings defensively systematic, some of his latest pieces have a visual clarity that positively purrs with confidence . . .'

John McEwen, *The Spectator*, 20 May 1978

'. . . There is still the sure sense of composition; but now it is as though it is a mark that is established, albeit in space and made of painted metal, against which another moves and another overlays or undermines . . .'

William Packer, *The Financial Times*, 12 March 1985

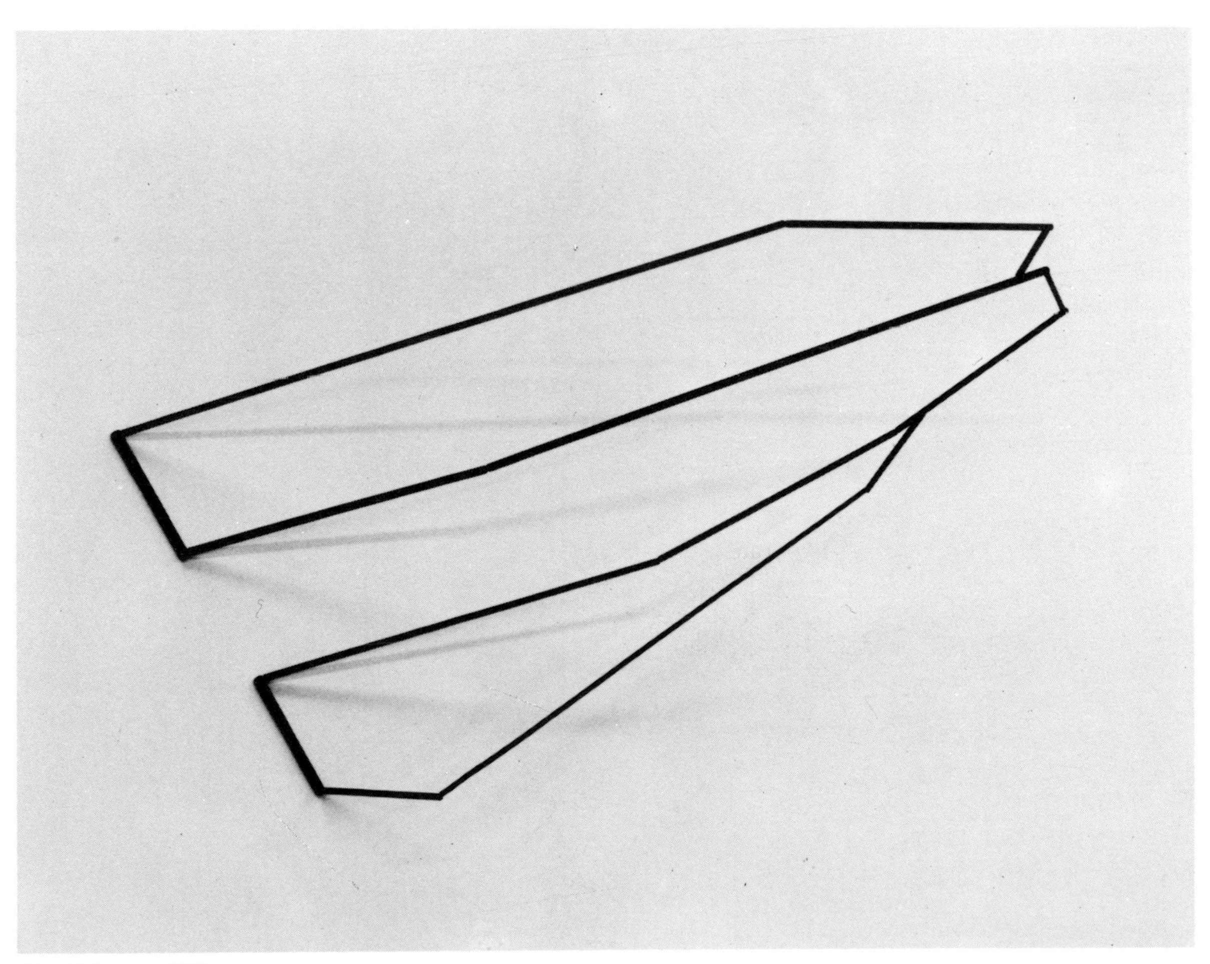

88 Trip 1976
painted aluminium
68.5 × 122 × 56 cm

Paul Huxley

89 Dead and Alive 1977/78
acrylic on canvas
203.2 x 203.2 cm

Phillip King

90 Sculpture '75 (0 Place) 1975
aluminium, sprayed steel, slate, wood and cord
202 × 104.1 × 217 cm and 29.2 × 83.8 × 78.7 cm

Peter Kalkhof

Born 1933 in Germany. Studied at the School of Arts and Crafts, Braunschweig; the Academy of Fine Art, Stuttgart; Slade School of Art, London and Ecole des Beaux-Arts, Paris 1953–60. Artist in residence, Osnabrück 1985. His first exhibition was at the Galerie am Bohlweg, Braunschweig 1962 and subsequently showed at the Galerie im der Garage, Stuttgart 1964 before showing at the Hamilton Galleries, London 1967 and at Annely Juda Fine Art 1970 and regularly since. Amongst other exhibitions he has shown in since then are Alexandra Palace, 1971; Galerie Wellmann, Dusseldorf, 1973; 'British Painting '74' Hayward Gallery 1974; Scottish Arts Council tour and Southern Arts Travelling Exhibition 1976; Kulturgeschichtliches Museum, Osnabrück and Galerie Loyse Oppenheim, Nyon, Switzerland in 1977; Kunstverein Marburg, 1979 and the Goethe Institute, London, 1981. His work is represented in several public collections including the Arts Council of Great Britain, Museum of Reading, European Parliament and the Leicester Education Committee.

. . . This exhibition of new work by Kalkhof is the best so far – a series of essays in the relationship of color and space to one another. More complex than before, they have a subtle way of compelling attention . . .'

Max Wykes-Joyce, *International Herald Tribune*, 18-19 May 1974

91 Colour and Space 'Centre Constellation' 1976
acrylic on canvas
198.1 x 182.9 cm

Richard Kidd

Born 1952 in Newcastle-upon-Tyne. 1970–74 Studied at Newcastle University, Department of Fine Art. 1976 Arts Council award. First London show 1977 Rowan Gallery and regularly since. 1980 Awarded a Harkness Fellowship to U.S.A. Among the group shows in which he has participated are 1975 'Mostra '75' Rome; 'Richard Kidd/Bruce Russell', Midland Group Gallery, Nottingham; 1983 'British artists in New York', Newhouse Gallery, New York. He is represented in a number of public collections that include Arts Council of Great Britain; Contemporary Art Society, London; Kunsthaus Zurich; Museum of Modern Art, Rio de Janeiro; Power Institute of Contemporary Art, Sydney; Ulster Museum, Belfast.

'. . . British artist Richard Kidd is shattering the generally-held belief that all the best abstract painting comes out of the United States. In fact while the famous American artists are mostly fading stars who did their best work in the sixties, excited young painters like Kidd are doing new things that are making the London art scene a world leader . . .'

Evening News, 16 February 1979

92 Still Life 1978
acrylic and graphite on cotton duck
123 x 133.5 cm

Mark Lancaster
93 Yellow I 1974
oil on canvas
183 x 122 cm

Francois Morellet

Born 1926 Cholet, France where he still lives and works. Self-taught. His first one-man show was in 1950 at Galerie Creuze, Paris and since then he has had numerous solo exhibitions worldwide including 1958 Galerie Colette Allendy, Paris; 1967 and 1971 Galerie Denise René, Paris; shows at Galerie Swart, Amsterdam in 1969, 1973, 1975, 1977 and 1979; Galerie M, Bochum in 1970, 1971, 1975 and 1980. 1970 Galerie Denise René & Hans Mayer, Dusseldorf, and numerous one-man exhibitions in 1971 at Galerie La Bertesca, Genoa; Stedelijk van Abbemuseum, Eindhoven; Kunstverein Hamburg; Schloss Morsbroich, Leverkusen. 1972 he showed at the Palais des Beaux Arts, Brussels; Kunstmuseum, Bochum; Lucy Milton Gallery, London; Musée des Beaux-Arts, Grenoble and Kunstmuseum, Dusseldorf. From 1972 to 1974 the C.N.A.C. organised a travelling exhibition which was shown at 18 museums in France. 1973 Musée des Beaux-Arts, Nantes; Galerie Arte Contacto, Caracas; Museum Sztuki, Lodz and Galerie D+C Müller-Roth, Stuttgart; where he showed again in 1976 and 1980. 1974 Galerie Lydia Megert, Berne; Galerie Cavallino, Venice; Kunsthalle Bielefeld. During 1974/75 the Lucy Milton Gallery, London organised a travelling exhibition which was shown at 11 English museums. 1975 Studio Marconi, Milan. 1977 Nationalgalerie Berlin; Staatliche Kunsthalle Baden-Baden; Musée d'Art Moderne de la ville de Paris; Kunsthalle Kiel; Galerie Gillespie-De Laage, Paris and his first show at Annely Juda Fine Art, London. He showed at Galerie Gilles Gheerbrant, Montreal in 1978 and again in 1981, as well as having another one-man show at the Musée d'Art Moderne de la ville de Paris, 1978. 1979 Galleri Mörner, Stockholm. 1980 Galerie le Coin du Miroir, Dijon; Galerie Nordenhake, Malmö; Musée des Beaux-Arts, Toulon. In 1981 he had his second show at Annely Juda Fine Art, London and also showed at the Helsingin Kaupungin Taidemuseo, Helsinki and Galerie Liliane et Michel Durand-Dessert, Paris. 1982 Musée Savoisien, Chambery; Musée des Beaux-Arts, Angers, France. 1983 Musée Municipal, La Roche-sur-Yon; Moderne Galerie Joseph-Albers-Museum, Bottrop which travelled to the Wilhelm-Hack Museum, Ludwigshafen, West Germany. 1984/85 Albright-Knox Art Gallery and U.S.A. tour. From 1943 onwards he has shown in innumerable important mixed exhibitions including the Moderna Museet, Stockholm; The Museum of Modern Art, New York; Centre Georges Pompidou, Paris; Stedelijk Museum, Amsterdam; Kunsthaus Zurich; Philadelphia Museum of Art; Musée d'Art Contemporain, Montreal; Rijksmuseum Kröller-Müller, Otterlo and the Hayward Gallery, London. He is represented in public collections worldwide.

94 Seule droite traversant 2 carrés dans 2 plans différents (Oeuvre No. 78042) 1978
acrylic on canvas (2 parts)
43.5 x 83.5 cm

Edwina Leapman

Born in Hampshire and studied at the Slade and Central School of Arts and Crafts. Won Arts Council awards in 1976 and 1979. First individual exhibition at the New Art Centre, London 1974. Exhibited at Annely Juda Fine Art in 1976 and regularly since. Other principal solo exhibitions include the Galerie Loyse Oppenheim, Nyon and Galerie Artline, The Hague 1979. Selected group exhibitions include 'Young Contemporaries' Arts Council touring exhibition 1954; Signals Gallery, London 1966; John Moores Exhibition, Liverpool 1972, 1974 and 1976; Hayward Annual, 1978, Hayward Gallery, London; 'The British Art Show', Mappin Art Gallery Sheffield and tour 1979–80; Eight + Eight, Annely Juda Fine Art, 1980. Private collections include the Arts Council of Great Britain; Power Institute, Sydney; Contemporary Art Society, London and the Israel Museum, Jerusalem. Lives and works in London.

'. . . Edwina Leapman's extraordinarily beautiful contemplative paintings at Annely Juda consist simply of horizontal stripes of white paint over a brownish background; variations in paint texture and surface produce sensitively modulated shadows. Absurd no doubt when noted in a few words; but wonderful to look at . . .'

Marina Vaizey, *The Sunday Times*, 28 November 1976

95 Untitled 1976
acrylic on canvas
167.7 x 183 cm

John McLaughlin

Born 1898 in Sharon, Massachusetts. Self-taught, travelled widely in Japan and the Far East studying language and art between 1935 and 1940 and during the Second World War he was an intelligence officer in China, Burma and India. He won the Tamarind Lithography Fellowship, Los Angeles in 1963 and the Visual Arts Award, National Endowment for the Arts, Washington D.C. in 1967. Died in 1976 in California. His first one-man show was with the Felix Landau Gallery, Los Angeles in 1953 and he subsequently had regular shows there. Other one-man exhibitions include the University of California, Riverside 1958; Long Beach Museum of Art, California 1960; 'Retrospective' at the Pasadena Art Museum, California 1963; Corcoran Gallery, Washington D.C. 1969; Nicholas Wilder Gallery, Los Angeles 1972; 'Retrospective' La Jolla Museum of Contemporary Art, California 1973; Whitney Museum of American Art, New York and André Emmerich Gallery, New York in 1974 and 1979; Felicity Samuel Gallery, London 1975; Galerie André Emmerich, Zurich 1976; Nicholas Wilder Gallery, Los Angeles 1979; Annely Juda Fine Art, London 1981; Gatodo Gallery, Tokyo 1983, 1984 and 1985. His work has been exhibited in numerous group shows, including 'Pacific Coast Art' which toured the Cincinnati Art Museum, San Francisco Museum of Art, Walker Art Center, Minneapolis 1955 and 'Four Abstract Classicists' which was shown at the Los Angeles County Museum; San Francisco Museum; I.C.A. London and Queens College, Belfast 1959-60. In 1962 'Geometric Abstraction in America', Whitney Museum of Art, New York which was a touring exhibition; 1965 'The Responsive Eye', Museum of Modern Art, New York; 1971 '11 Los Angeles Artists', Hayward Gallery, London (toured Britain) and in 1975 the international travelling exhibition 'Color as Language', Museum of Modern Art, New York. Amongst the public collections he is represented in are the Metropolitan Musum of Art and the Museum of Modern Art in New York; the Smithsonian Institute and the Corcoran Gallery of Art in Washington D.C.; the County Museum of Art, Los Angeles; Musum of Modern Art, Pasedena; University of California, Berkeley and the Wadsworth Atheneum Connecticut.

96 Untitled 1974/75
acrylic on canvas
122 x 152 cm

Jeremy Moon

97 No. 2/73 1973
acrylic on chipboard
104 x 112 cm

Martin Naylor

Born 1944 in Yorkshire. 1961–66 Studied at Dewsbury and Batley Art School and Leeds Art College. 1967–70 Studied at the Royal College. 1973–74 Gregory Fellow in Sculpture, University of Leeds; 1975 Gulbenkian Foundation Visual Award; 1979 Arts Council Award. 1972 First London show in the Serpentine Gallery. 1974 First show Rowan Gallery and regularly thereafter. 1975 Leeds City Art Gallery; 1976 'Sculpture and Drawings 1973–76', Sunderland Arts Centre and M.O.M.A. Oxford; 1977 Sao Paulo Bienal; 1982 Arcade Gallery Harrogate; 1985 'Between Discipline and Desire' Galerie Artem, Quimper, France. Among the many group shows in which he has participated are 1972 'British Sculpture '72', Royal Academy, London, 1975; 'British Art of the mid-70's' Forum Kunst, Leverkusen; 1979 Elise Meyer, New York and 'British Art Show', Arts Council exhibition touring museums in Britain; 1982 'British Sculpture in the 20th Century Part 2', Whitechapel Art Gallery, London; 1984 'Private View', Ecole des Beaux Arts Nantes; 1985 Everard Read Gallery, Johannesburg. Among many other public collections he is represented in those of the Arts Council; British Council; Government Art Collection; Iwaki Museum of Modern Art, Japan; National Collection of Brazil, Rio de Janeiro; Victoria and Albert Museum, London.

'. . . Naylor's translation of this vision is a remarkable achievement; it reveals an imagination with a long reach reined by rigorous craftsmanship and fastidiousness. He can pump nostalgia into a nail . . .'

Nigel Gosling, *The Observer*, 17 February 1974

'. . . Whatever medium he uses it is a vehicle for the expression of ideas, of man's place in the world and the fragility of human existence . . .'

Mary Rose Beaumont, *Arts Review*, 1 April 1983

98 A view beyond the City 3 1978
mixed media
180.5 x 61 x 53.3 cm

Bridget Riley

99 Orphean Elegy 7 1978
acrylic on canvas
140.5 x 130.5 cm

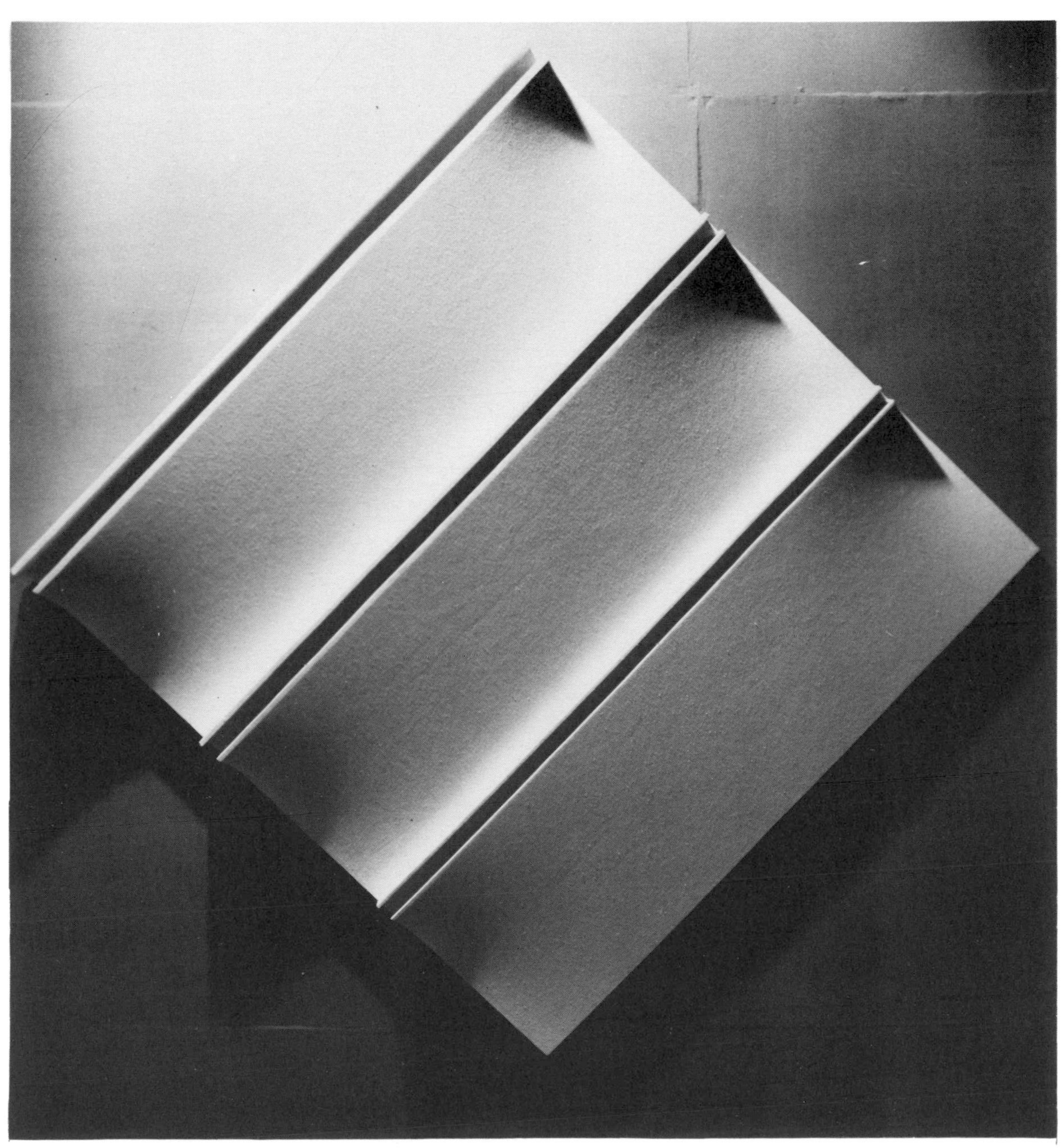

Michael Michaeledes

100 Three Grooves 1976
cotton duck on raised stretcher
182 × 182 × 12.5 cm

Alan Reynolds

Born 1926 in Newmarket, Suffolk. In 1946 had his first encounter with modern art when he saw first post-war exhibitions of the Twenties and Thirties in Germany and was particularly influenced by the paintings and writings of Paul Klee. From 1948 to 1952 he studied at Woolwich Polytechnic School of Art and in 1952 was awarded a scholarship to the Royal College of Art where he received a medal for painting in his first year. Between 1954 and 1961 he taught drawing at the Central School of Arts & Crafts in London and has been teaching at St. Martin's School of Art since 1961, where he is now Associate Lecturer of Painting. Until 1958 he painted landscapes. From then until 1966 he did abstract paintings and watercolours with emphasis on pictorial construction and in 1969 constructed his first group of reliefs in painted wood, curvilinear in form which were influenced by the work of Sophie Täuber-Arp. In 1975 he began making constructional reliefs, orthogonal in form and the following year he went on to free-standing, painted wood constructions. In 1978 he started doing modular constructions and drawings. He has had ten one-man exhibitions at the Redfern Gallery, London during the 1950's, the 60's and early 70's. Also at the Durlacher Gallery, New York in 1954 and 1958; Leicester Galleries, London 1958; Annely Juda Fine Art, London 1978; Galerie Renée Ziegler, Zurich 1980; Juda Rowan Gallery, London 1982. Among the group exhibitions he has participated in are the Pittsburgh International in 1952, 1955, 1958 and 1961; 'International Watercolour Exhibition' Brooklyn 1953. In 1955 he took part in several group shows at the Musée National d'Art Moderne in Paris; Palais des Beaux Arts in Brussels and the British Council exhibition 'British Contemporary Painting' in Oslo and Copenhagen. 1957 and 1960 'Critic's Choice' Arthur Tooth and Sons London. 1971 'Spectrum Exhibition' Arts Council of Great Britain and 'British Painting 1952–77' at the Royal Academy, London. 1977 Galerie Loyse Oppenheim, Nyon, Switzerland. 1980 'Eight + Eight' Annely Juda Fine Art, London. His work is represented in numerous British public collections including the Arts Council, British Council, Tate Gallery and Victoria & Albert Museum, London and in international collections such as the Museum of Modern Art, New York; The Cleveland Museum of Art; the National Gallery of Canada in Ottawa and in Australia the National Galleries in Adelaide, Melbourne and Sydney. He lives and works in Kent.

'. . . Alan Reynolds, once a realist, has taken the long haul to non-representation in a pure, intense exhibition of drawings, prints and constructed reliefs all in black and white at Annely Juda's. They are remarkably beautiful and compelling to look at in their almost infinite variations on a basic four-part theme. These are immaculately crafted columns, bars and planes in which continual play with proportions produce something akin to the pleasures to be found in classical architecture . . .'

Marina Vaizey, *The Sunday Times*, 19 February 1978

101 Structures–Group II (K) 1979/80
relief contruction–prepared card on wood base
120.7 × 95 × 1.5 cm

Sean Scully

Born 1945 in Dublin. Studied at Croydon College of Art and Newcastle University, 1965–71. Has held teaching posts at Harvard, Princeton and Newcastle Universities and Chelsea and Goldsmith's Schools of Art 1971–83. 1973 First one-man show at Rowan Gallery and regularly since. He won a Harkness Fellowship in 1975 and moved to New York, where he also had a solo exhibition at the La Tortue Gallery, Santa Monica, the same year. Since then, he has had more than eight one-man shows in New York and elsewhere in the United States including Susan Caldwell, Inc., New York, 1979/81, William Beadleston Gallery, New York, 1982. In 1981, the Ikon Gallery, Birmingham, organized an important survey exhibition of his work of the last decade which toured to Sunderland, Dublin, Belfast and London. From 1983 he showed regularly at David McKee Gallery, New York. Also in 1983 he became an American citizen and won a Guggenheim Fellowship. In 1985, a major exhibition of paintings 1981–84 was organised by the Carnegie Institute, Pittsburgh and the Boston Museum of Fine Arts. His work has been included in numerous group exhibitions including 'La peinture anglaise aujourd'hui', Museum of Modern Art, Paris, 1973; 'British painting 1952–1977', Royal Academy, London 1977; 'Certain Traditions' 1978/79, touring Canada and the U.K.; 'The British Art Show', Sheffield and tour, 1979; ROSC, Dublin, 1980 and 1984 and 'A Survey of Contemporary Painting and Sculpture', Museum of Modern Art, New York, 1984. His work is represented in several major public collections including the Victoria and Albert Museum, London; Boston Museum of Fine Arts; Dallas Museum of Fine Arts; Manchester City Art Gallery; Felton Bequest, Melbourne; Fitzwilliam Museum, Cambridge and the Metropolitan Museum, New York. Currently he lives and works in New York.

'. . . Sean Scully's work has devasting richness to it – a kind of miasmic determination to let the imagination flood in, around, above, over and under the intertwining vertical and horizontal bands which form the structural basis of his canvases . . .'

Peter Fuller, *Arts Review*, 17 November 1973

'. . . Sean Scully is a young artist who has gone his own way at his own pace, as free from hurry as from hype, and has turned himself into one of the best abstract painters in the country . . .'

John Russell, *New York Times*, 30 September 1983

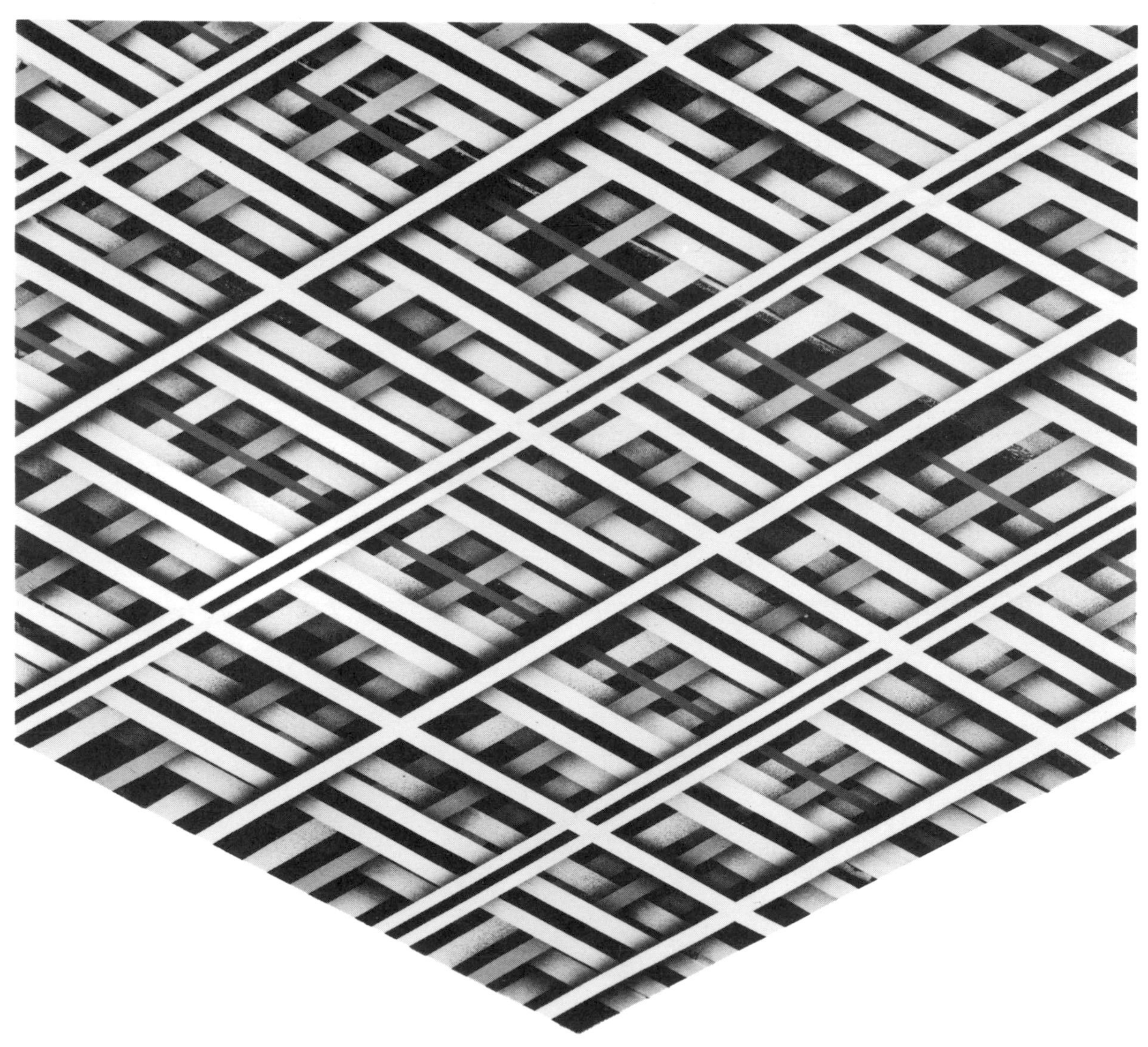

102 East Coast Light 2 1973
acrylic on cotton duck
213.5 x 244 cm

Amikam Toren

Born in Jerusalem 1945. Resident in England from 1968. His first one-man exhibition was at the Maserik Gallery, Tel Aviv, 1967. He showed at the Edinburgh Festival 1968; Annely Juda Fine Art, London, 1973; the Serpentine Gallery, London, 1976; I.C.A. and Barry Barker Ltd. 1979; Riverside Studios, London 1981; Lewis Johnston Gallery in 1982/1983; Galeria Akumulatory, Poznan, Poland 1983 and Matts Gallery London 1984. He has exhibited in the following group exhibitions, 1967 Paris Biennale; 1971 Art Spectrum, London; 1972 'Sculpture and Sculptors' Drawings', Annely Juda Fine Art, London; 1974 'Off the Top of their Heads', Artists Meeting Place, London; 1975 Garage Art Ltd., London; 1977 'On Site', Arnolfini Gallery Bristol; 1978 'London Calling', Acme Gallery; 1981 'The Garden of Knowledge', Critics Gallery, Warsaw; 1982 'Un nuovo Classicismo Premio Cubiam', Padua; 1983 'Photo(graphic) Vision', Winchester Gallery, Winchester; 1984 Venice Biennale; 'Problems of Picturing', Serpentine Gallery, London; 1985 'New Art', Anthony Reynolds Gallery, London. He has published the following 1979 'Replacing' photo/text by Amikam Toren, published by I.C.A., London; 1984 'Actualities', photo/text by David Coxhead and Amikam Toren, published by Matts Gallery. His work is in the collection of the Arts Council of Great Britain and he lives and works in London.

103 Untitled 1973
wood and screws
47 x 68.3 cm

Friederich Werthmann

Born 1927 in Barmen, Germany. Self-taught, began doing figurative sculpture in wood and stone in 1948, going on to abstract work in 1952. In 1956 he made structures in fortified cement, made his first spheres in 1959 and works moved by wind in 1965. From 1975 he has been doing dynamite blasted sculpture. His numerous one-man exhibitions include Galerie Parnass, Wuppertal 1956; Galerie Apollinaire, Milan 1957; Galerie Riehentor, Basle and Kunstverein Freiburg 1959; The Wilhelm-Lehmbruck-Museum, Duisburg in 1960 and 1978; Galerie 22, Dusseldorf 1960; Galerie Niepel, Dusseldorf and Galerie Sopho, Lyon 1963; Hamilton Galleries, London in 1964, 1965 and 1966; Galerie Semiha Huber, Zurich; Galerie Ad Libitum, Antwerp and the Folkwang-Museum, Essen in 1968; Karl-Ernst-Osthaus-Museum, Hagen 1969; Rheinpark, Emmerich 1970; Annely Juda Fine Art, London 1973 and again in 1977/78; Museum Wiesbaden 1976; Stadtmuseum Dusseldorf, 1982/83. Amongst the group exhibitions he has shown in are 'Gruppe 53' Kunstverein Dusseldorf, 1955–59; the Biennale Middelheim, Antwerp in 1957, 1959, 1961 and 1965; Musée Rodin, Paris in 1961, 1963 and 1964; Opening of the Kunsthalle Dusseldorf 1967; Biennale, New Delhi 1968; 'Sculpture and Sculptor's Drawings' Annely Juda Fine Art, London 1972; Amnesty Sculpture Exhibition, Bristol Cathedral, St. Paul's Cathedral and the Institute of Education, London 1979. His work is represented in several major public collections including the Peter Stuyvesant Collection, Amsterdam; Museum Ehrenhof, Dusseldorf; Von der Heydt-Museum, Wuppertal; Stadt Museum Wiesbaden; Wilhelm-Lehmbruck-Museum, Duisburg; Ensor Museum, Ostend; Openluchtmuseum Middelheim, Antwerp; Municipal Museum of Modern Art, Dublin and the Bank of Scotland, London. Lives and works in Dusseldorf.

104 Steelhenge 1977
stainless steel
200 × 20 × 20 cm

THE EIGHTIES

My profession in a capitalist society is similar to that of a tight-rope walker.
George Grosz

It is difficult to write a paradise when all the superficial indications are that you ought to write an apocalypse.
Ezra Pound

I seek no quick effects . . . what I want to create is meditation pictures of the 20th century.
Josef Albers

If Julian Schnabel had come into this gallery asking for a show I would have told him to come back in five years.
David Juda

My career as an art critic at *The Guardian* has coincided almost exactly with the period of artistic activity which we are here to celebrate: The Eighties. The first review I wrote of an Annely Juda exhibition was of a Christo show held in the Spring of 1979, in tandem with a big I.C.A. tribute to his Running Fence project. I don't know if it is fair to think of Christo as an Eighties artist. I suspect not. His heart lies surely in the mad dreams, the schemes, the impossible plans of the seventies, when 90% of so much art seemed to consist of aspiration. It was as if the pure aspirations of twentieth century artists had reached some sort of baroque finale in the art of Christo: Angels appear blowing their trumpets, dry ice swirls in, searchlights skim the sky like the opening of a Twentieth Century Fox film, and there he is, the little man from Bulgaria, who looks like Woody Allen and dreams these impossible dreams of wrapping mountains and making a package out of the Reichstag.

Christo, in his rather over-the-top, operatic way seemed to me to symbolise the power of the twentieth century artist. In that first exhibition that I reviewed, there was a photograph by Wolfgang Volz of the Wrapped Walk Ways in a park in Kansas. The photograph was taken from a helicopter. Volz looked down on shimmering rivers of gold that appeared to have flooded the lawns of the park like lava coming down a mountain. It could only have happened in art. How spectacularly beautiful were those rivers of gold cloth rippling in the wind!

Having seen the photographs, watched the film, read the books, studied the maps, examined the diagrams, bid, unsuccessfully, for the drawings at auction, felt the power of the myth and laughed a little, from a distance, at the exploits of its maker, I now learn that I will soon be able to see a Christo project in the flesh. The reckless citizens of Paris have allowed him to wrap Pont Neuf this Autumn. I will be there.

Although Christo is not, essentially, an Eighties artist, the colour of the cloth with which he wrapped a set of islands off the coast of Florida was very much an Eighties colour, baby pink, lurid and artificial, demanding to be noticed. It is the sort of colour which by and large has been conspicuous by its absence from 11 Tottenham Mews over the past five years.

The most important event to have occurred at the gallery in the past five years has been a physical rather than an aesthetic disruption. In 1982 Annely Juda Fine Art merged with the Rowan Gallery to form the Juda Rowan. Overnight the gallery doubled in size. Upstairs it remained unmistakably Annely Juda's in spirit. But downstairs, in the new space, all that unsullied modern purity (which probably existed more in the mind than in reality) was messed up a little, dare I say fertilised; certainly invigorated.

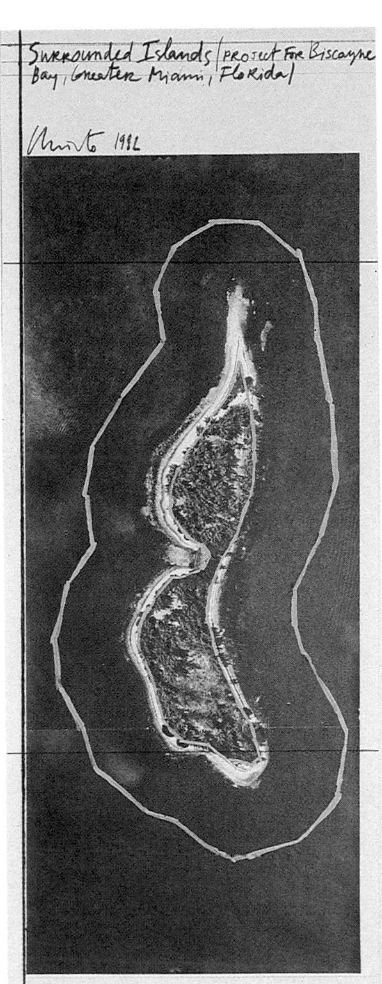

Christo, Surrounded Islands, project for Biscayne Bay, Florida 1982 collage in 2 parts 71 x 56 cm and 71 x 28 cm

The Rowan Gallery was another of London's oldest established galleries, a swinging sixties gallery that had gone on to share in some of the most significant developments in British art. This was afterall Bridget Riley's gallery. Phillip King was a gallery artist and one of the best shows I remember after the merger was the exhibition in which he unveiled his new colourful face for The Eighties. The Rowan Gallery had nurtured Barry Flanagan right up to the point at which he made his great imaginative leap into the kingdom of the hares. Michael Craig-Martin was a former gallery artist.

The identity of the Rowan Gallery was hard to pinpoint. It too enjoyed a certain painterly and sculptural purity. But it was a purity that knew how to relax: The joyous colours of Bridget Riley; the impish aesthetics of Barry Flanagan. At the Rowan you found not only integrity, but also wit and joie de vivre of a distinctly British variety. During that great phoney war between abstractionists and figurationists that raged at the end of the Seventies, the Annely Juda Gallery would undoubtedly have thrown in its emotional lot with the abstractionists. I'm not so sure about the Rowan.

Early in 1981 I reviewed Bridget Riley's last exhibition at the Rowan Gallery: 'Bridget Riley has always claimed less abstraction for herself than was discovered in her work by her admirers. She has never thought of herself as an Op-artist, content to make your eyes shimmer and your head spin. She has long claimed that her work should be seen as a response to Post-Impressionism and particularly to Seurat. Until recently that claim seemed faintly ludicrous . . .' But in that glorious last show at Bruton Place, her paintings did indeed twitch and hover, glisten and vibrate like the air above a road on a hot day.

Some of the artists who now come under the mantle of the Juda Rowan Gallery would have settled easily enough into the old Annely Juda Fine Art – Paul Huxley, Bridget Riley, the early work of Sean Scully. But others clearly belonged on the other side of the aesthetic fence. In his last show Antony Donaldson gave us a nude sitting on a rock. Was she the first obvious nude shown at 11 Tottenham Mews? (I say obvious because in *his* last show, Michael Kenny revealed very clearly that he has been sculpting nudes all along!)

Then what were we to make of the manic suburban romps of Anthony Green R.A.? Chasing his wife in and out of tents, across living rooms, over the mantlepiece clock, out onto the lawn and into the back of a small Morris Minor where the two of them seemed to be permanently consumating their long and enthusiastic marriage? Anthony Green is an aesthetic law unto himself.

The merger with the Rowan Gallery brought many strong artists to 11 Tottenham Mews. It brought new blood, new energy, a shower of new directions and undoubtedly new headaches: twice as many exhibitions to be organised, twice as many catalogues to be written, twice as many trips to be made, a hundred times as many problems to be sorted out.

The Rowan's proprietor, Alex Gregory-Hood, is a tall, grey, polite Englishman, who although in his seventies, sometimes gives the impression of not having quite outgrown his schooldays. The sense of playfulness which tickles the aesthetics of some of his artists is undoubtedly his. And yet apart from their great age, he and Annely Juda have two important things in common. Both have reputations for outstanding loyalty to their artists. Both have refused to rush out and sign up representatives of the fashionable Eighties style.

'If Julian Schnabel had come into this gallery asking for a show,' David Juda said to me recently 'I would have told him to come back in five years.'

Expressionism: The human spirit trying to knot brushstrokes into a metaphor for its own confusion. Alex Gregory-Hood has the Englishman's traditional mistrust of gratuitous displays of emotion. Annely Juda was brought up with Expressionism, not today's facile, second-hand variety, but the original German kind, an Expressionism born of necessity rather than style.

Annely Juda knows all about Die Brucke in Dresden, about Kirchner, Schmidt-Rottluff, Heckel, ushering in the new century with wild displays of colour that symbolised their raw anxiety. She knows about Der Blaue Reiter, Kandinsky, Campendonk, Macke and Marc, their art trembling with the passion of being in Munich in 1911, feeling the war over their shoulders. After the war came Grosz, Dix and Beckmann, whose anger and despair spilled out from the busy pavements of Berlin into the rest of T. S. Eliot's Europe: 'Under the brown Fog of a winter dawn/A crowd flowed over London bridge, so many/I had not thought that death had undone so many . . .'

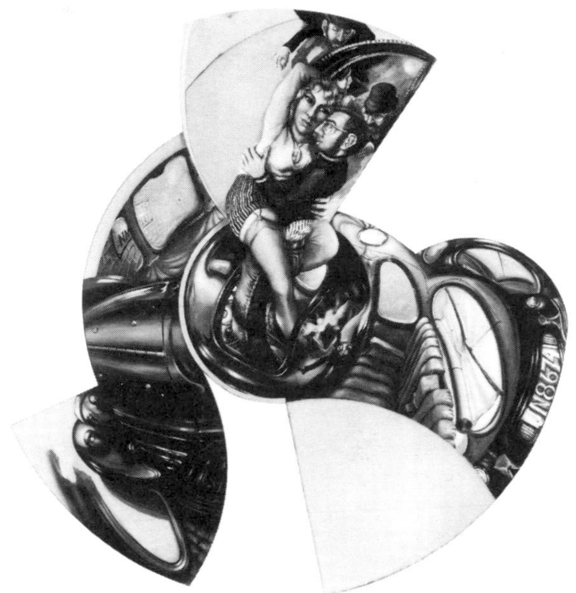

Anthony Green, JN 8674, Je t'adore –The Engagement 1983/4
oil on board 198 cm diameter

Expressionism: The official language of human despair. Why has it become the official language of The Eighties? Why has the Juda Rowan Gallery completely ignored it?

The original Annely Juda gallery always seemed different to me from other London galleries. Even in the gloom of late afternoon at Tottenham Mews it could not pass for a fashionable go-ahead place. There was something too worn about the gallery, too many feet had rounded off the corners of those rickety stairs. The eyes of its proprietor had seen too much. She was much too set in her good ways to go jumping on and off bandwagons.

When I think of Annely Juda, I think of the old style of art dealer. Of Kahnweiler, of Vollard, their likenesses taken apart by Picasso and put back together as Cubist icons of the new kind of patron. With her slightly mysterious central European roots, her great age (I'm sorry Annely but rather like Walter Pater's Mona Lisa you always seemed to me to be as ancient as the rocks among which you sat), with her thoughtful face, she appeared to be a real link with the great days of Modernism.

This is not something you can say of any other major London dealer. When I look at Leslie Waddington, I can, if I try hard, imagine back as far as Pop Art. When I look at Anthony d'Offay I'm afraid I cannot really see further back than the mid-Seventies. But when I am in the presence of Annely Juda I feel myself to be, somehow, in touch with the birth of Cubism, with Kandinsky and Malevich, with the Bauhaus and the clean white hope of the Viennese Secessionists.

I recently came into the gallery and began talking about a show of magical watercolours at the Goethe Institute by that hunted and haunted twentieth century ghost, the artist Wols. His work glowed with such innocent colour, like a tempera by Botticelli. Annely had not seen the show. But she knew of course, someone who knew Wols and she told me the story of how the poor drunken man used to stand outside cafes in Paris offering to swop four of these glowing, magical watercolours for a single glass of wine . . ..

In the great sad face and comfortable Jewishness of Annely Juda I imagine I can still sense the war, the great re-drawing of the map of Europe, artists criss-crossing hither and thither, searching for a quiet spot in which to work. When I consider the presence of Annely Juda in an absurd little side-street off the Tottenham Court Road I think of the equal absurdity of Kurt Schwitters living and dying anonymously in the Lake District. I think of the Hungarian, Laszlo Moholy-Nagy designing the Parker '51. I think of Naum Gabo coming to London from Russia; of Pevsner and Gombrich; I think of Mondrian living in Hampstead; I think of Modernism as something white and pure and precious, smuggled out of the rubbish-strewn cities of Central Europe under the coats of artistic refugees. For me the Juda Rowan Gallery is, or perhaps was, a kind of shrine to those lofty ideals which are no longer held by many; are no longer held by enough.

I remember well my first visit to the gallery. I had seen the name in print and it had conjured up all sorts of grand visions, marble floors and designer desks, gallery girls with superior stares who look you up and down and decide whether you are worth smiling at or not. I had seen such creatures in other galleries. As a scruffy first year art history student I wasn't usually worth the smile. So I had tried to buy their acceptance by investing a considerable chunk of my student grant in their glossy catalogues, full of colour plates of Picasso, Braque, Matisse, but no text to speak of. (Annely Juda catalogues weren't like that. They were always impressively wordy and worthy).

My twentieth-century art history tutor at Manchester University, Andrew Causey, had recommended Michael Kenny to me in his usual tight-lipped and inscrutable way. 'Michael Kenny is rather important. Don't you think?' I didn't think, because I didn't know Michael Kenny from Kenny Ball. Like the course I was on, my knowledge of twentieth-century art braked to a dramatic halt with the Pop Artists. It was not until much later that I found myself in London one week-end and noticed that Michael Kenny had a show at a gallery with an exotic name that you could roll around in your mouth like a bon-bon: Annely Juda Fine Art. What on earth could it mean?

Inside was cosy. A pair of rickety steps led up to an equally rickety Michael Kenny exhibition. It too seemed to be made of worn floorboards, marked and measured with a protractor, stately and mysterious. Upstairs, behind a cluttered desk, it wasn't a sweet young thing with hurried eyes who greeted me but a woman old enough to be my mother, chattering away on the telephone in a thickish European accent. I felt at home immediately. Years later when I became the art critic of *The Guardian*, the Annely Juda gallery was the first place I made for, with the instinct of a lonely homing pigeon.

Annely Juda tells a funny story about the setting up of her gallery. Since her mother had been a pupil of Kokoschka's it was to Kokoschka that she went when she decided that she would like to start a gallery in London. She wanted him to recommend names, artists she should see, people she should meet. Kokoschka gave her the names of former pupils based in London. Annely, full of reverence, went to see their work . . . and hated it.

It was not that she was against Expressionism *per se*, it was just that she had seen the real thing done before by the real masters. When the New Spirit in Painting came to London it was not a new spirit to her.

Expressionism: According to Donald Judd it is 'not an important' form of artistic language. But it has been the most often heard language of recent times, the official language of Eighties art. Annely Juda herself knows all about Expressionism. I recently saw a work by her mother, a house in a garden shaped quickly and crudely out of swirling brushstrokes. Someone joked that it would not look out of place in an exhibition today. The joke was too near the mark to be truly funny.

Expressionism: A generation starved of content, starved of emotion, starved of that most basic ingredient of art – the human figure – threw itself into the new painting like a hungry hyena coming across a sad old buffalo in the desert. I must confess that I threw myself in there with them. So, I notice, did John Edwards, who recently had a show at 11 Tottenham Mews, and who could be seen trying to make the difficult transition from abstraction to figuration. He is the only Juda Rowan artist I can think of who has attempted it.

Expressionism: The basest form of artistic language or a short cut to meaning, an easy route to reality? What was it that the art of the Seventies had given so little of to its artists that, come the Eighties, they would gorge themselves on its alternative? It was, I think, a quality that we could call many things – corporeality, love, the object – but which I will call *contact*, an art you could touch, an emotion you could hold, paint you could feel and mould. The art of the Seventies had spent too long distancing itself from its own produce, nourished on concepts. In times of economic recession investors put their money into gold; in times of artistic uncertainty, artists put their uncertainty into paint.

So away they rushed: Conceptualists who had not held a paintbrush since their A-levels, sculptors who had never touched a block of stone, performance artists, land artists, video artists, serial artists, artists who worked, conceptually, in pairs, Ritual artists and MAIL artists, all of them rushed out to find an aesthetic they could touch . . ..

Juda Rowan ignored the lot of them. They continued showing the artists they had always shown. Artists they had supported loyally and bravely for so long. Even when I didn't admire the artists, how I admired the way the gallery stuck by them. This was art with time on its hands. Art that was not about to rush into the nearest Windsor and Newton paint store and buy up the lot simply because the calendar had clicked over from 1979 to 1980.

In November 1980 I wrote in *The Guardian* about a wonderfully tranquil and determined show by Edwina Leapman: 'We have already seen how the Eighties seem intent on having their say quickly. Eighties artists will often be seen responding to the call of Matisse, the lure of sensational colour, the satisfaction of the big brushstroke, the need to tell everyone about themselves. Who has time to become a Poussin, a Seurat, a Braque, an organiser of pictures rather than an instant communicator? Edwina Leapman has time . . ..'

Time: It is something precious that both Annely Juda and Alex Gregory-Hood have always lavished on their artists. Michael Kenny, Bridget Riley, Phillip King, Alan Green and others have all been with the Juda or the Rowan for the best part of two decades or more. Such loyalty from dealers is as rare today as it is valuable.

In December 1980 I was asked to write a catalogue introduction for an Alan Green exhibition in Japan. Reading it now I am surprised by its continuing relevance. 'When you look around at the paintings collected here you are not confused by surfaces soaked in atmospheric colours, colours pretending to be what they are not; you are not pointed in a hundred directions in the hope that one of them will apply directly to you. The surfaces you see are not the result of some sudden expressive whim on the part of the artist, nor do they pamper to our lowest common denominator, the visible world around us. These paintings have been carefully arrived at over time.'

Much the same can surely be said of the identity of the Juda Rowan Gallery. It has been arrived at over a time that stretches back beyond the actual years in which both galleries have existed, back to the birth of Modernism, back to the moment when the calendar clicked over from 1899 to 1900, and art found itself in the new world. If I had to select an exhibition which summed up for me the identity of the gallery it would not be a show of new work at all, but one of those

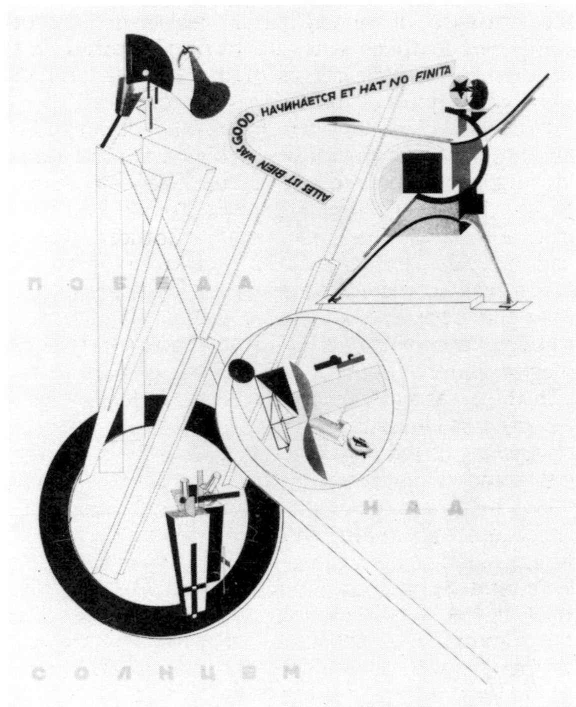

El Lissitzky, The Plastic Realization of the Electro-Mechanical Spectacle 1923 title page of 'Victory over the Sun' colour lithograph 53.5 x 45.4 cm

marvellous summer exhibitions full of bits and pieces by El Lissitzky, Mondrian, Malevich and the rest, which have added so much to London's annual art calendar. Indeed if I had to single out one work from any summer show I have seen in London since I began writing about art, a work I would like to possess above all others, it could, I think, be the extraordinary soaring suite of ten lithographs by El Lissitzky that celebrated the Victory Over the Sun. The title alone makes me giddy. I would visit the gallery once a week just to see it. The optimism of Bridget Riley, the vigour and toughness of Sean Scully, the faith of Alan Green, all appear in an earlier form in El Lissitzky.

And so while the aesthetics of the outside world seemed to grow younger and younger as the Eighties progressed, wilder and wilder, quicker and quicker, more and more colourful, sillier and sillier, inside the Juda Rowan Gallery time sometimes gave the impression of standing still. Upstairs in particular became a kind of refuge for the clean, clear white abstraction of the Seventies. They won't like me saying it. But it is true.

I have heard young artists complain that the art-identity of the gallery is too minimal for the Eighties, too quiet for modern times. I turn again to the Alan Green catalogue I wrote in 1980 for a reply: 'What is minimal

Alan Green, Three Blues 1980 oil on canvas 193 x 155 cm Private Collection, Wakayama, Japan about working within a set of limits in order to be able to understand those limits to the full? What is minimal about the freedom to make a thousand specific choices rather than a handful of general ones?' But when all is said and done, it must be admitted that there have been times when the gallery has given the impression of wanting to keep the Eighties at bay.

I remember, none too distinctly I have to say, a clutter of Japanese artists whose work could be found nowhere else in Britain: Yoshikuni Iida, whose stainless steel blocks were held in a precarious balance by coiled springs: Noriyuki Haraguchi, the maker of simple metal squares. How did these exotic Japanese artists emerge? They were not written about in the magazines I read. They were not winning prizes at the international exhibitions I attended. They were never mentioned in the artistic mainstream that I followed. With its simple geometric formulae, its determined Minimalism, their art was surely a nostalgic echo of the Seventies. This was not so much ignoring fashion as gritting your teeth and turning your back on it. They appeared, it seemed to me, out of nowhere at Annely Juda's. They settled briefly for a display of old-fashioned aesthetics and delicate geometry. Then they disappeared, not to be heard of again, until their next Juda Rowan show.

It seemed that the pure white, precarious package smuggled out of the smouldering cities of wartime Europe under the coats of artistic refugees, had been planted, and was flourishing in Japan where the climate and national temperament so clearly suited it. The Juda Rowan Gallery enjoyed reminding us that outside the tiny art circles of London there remained vast stretches of the art world where fashions did not change overnight, where aesthetics were stable and could be passed on from generation to generation, like a ripple in a Bridget Riley painting.

When the calendar clicked over from 1979 to 1980, Modernism did not die everywhere. Not in Japan. Not in the Zurich of Gottfried Honegger. Not in that little piece of classical Greece that is the studio of Michael Michaeledes. Not in the Bauhaus ambitions still displayed by Peter Kalkhof. Even when I did not feel moved by their work – which was regrettably often because my own temperament favours tears, loudness and passion – I was always impressed by their determination not to jump aboard the bandwagon. *Expressionism:* It's where the money was.

Juda Rowan bring a rare and insistent internationalism to London. Christo, the Bulgarian; Haraguchi, the Japanese; Sean Scully, the Irishman now living in America, take us far, far away from the lineage of the English art school system. The last show by Sean Scully featured a tough and vigorous abstraction, which looked all the tougher, all the more vigorous for having seen something of the world. It was an abstraction which had taken on board not only the energy of the Eighties, but also some of New York's squalor. It was an important show, a show that pointed forwards.

Not surprisingly, given its unmistakeably international outlook, the Juda Rowan Gallery has pioneered the involvement of British art galleries at international art fairs. In Basel, Chicago, Paris and now, London, the gallery always seemed to have a stand in which, for once, time and movements were ignored. Here you could find those thrilling lithographs in which El Lissitzky celebrated The Victory Over the Sun, hanging next to the large 'sensitized' surfaces of Alan Green or Bridget Riley, shimmering with colour, brimming with ambiguity. I admire them enormously.

But it was on occasions like these that you became aware of how much of the gallery's activity went on beneath the surface. Exhibitions of new art were only the tip of the iceberg. I have often wondered where Annely Juda finds her El Lissitzky lithographs, the paintings by Rodchenko and Puni, Vantongerloo and Moholy-Nagy. Were they smuggled out of Russia? Is there a vast collection of Constructivist work that is periodically tapped? With any luck we'll never know and that rather mysterious Central European shroud will continue to remain drawn around the inner sanctum of the Juda Gallery.

Let us not forget either that the Eighties have been a boomtime for dealers, and that Juda Rowan has boomed with the rest of them. In 1982 I interviewed Leslie Waddington for *The Guardian*. Already by then it was clear that as the state retreated further from its artistic obligations and the Arts Council washed its hands ever more vigorously of art, so private dealers were stepping gleefully into the resulting spaces:

Having spent most of the Seventies stuck on Go, London's dealers are on the move again. Waddington's Galleries are spreading around the Monopoly Board like Seurat's dots. They now have four spaces on Cork Street and the owner is already thinking about a fifth. 'We're booming beyond belief,' thunders Leslie Waddington with a boom worthy of a bittern. 'I'm not going to give you crap.' I don't expect him to – Waddingtons didn't get where they are now by giving away *anything*. And neither of course did the Juda Rowan Gallery.

Joking apart, it is clear that the Eighties have been a period of prodigious success for dealers. The decade might have begun with a few unfortunate closures, but now hardly a month goes by without some new gallery opening. Art has suddenly become fashionable in a way that I for one have never felt it to be before. A new breed of go-ahead collector has emerged, young, flashy, usually ignorant. Dealers can be seen advertising their wares on the pages of *Harpers and Queen*. When they are feeling intimate, they will confess that they have never had it so good.

As a result, art has often cut its cloth to fit this demand. It has become young, flashy, usually ignorant.

It beckons with bright colours and amuses with silly jokes. When I asked Alex Gregory-Hood what the biggest change was that he had noticed in the Eighties he replied that the journey from art school to gallery was now taking no time at all. The paint was hardly dry on their degree shows before the students of yesterday have become the masters of today. The art world is swinging even more frantically than it swung in the Sixties.

Personally, I am grateful that both Alex Gregory-Hood and Annely Juda are clearly too old and wise and set in their good ways to wish to become swingers again. The same must be said of most of their artists. Garth Evans and Anthony Green joined in 1962. Paul Huxley and Antony Donaldson in 1963. Phillip King in 1964. Michael Kenny in 1966. Bridget Riley in 1967. Is such loyalty to each other on the part of both dealer and artists a luxury which the future will be able to afford? My heart says yes. But my head shouts no.

There were ghosts stalking both Annely Juda Fine Art and The Rowan Gallery in the Eighties. At the Rowan there were artists who for one reason or another had gone elsewhere. Keith Milow, Michael Craig-Martin, Barry Flanagan are with different galleries. Jeremy Moon was killed all that time ago in a motor cycle crash, but is still remembered. At Annely Juda Fine Art there are ghosts of artists nurtured by the gallery but never exhibited: John Davies, Tim Head.

The first time I officially encountered the internationalism of the Juda Rowan Gallery was at the Venice Biennale in which Tim Head was showing at the British Pavilion. At the time he was with Annely, but his first show had been at the Rowan. I remember his Venice exhibition clearly. Using only the light of a handful of carefully positioned projectors he fashioned a new interior for the British Pavilion, a cool sequence of spaces, somehow neo-classical, as if David's Horatii Brothers had been sent out leaving only the room in which they took their famous oath. That cool light-filled space, full also of aesthetic optimism, full of international zeal, yet consisting almost entirely of aspiration, seemed to embody all that was best about the Juda Rowan's ambitions.

I asked Alex Gregory-Hood if he hated the Eighties. 'Not at all.' he replied. 'It was the Seventies I hated. The Eighties are much more cheerful.'

And, lest we forget, of course they are: More cheerful. More productive. More human in scale. More emotional in outlook. More encouraging to the young artist. More flexible. Less daunting. There were too many times, and exhibitions, in the Seventies when the doors of appreciation were slammed shut on anyone who wasn't a monk in a hairshirt.

But the Eighties are also more cynical, more facile, more mercantile, more frantically happy on the surface, more deeply depressed at the core, more thoughtless, cheaper, quicker, shoddier, seedier and more selfish. We are living through a second Rococo.

Behind the scenes at Juda Rowan it has also been a period of rapid growth. At the end of the Seventies there were four full-time members of staff. Now there are eleven. The number of artists has doubled. The number of exhibitions, here and abroad, has quadrupled.

And yet, on the surface, where other London galleries have thrown themselves enthusiastically into the spirit of the Eighties, the Juda Rowan Gallery has given the impression of holding back. No major new young artists have emerged. Faces already familiar from the Sixties and the Seventies have continued to rule the roost. Not much has happened at the gallery to proclaim a new decade which is now halfway through. It has clearly been a period of consolidation.

Now that period of consolidation seems to be over. David Nash has become a gallery artist and will have a show next year. John Atkin, the only sculptor ever to be given a scholarship to the Royal College by Henry Moore himself, has embarked upon what I hope will be a long, unhurried association with the gallery and will also have an exhibition next year. Atkin was a pupil of Phillip King's. Thus tradition will be continued. But through tradition comes renewal. That is as it should be.

Waldemar Januszczak
July 1985

Waldemar Janszczak is an art historian and author of *Understanding Art*, McDonald Education and *Techniques of the Great Masters*, Phaidon Press. Since 1979 he has been the art critic of *The Guardian*.

The Eighties

Exhibition

Abbreviated artists' biographies are to be found in the initial decade their work appears.

John Atkin

Born in Darlington in 1959. Studied at Teeside and Leicester Colleges of Art 1977–81. Won a Northern Arts 'Major Award' and taught at Teeside College of Art 1981. Awarded a Henry Moore Foundation Scholarship to enable him to study at the Royal College of Art 1982–85. Won Royal College of Art Drawing Prize 1985 and Picker Fellowship, Kingston Polytechnic 1985/86. First one-man exhibition at the Hatton Gallery, University of Newcastle-upon-Tyne 1985. His work has been included in several group exhibitions including the 'Northern Open', Ceolfrith Art Centre, Sunderland 1981; 'Current Issues', Royal College of Art Gallery; 1982; 'Sculptor's Drawings', Ruskin School of Art, Oxford, 1983. He has undertaken a number of commissions including a large sculpture for 'Tskuba Expo '85', Japan 1984/85. He lives and works in London. John Atkin will be having a one-man show of his work in the Juda Rowan Gallery in 1986.

105 Dolce et Decorum Est Pro Patria
Mori 1985
plaster, found objects, flashband, dye and oil
179 x 66 x 18 cm

Martyn Chalk

Born in Trowbridge, Wiltshire 1945. Graduated from Portsmouth College of Art in 1966. Currently teaches at the School of Fine Art, Humberside College of Higher Education, Hull. He has made eight reconstructions of Tatlin reliefs which have been widely shown in museum exhibitions and are in numerous public and private collections. His own work has been shown, amongst other one-man exhibitions, in a touring exhibition, Nottinghamshire County Libraries Service 1972-73 and at the Juda Rowan Gallery, London 1984. Group exhibitions in which his work has been shown include the 'Winter Exhibition', Ferens Art Gallery, Hull 1968 and 1969; 'Open Air Sculpture', Mid-Pennine Association for the Arts, Haworth Gallery, Accrington and Abbot Hall Gallery, Kendal 1970; 'Art Spectrum North', touring Arts Council exhibition 1971-72; 'Artists' Envelopes', touring exhibition 1975-76; 'Winter Exhibition', Ferens Art Gallery, Hull and 'Harleys Boston Open Exhibition', (prizewinner) Blackfriars Art Centre, Boston and Usher Gallery, Lincoln 1982; 'Sculptors from Hull', Crescent Arts Workshop, Scarborough; 'Recent Reliefs and Drawings' (with Yvonne Peake), Ferens Art Gallery, Hull 1985. His work is represented in the public collections of the Contemporary Art Society, London and the East Riding County Council. He lives and works in Hull.

106 Relief on a Square March 1985
steel, wood and paint
60 x 55 x 19 cm

Christo
The Umbrellas

Project for Japan and Western U.S.A.

Thousands of umbrellas, 18 feet high and 24 feet in diameter will meander in the landscape for several miles, simultaneously in Japan and the Western part of the United States, as a two-site project.
The octagonal shape umbrellas will run alongside roads and river banks, crossing rural areas, fields and intersections in suburban areas in both countries.
Sometimes in clusters, then in a line or spaced from each other, 'The Umbrellas' occasionally will slightly tilt according to the slope of the terrain on which they rest.

As I have done for all my other temporary works of art, 'The Umbrellas' shall be entirely financed by me through the sale of my preparatory drawings, studies and early works.
For a period of two weeks 'The Umbrellas' will be seen, approached and enjoyed either by car from a distance and closer as they border the road, or in a promenade route under the 'Umbrellas' in their luminous shadows.

Christo
April 1985

107 The Umbrellas (Project for Japan and West U.S.A.) 1985
collage
66.7 x 77.5 cm

108 The Pont Neuf Wrapped (Project for Paris) 1985
2-part collage
30.5 × 77.5 cm and 66.7 × 77.5 cm

June Green

Born 1935 in County Durham, England. 1951–55 Sunderland College of Art. 1955–58 Royal College of Art, London. Her first one-man exhibition was at the London Press Exchange Gallery 1968 and since then she has had one-man exhibitions at Galerie Hervé Alexandre, Brussels 1975; Annely Juda Fine Art, London 1979; Gimpel-Hanover & André Emmerich Galerien, Zurich, 1984. Among the group shows she has participated in are 1960 'London Group' R.B.A. Galleries, London; 1963 'The Teaching Image' Leeds City Art Gallery; 1968–69 John Player Open Exhibition and subsequent tour; 1971 'Art Spectrum' Alexandra Palace, London; 1973 'Aerial Structures' Sunderland Arts Centre; 1974 'Soft Art' Camden Arts Centre, London; 1980 Annely Juda Fine Art, London; 1984 'Five Sculptors' and 1985 'Small Works', both at the Juda Rowan Gallery, London. June Green lives and works in Kent.

109 1/85 Ginkgo 1985
grey riven slate (4 parts)
overall size: 4 x 98 x 98 cm

Anthony Green

110 3rd Working Drawing for The Lunch Party being the final working drawing for 'Afternoon Tea' 1983
mixed media on paper
50.5 x 35 cm

111 Afternoon Tea 1985
(not illustrated)
oil on board
228.5 x 190.5 cm

Alan Green

112 Red-Pink 1985
oil on canvas
161 x 145 cm

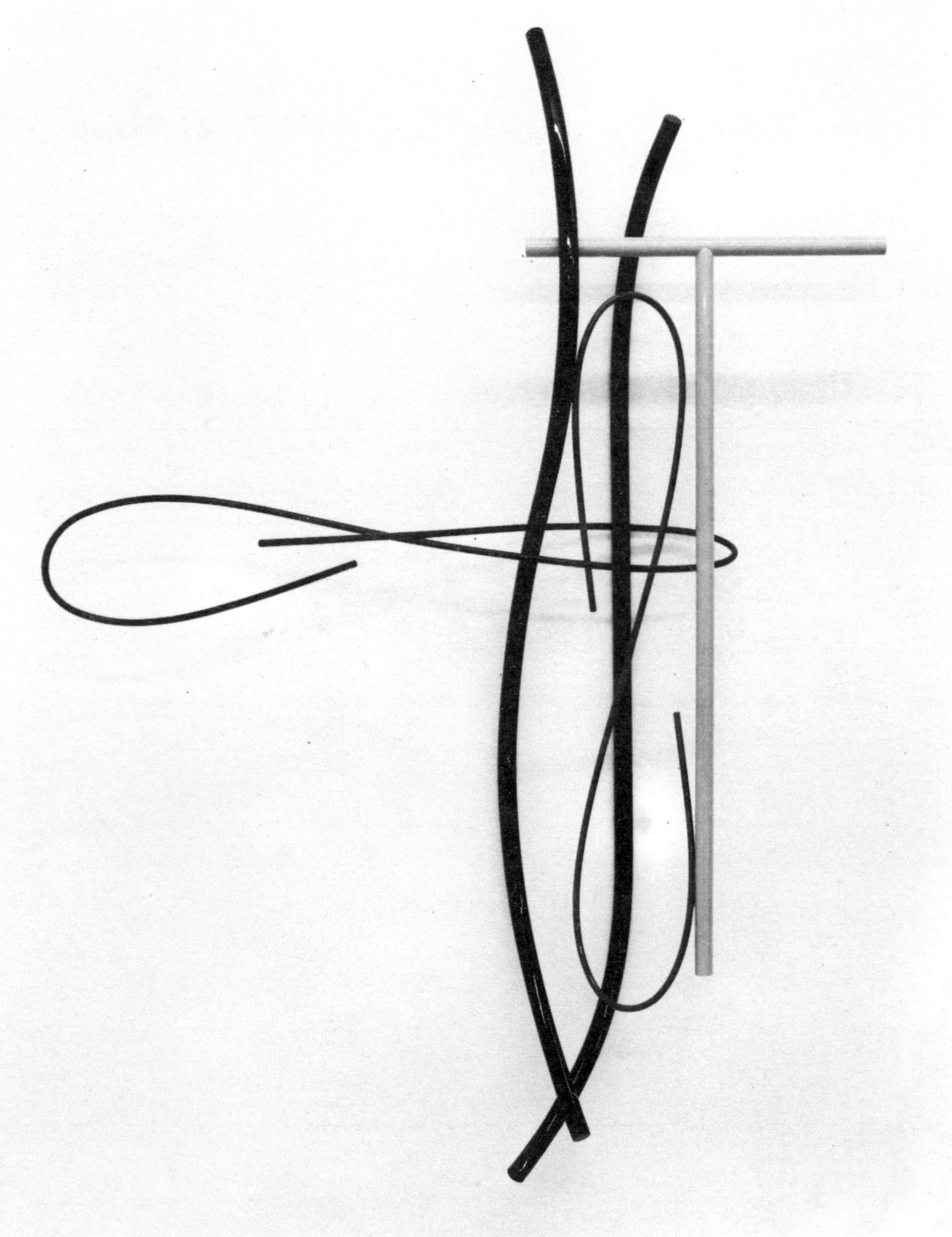

Nigel Hall
113 K 5 1985
painted aluminium
131 x 95.5 x 26.5 cm

Noriyuki Haraguchi

Born 1946 in Yokosuka, Japan. 1970 Graduated from the Faculty of Arts, Nihon University. First one-man exhibition in 1968 at Muramatsu Gallery, Tokyo. Regularly had one-man exhibitions at Tamura Gallery, Tokyo, first in 1969, then in 1973, 1974 and 1975. Other solo shows include 'Square-Paper Materials' Kaneko Art Gallery, Tokyo 1977; Galerie Alfred Schmela, Dusseldorf 1978; Sakura Gallery, Nagoya 1979 and 1981; Annely Juda Fine Art, London and Galerie Art in Progress, Dusseldorf 1980; Juda Rowan Gallery, London 1983 and Karin Bolz Galerie, Mulheim 1985. Has been showing at the Akira Ikeda Gallery in Nagoya and Tokyo since 1981. Amongst his numerous group exhibitions are the '7th Contemporary Art Exhibition of Japan' at the Metropolitan Art Museum, Tokyo in 1966; '5th International Young Artist Exhibition', Seibu Department Store, Tokyo; '4th Japan Art Festival' National Museum of Modern Art, Tokyo; 'Trends in Contemporary Art', National Museum of Modern Art, Kyoto which were all in 1969; '10th Contemporary Art Exhibition of Japan' Metropolitan Art Museum, Tokyo 1971; 'Contemporary Artists '72' Yokohama Public Gallery 1972; '8th Japan Art Festival' Central Art Museum, Tokyo (Award for Excellence); 1st Hakone Open-Air Museum Exhibition, Hakone 1973; 'Japan-Tradition und Gegenwart', Kunsthalle Dusseldorf 1974; 'Kyoto Biennale 1976' Kyoto Municipal Art Museum 1976; Documenta 6, Kassel 1977; 'Biennale de Paris' Musée National d'Art Moderne, Paris 1977; Galerie Alfred Schmela, Dusseldorf 1977; '6th Contemporary Sculpture Exhibition' Suma Detached Palace Garden, Kobe 1978; 'Vision for the 80's' Hara Museum of Contemporary Art, Tokyo 1980; 'Schwarz' Kunsthalle Dusseldorf and 'Contemporary Japanese Art' Seoul 1981; 'A Panorama of Contemporary Art in Japan', The Museum of Modern Art, Toyama 1982. Haraguchi lives and works in Japan.

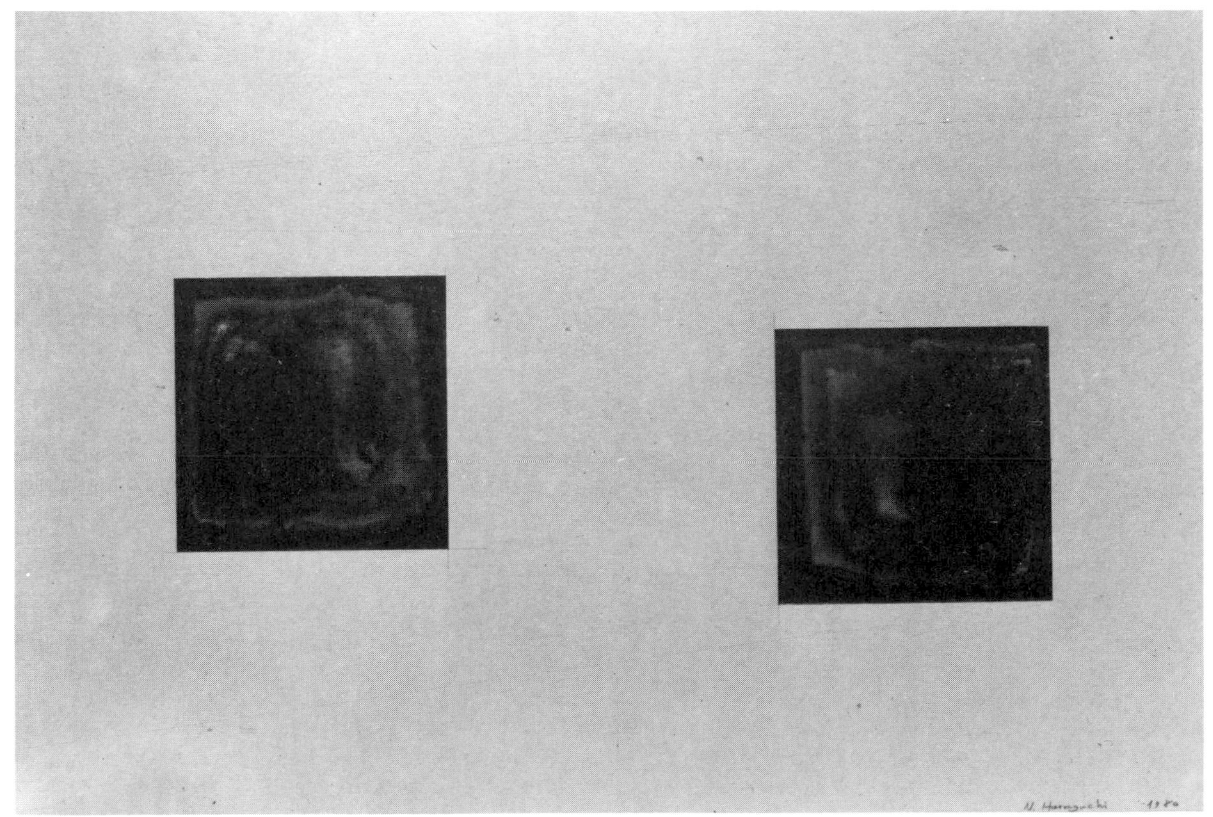

114 Untitled 27 1980
lead collage on Japanese hand-made paper
69 x 103 cm

John Golding
115 I (Splintered Light – Toledo Blue) 1985
acrylic and mixed media on cotton duck
152 × 208 cm

Gottfried Honegger

Born 1917 in Zurich where he studied art. 1939 went to Paris to paint. Returned to Switzerland at outbreak of War. First one-man exhibition at Chichio Haller, Zurich, 1950. Travelled extensively and lived in New York from 1958 to 1960 when he first showed at the Martha Jackson Gallery and again in 1964. Since 1963 regular one-man exhibitions at Gimpel & Hanover Galerie, Zurich and at Gimpel Fils, London in 1964 and 1968. First showed at Annely Juda Fine Art in 1979 and at the Juda Rowan Gallery in 1983. Amongst his other important one-man exhibitions are those at the Württembergischer Kunstverein, Stuttgart 1966; Kunsthaus, Zurich 1967; Museum am Ostwall, Dortmund 1968; Valley House Gallery, Dallas 1969 and 1972; Galerie Swart, Amsterdam 1972; Badischer Kunstverein, Karlsruhe 1972; Galerie Teufel, Cologne 1972; Galerie d'Art Moderne, Basle 1974; Galerie Denise René, Paris 1974 and 1975; XIII Bienal de Sao Paulo, Brazil 1975; Musée d'Art Moderne de la Ville de Paris 1978; Galerie Nouvelles Images, The Hague 1978 and 1983; Ulmer Museum, Ulm 1981; Galerie Müller-Roth, Stuttgart 1983; Kunsthaus Zug, Zug 1984. He is represented in numerous public collections, Centre National d'Art Contemporain, Paris; Israel Museum, Jerusalem; Carnegie Institute, Pittsburgh; Dallas Museum of Fine Arts, Texas; Hirshhorn Museum, Washington D.C.; Museum of Modern Art, New York; Louisiana Museum, Humlebaek; Musée National d'Art Moderne, Centre Georges Pompidou, Paris; Staatsgalerie Stuttgart; Albright-Knox Art Gallery, Buffalo. Monograph on his paintings and sculpture by Serge Lemoine, published by Waser, Zurich 1984. Since 1961 he has lived and worked in Paris and Zurich.

116 Tableau-Relief P 870 1982
acrylic on canvas
200 x 50 cm

Julian Hawkes

Born 1944 in Gloucestershire. 1963–69 Studied at the West of England and Slade Schools of Art. 1969–75 Assistant to Phillip King. 1975 Awarded the Gulbenkian Visual Arts Award. 1978 First showed at the Rowan Gallery and regularly thereafter. 1984 'Julian Hawkes Sculpture', Wells Castle, Norfolk. Among other group exhibitions 1973 Serpentine Gallery; 1975 'The Condition of Sculpture', Hayward Gallery; 1976 'Arte Inglese Oggi', Palazzo Reale, Milan and the Sydney Biennale, Art Gallery of New South Wales; 1980 'Nature as Material', Arts Council touring exhibition; 1982 'Maquettes for Public Sculpture', Welsh Sculpture Trust, Margham Park; 1985 'The Crafts Factor in Architecture and Building' RIBA, London. He is represented in the collections of the Arts Council of Great Britain; Eastern Arts Association; Mildura Arts Centre, Victoria, Australia; Peterborough City Council.

'. . . No pretentious claims made, but it does not require much perception to see that, where the essentials are concerned, Hawkes's sculpture is like Sister Kate's shimmy: quite simply, he does it, and does it good . . .'

John Russell Taylor, *The Times*, 25 October 1983

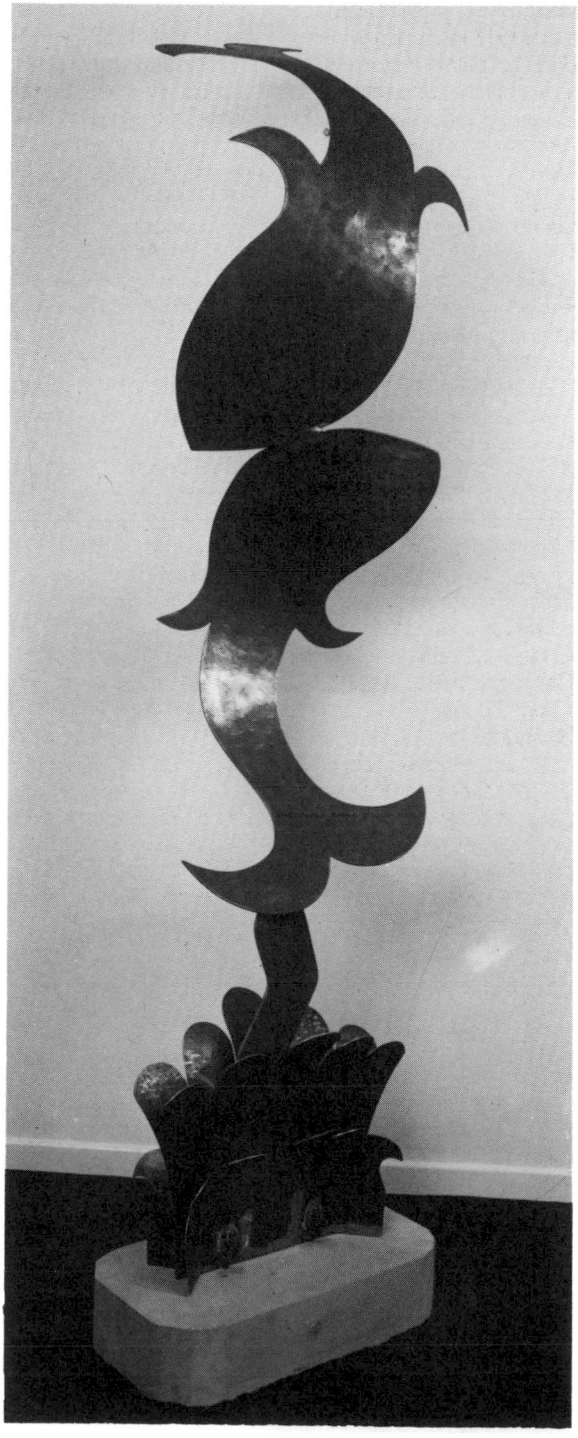

117 Splash 1985
mild steel and York stone
223.5 x 61 x 63.5 cm

Malcolm Hughes

Born in Manchester in 1920. Studied at Manchester and Royal College of Art. Taught at Bath Academy of Art, Corsham, Chelsea and Slade School of Art. 1969 co-founded the Systems Group. 1982 Emeritus Reader in Fine Art, University of London. 1984 Honorary Fellow, University College of Wales. First one-man exhibition was at the I.C.A. Gallery in 1965. 1967 Axiom Gallery; 1972 Lucy Milton Gallery; 1983 Juda Rowan Gallery; 'Working Drawings', University Gallery, Leeds, 1985. Amongst the group exhibitions that have included his work are 1967 'Constructions', Arts Council U.K. touring exhibition; 'Four Artists: Reliefs, Constructions and Drawings', Victoria and Albert Museum, 1971; 'Systems', Whitechapel Art Gallery and U.K. tour 1972; 'Art as Thought Process', Serpentine Gallery, 1974; 'New Work 2', Hayward Gallery, London 1975; 'Arte Inglese Oggi', Milan 1976; 'British Artists of the Sixties', Tate Gallery and Annely Juda Fine Art (with Dilworth, Lowe and Steele) 1977; 'Constructive Context', Warehouse Gallery and U.K. tour, 1978; '8 + 8', Annely Juda Fine Art, 1980; 1983 'Concepts in Construction', selected by Irving Sandler and touring U.S.A.; 1984 'Constructive Tendencies in Europe', Galerie Konstructiv Tendens, Stockholm, Sweden.

118 PX1, PX2 1985
oil on canvas (2 parts)
each part 61 x 61 cm

Michael Kenny

119 Vice-wore fool's dress 1985
work in progress at Portland Quarry

Phillip King

120 Fire in Taurus 1984
painted steel
188 x 153 x 136 cm

George Meyrick

Born in London 1953. 1971–72 St. Martin's School of Art. 1972–75 Brighton Polytechnic. 1975–76 Chelsea School of Art. 1980 Greater London Arts Association Visual Arts Award. 1981 first one-man show at S. East Gallery, London; 1982 Spectro Gallery, Newcastle-upon-Tyne and in 1984 at The Henry Moore Centre for the Study of Sculpture, Leeds City Art Gallery. Among his group shows are the touring show of Six Young British Sculptors in 1978; 'Small Works' Newcastle Polytechnic Gallery 1979 and 1982; S. East Gallery, London 1979 and 1980; 'New Sculpture' Midland Group, Nottingham 1981; House Gallery, London 1981; 'Works from the S. East Gallery' at the St. Paul's Gallery, Leeds 1982; 'Jesmond House Show' Newcastle-upon-Tyne 1982; Galerie Hoffmann; Friedberg, Germany 1983; Studio-Odd, Hiroshima 1983; 'Five Sculptors' Juda Rowan Gallery, London 1984; 'Small Works' Juda Rowan Gallery, London; 'Drawing' Exhibiting Space, London; 'Colour and Systems' Arts Council of Great Britain touring exhibition and 'Die Ecke' Galerie Hoffmann, Friedberg, Germany, 1985. He is represented in the public collections of The Arts Council of Great Britain, The British Council, The Henry Moore Centre for the Study of Sculpture, Leeds City Art Gallery and Lotherton Hall, Leeds. He lives and works in London.

121 Untitled (bright green solid) 1985
painted wood
32.5 x 23 x 16.5 cm

David Nash

Born Esher, Surrey, 1945. Studied at Kingston and Chelsea Schools of Art. Since 1967 he has lived and worked in Blaenau Ffestiniog, North Wales. He was awarded a Welsh Arts Council bursary in 1975 and in 1978 he was resident sculptor at Grizedale Forest. His first one-man exhibition 'Briefly Cooked Apples' was held as part of the York festival in 1973. Since then he has had solo exhibitions of his work worldwide mainly in publicly funded spaces or at museums and only occasionally in commercial galleries. These exhibitions include 'Loosely held Grain', Arnolfini Gallery, Bristol, 1976; 'Fletched over Ash', AIR Gallery, London; 'Wood Quarry', Elise Meyer Gallery, New York, 1980; 'Pyramids and Catapults', St. Paul's Gallery, Leeds; 'Fellowship 81–82', Yorkshire Sculpture Park and 'Wood Quarry, Otterlo', Kröller-Müller Museum 1982; 'Sixty Seasons', Third Eye Gallery, Glasgow and tour 1983 and most recently his Museum tour in Japan that was organized by the Tochigi Prefectural Museum 1984/85. Amongst the major group exhibitions that his work has been included in are 'The Condition of Sculpture', Hayward Gallery, London, 1975; 'British Art Now', Guggenheim Museum, New York and Royal Academy, London, 1980; 'Aspects of British Art Today', Tokyo Metropolitan Museum and tour 1982; ROSC, Dublin and 'International Survey of recent painting and sculpture', Museum of Modern Art, New York, 1984. His work is included in several major international collections including the Tate Gallery, London; Kröller-Müller Museum, Otterlo; Guggenheim Museum, New York; Tokyo Metropolitan Museum and Tochigi Prefectural Museum, Japan. David Nash will be having a one-man show of his work in the Juda Rowan Gallery in 1986.

122 Crack and Warp – stacked table 1985
ash
142.2 x 71 x 50.8 cm

Martin Naylor

123 Le Bateau Ivre 1985
mixed media
45.7 x 91.5 x 7.5 cm

Bridget Riley
124 Shahnama 1984
oil on linen
206 x 169 cm

Keir Smith

Born 1950 in Kent. Senior lecturer in sculpture at Birmingham Polytechnic. His first one-man show was in 1976 at the Oriel Gallery, Cardiff and in 1977 he had one-man exhibitions at the Hays Gallery in Sheffield, the AIR Gallery in London and the Hatton Gallery at the University of Newcastle-upon-Tyne. Other one-man shows include 1980 Acme Gallery, London; 1982 Ceolfrith Gallery at the Sunderland Arts Centre and the Ikon Gallery, Birmingham; 1983 Richard Demarco Gallery, Edinburgh and from 1984–85 a show which toured to the Rochdale Gallery; Aspex Gallery, Portsmouth; Ramsgate Library Art Gallery and the Chapter Arts Centre in Cardiff; 1985 Bluecoat Gallery, Liverpool. He has been in numerous group shows, including 1973 'Northern Young Contemporaries' and 1974 'New Contemporaries' at both of which he was a prize-winner; 1978 'Eight Artists at the Edinburgh Fruitmarket'; 1981 'Art and the Sea' Southampton Art Gallery and I.C.A., London; 1983 'Drawing in Air' Ceolfrith Gallery, Sunderland and national tour; 1984 'Sculptors and Modellers' Tate Gallery, London and 'Sense of Place', Sunderland Arts Centre and national tour. In 1979 he was the resident sculptor at Grizedale Forest, Cumbria where one of his sculptures is now sited. He has sculpture sited at various other places, including Portland Clifftop Sculpture Park (1983), Yorkshire Sculpture Park (1983), Ramsgate Library Gallery (1985) and University of Bath (1985) which won a prize at the Bath Festival Sculpture Competition. Keir Smith currently lives and works in London.

125 Tattered Sail 1984
oak
51 x 234 x 5 cm

Sean Scully
126 Shadowing 1984
oil on canvas
213.4 x 182.9 x 14 cm

Yoshishige Saito

Born in Tokyo, 1904. Studied at Nihon Middle School, Tokyo 1918–24. Worked as Managing Editor of general magazine, Tokyo 1945–48. Travelled to France, England, Italy, Greece, Spain, Turkey, Egypt and U.S.A. Professor of Art, Tama College of Art, Tokyo 1964–73. Awarded painting prize, 5th Bienal, Sao Paulo 1959; Honorable Mention for Painting, Guggenheim International, New York 1960; International Painting Prize, 6th Bienal, Sao Paulo 1961. First one-man exhibition, Tokyo Gallery, 1958 and then regularly thereafter. Galerie Friedrich and Dahlem, Munich 1964 and Galleria d'Arte del Naviglio, Milan and Freiburg Kunstverein, West Germany 1965. In 1967 he showed at Galleri Haaken, Oslo, and in 1978 The National Museum of Modern Art, Tokyo. In 1983 he had one-man shows at the Juda Rowan Gallery, London and Galerij S65, Aalst, Belgium. Amongst the many group exhibitions he has participated in are 1958, Carnegie International, Pittsburgh; 1959 Sao Paulo Bienal, Brazil (and 1961); 1960 30th Venice Biennale and Guggenheim International, New York; 1963 1st Salon International de Galeries Pilotes, Lausanne; 1965 'Moderne Malerei aus Japan', Kunsthaus, Zurich; 1966 'New Japanese Painting and Sculpture', Museum of Modern Art, New York; 1967 '2nd Japan Arts Festival', toured U.S.A.; 1973 'Contemporary Art Exhibition of Japan–20 years of Contemporary Art in Retrospective', National Museum of Modern Art, Tokyo; 1974 'Japan – Tradition und Gegenwart', Dusseldorf Kunsthalle, West Germany; 1975 'Louisiana pa Japan', Louisiana Museum of Modern Art, Denmark; 1977 'Contemporary Japanese Art', Modern Art Museum, Tochigi; 1979 'Contemporary Art Post-war', Modern Art Museum, Kanagawa; 1980 'Japanese western-style painting-course of 20 years post-war', Kyoto Municipal Art Museum; 1981 'Trends in Contemporary Art', Tokyo Metropolitan Art Museum, Japan; 1982 Carnegie International, Pittsburgh. His work is included in the collections of the Museum of Modern Art, Kamakura; the National Museum of Modern Art, Tokyo; the Museum of Contemporary Art, Nagaoka; the Museum of Fine Arts, Houston; the Rockefeller Collection, New York and the Kröller-Müller Museum, Otterlo.

127 Triangularly H 1982
painted wood and bolt
137 x 104 x 25 cm